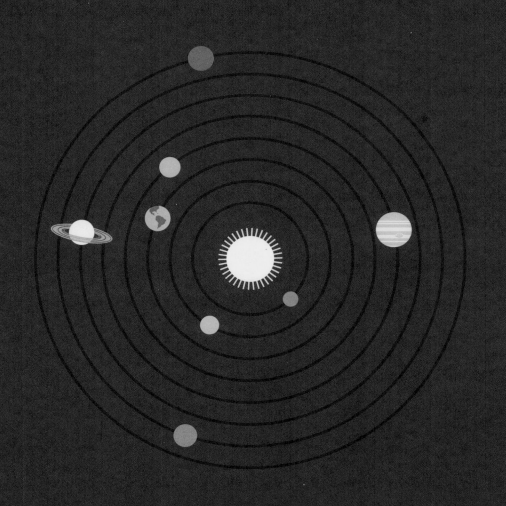

Dedicated to the memory of Ian Batty, who was wise and kind in equal measure.
—Isabel Thomas

For Meagan, master of the elements of grace, harmony, and style.
—Sara Gillingham

Dear Reader,

If you had to pick the most amazing discovery ever made by science, it might be this: everything in the universe is made of just 92 basic building blocks. They are known as the elements. How is it possible that just 92 ingredients can build so many different things? How can objects as different as a rock, a tree, and a human brain be made out of the same stuff? As you explore this book, you'll begin to find out. You'll meet each of the elements found in nature, and some that have been created by humans.

For the last 150 years, scientists have used a chart called the periodic table to help them explore and understand the elements. This book uses the periodic table as a map too—a way to organize your journey of discovery. It's possible to find hundreds of different versions of the periodic table in books and online. We have used the American Chemical Society (ACS) and the International Union of Pure and Applied Chemistry's (IUPAC) periodic table of the elements as our primary reference for names, terms, and categories used in this book. You'll notice that many of the measurements are expressed using the International System of Units (SI). SI units, such as meters and kilograms, are used by scientists around the world, including in the US, so that they can communicate information universally without any confusion. In some cases we have converted data into units used in everyday life in the US, to help you compare the facts in this book to things you come across every day.

As you explore, remember—we have not yet discovered everything there is to know about the elements. The periodic table will continue to change. Perhaps you will discover some of the secrets that still lie hidden within its rows and columns.

—Isabel Thomas

ACKNOWLEDGMENTS

Thank you to Maya Gartner, Sara Gillingham, and Meagan Bennett for making me part of your fantastic team. Special thanks to the American Association of Chemistry Teachers at the American Chemical Society. To Robin Pridy for your meticulous fact checking. To Kate Shaw for encouragement. And to Nick, Harry, Joey, and Oscar for exploring the periodic table with me.
— I.T.

With deepest thanks to Maya Gartner, Isabel Thomas, Michelle Clement, Amy Rennert, and Caskey McFerrin.
— S.G.

Exploring the Elements

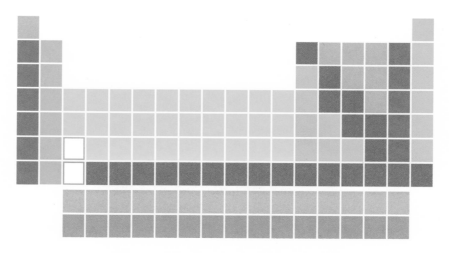

A COMPLETE GUIDE TO THE PERIODIC TABLE

Words by ISABEL THOMAS   Pictures by SARA GILLINGHAM

CONTeNTs

C Carbon	**O** Oxygen	**N** Nitrogen	**Te** Tellurium	**N** Nitrogen	**Ts** Tennessine

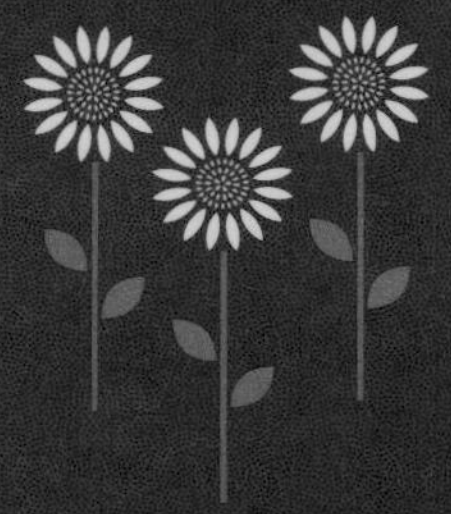

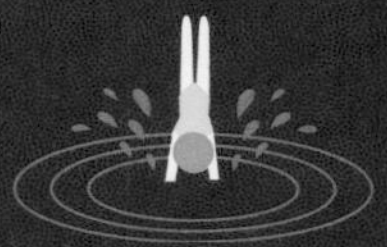

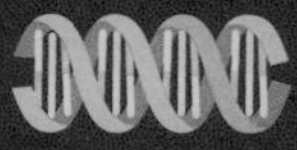

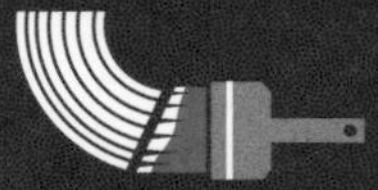

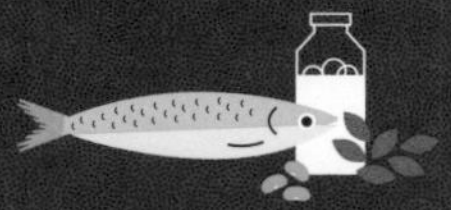

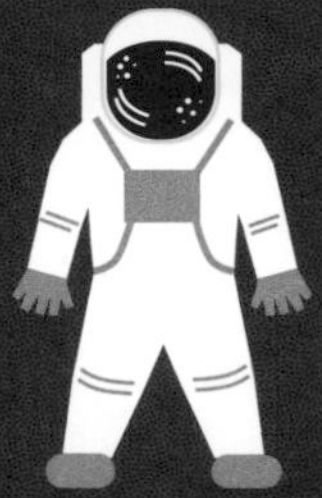

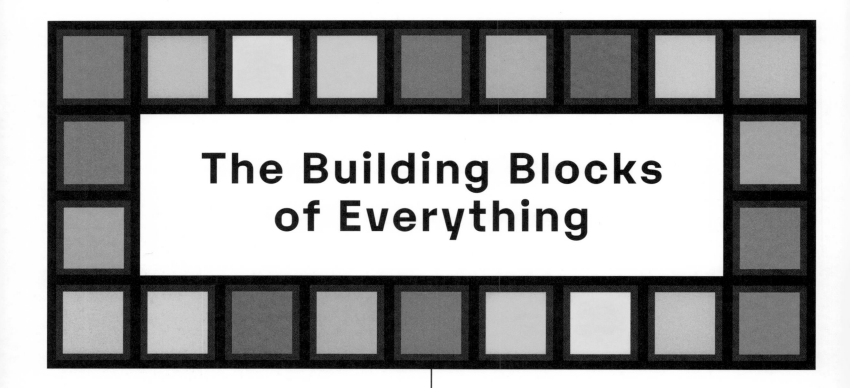

The Building Blocks of Everything

ELEMENTS ARE THE BUILDING BLOCKS OF EVERYTHING, FROM DISTANT STARS TO THE GROUND UNDER YOUR FEET, FROM THE PAGES OF THIS BOOK TO THE PERSON READING IT.

WHAT ARE THINGS MADE OF?

Humans have been asking and trying to answer this question for thousands of years. The best way to find out what something is made of is to take it apart—to split it up into smaller and smaller pieces, until you can't split it up anymore. Scientists have done this with everything around us—from plants and animals to rocks and the air, from leaves and lava to gemstones and eyelashes. Scientists have even split apart the light from distant stars, to find out what those stars are made of. What they have discovered is fantastic, amazing, and mind-boggling.

Everything in the universe is made of just 92 basic ingredients. These "building blocks of everything" are known as the elements.

How is it possible that just 92 ingredients can build so many different things? How can objects as different as a toad, a tree, and a human brain be made out of the same stuff? To understand how this is possible, you can think of the elements as being a bit like different kinds of Lego® bricks. Mathematicians have calculated that it's possible to combine just six different Lego® bricks in 915,103,765 different ways! Nature has 92 different building blocks to play with and has combined them in different ways to form billions of different substances and objects.

In this book you'll meet the 92 elements found in nature, and an extra 26 elements that have been created by humans. You'll find out what makes each element unique, their roles in the natural world, and the ingenious uses that we have found for them.

WHAT ARE ELEMENTS?

Each element is a substance that cannot be split into simpler substances. For example, if you had a lump of the element gold, you could cut it into smaller pieces, but those small pieces would still be pieces of gold! You could cut those small pieces of gold into tiny pieces, but they would still be pieces of gold! The smallest possible piece of an element is called an atom. One atom of gold is about 166 picometers wide. A picometer is a trillionth of a meter, so a gold atom is far too small to see with your eyes. In fact, you could line up about a million gold atoms across a single human hair!

In order to see individual atoms of gold, you'd need to use one of the world's most powerful microscopes. Under these microscopes, gold atoms look like tiny balls, neatly lined up. However, atoms are not just tiny balls. They are more complicated than that.

Each element is made of a different type of atom. So, to really understand what elements are, and what makes them different from one another, we need to imagine our way *inside* atoms.

WHAT ARE ATOMS MADE OF?

Atoms are made of tiny **particles**, called **protons**, **neutrons**, and **electrons**. Each atom is a bit like a tiny version of our solar system: Just like the real solar system, most of the "stuff" in an atom is concentrated at the very center, in a clump called the **nucleus**.

Protons and neutrons are so small, you could line up a trillion of them on the period at the end of this sentence. Electrons are even smaller.

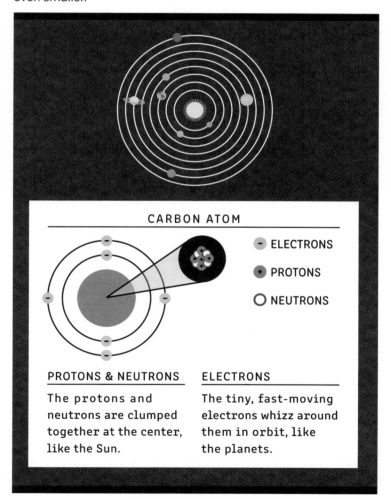

CARBON ATOM

- ELECTRONS
+ PROTONS
O NEUTRONS

PROTONS & NEUTRONS

The protons and neutrons are clumped together at the center, like the Sun.

ELECTRONS

The tiny, fast-moving electrons whizz around them in orbit, like the planets.

Each element is made from a different type of atom. The differences between their atoms is what makes the elements look and behave differently from one another. What makes the atoms different is the number of protons and electrons they contain. The element hydrogen has the smallest, simplest atom. Each hydrogen atom has just one proton and one electron. The atoms of other elements have a different number of protons and electrons. For example, oxygen atoms have eight protons and eight electrons, while iron atoms have 26 protons and 26 electrons. Sometimes the number of neutrons in an atom matches the number of protons and electrons. Sometimes it is different. The **atomic number** of an element tells you the number of protons and electrons inside every atom of that element. Every element has a different atomic number.

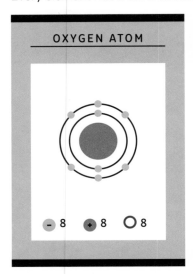

OXYGEN ATOM

- 8   + 8   ○ 8

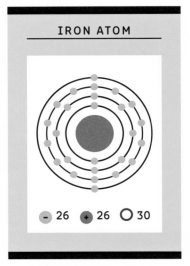

IRON ATOM

- 26   + 26   ○ 30

So far, humans have discovered 118 different types of atom, which means that we can name 118 different elements.

ORGANIZING THE ELEMENTS

Each element has a unique set of properties. An element's physical properties include the temperature at which it melts or boils, its **density** (how closely packed its atoms are) and hardness, and whether or not it **conducts** heat and **electricity** (lets heat and electricity flow through it). These physical properties help to explain how each element looks and feels in our hands. An element's chemical properties describe how it behaves when it gets near other elements—whether it will react with them, and how quickly this **reaction** happens. These chemical properties help to explain the taste, smell, and **toxicity** of an element.

There are 118 elements, and each element has dozens of different properties. Around 150 years ago, scientists began looking closely at the similarities and differences among elements and began to spot patterns. These patterns were used to organize the elements into a chart called the periodic table. The periodic table is a brilliant tool for exploring the elements, and for helping us to understand them better.

THE PERIODIC TABLE

The periodic table is a chart that lists all the elements in order of atomic number—starting with hydrogen (the smallest atom, with just one proton) and ending with oganesson (the largest atom, with 118 protons). The elements aren't just listed in one long line, but arranged in rows, called **periods**, and columns, called **groups**. Elements in the same group share similar properties. For example, all the elements in group 1 are soft, shiny metals that react very easily with other elements. All the elements in group 18 are colorless, non-metal gases that barely react with anything.

When the Russian scientist Dmitri Mendeleev first spotted these repeating patterns 150 years ago, he could not explain why they came about. Today we know the elements in the same group have similar properties because of similarities among their atoms. When you look at the periodic table, you are looking at repeating patterns in the structure of atoms themselves! You can find out more about the history of the periodic table on page 207.

CATEGORIES

Alkali Metals	Metalloids	Lanthanides
Alkaline Earth Metals	Non-Metals	Actinides
Transition Metals	Halogens	Superheavy Elements
Post-Transition Metals	Noble Gases	

In this book, we have used colors to highlight categories of elements that have certain things in common. Sometimes these categories include a single group from the periodic table. Other times, they form a block in the periodic table that includes elements from several groups. These categories are the basis of the chapters in this book.

GROUPS & PERIODS

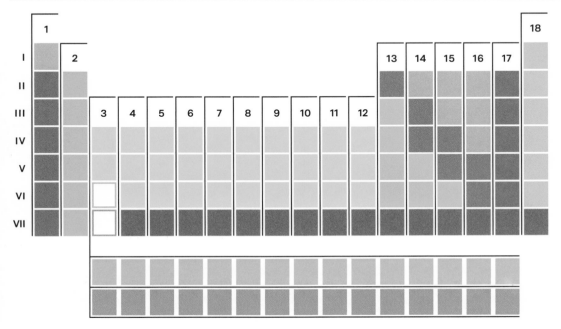

Groups 1–18

Each column of the periodic table is known as a group. Elements in the same group have the same number of outer electrons, so they share similar chemical properties.

Periods I–VII

Each row of the periodic table is called a period. As you read across each period, the atomic number of the elements increases and the structure of their atoms changes. It's these differences in atoms—invisible to human eyes—that explains why elements behave as they do, and explains the shape of the periodic table.

Periodic Table of Elements

1										
1 **H** Hydrogen	**2**									
3 **Li** Lithium	**4** **Be** Beryllium									
11 **Na** Sodium	**12** **Mg** Magnesium	**3**	**4**	**5**	**6**	**7**	**8**	**9**	**10**	**11**
19 **K** Potassium	**20** **Ca** Calcium	**21** **Sc** Scandium	**22** **Ti** Titanium	**23** **V** Vanadium	**24** **Cr** Chromium	**25** **Mn** Manganese	**26** **Fe** Iron	**27** **Co** Cobalt	**28** **Ni** Nickel	**29** **Cu** Coppe
37 **Rb** Rubidium	**38** **Sr** Strontium	**39** **Y** Yttrium	**40** **Zr** Zirconium	**41** **Nb** Niobium	**42** **Mo** Molybdenum	**43** **Tc** Technetium	**44** **Ru** Ruthenium	**45** **Rh** Rhodium	**46** **Pd** Palladium	**47** **Ag** Silve
55 **Cs** Cesium	**56** **Ba** Barium	**57-71** Lanthanides	**72** **Hf** Hafnium	**73** **Ta** Tantalum	**74** **W** Tungsten	**75** **Re** Rhenium	**76** **Os** Osmium	**77** **Ir** Iridium	**78** **Pt** Platinum	**79** **Au** Gold
87 **Fr** Francium	**88** **Ra** Radium	**89-103** Actinides	**104** **Rf** Rutherfordium	**105** **Db** Dubnium	**106** **Sg** Seaborgium	**107** **Bh** Bohrium	**108** **Hs** Hassium	**109** **Mt** Meitnerium	**110** **Ds** Darmstadtium	**111** **Rg** Roentge

The lanthanides and actinides are often shown at the foot of the periodic table, like this, so that it isn't too long to fit on a page.

57 **La** Lanthanum	**58** **Ce** Cerium	**59** **Pr** Praseodymium	**60** **Nd** Neodymium	**61** **Pm** Promethium	**62** **Sm** Samarium	**63** **Eu** Europium	**64** **Gd** Gadolinium	**65** **Tb** Terbi
89 **Ac** Actinium	**90** **Th** Thorium	**91** **Pa** Protactinium	**92** **U** Uranium	**93** **Np** Neptunium	**94** **Pu** Plutonium	**95** **Am** Americium	**96** **Cm** Curium	**97** **Bk** Berkeli

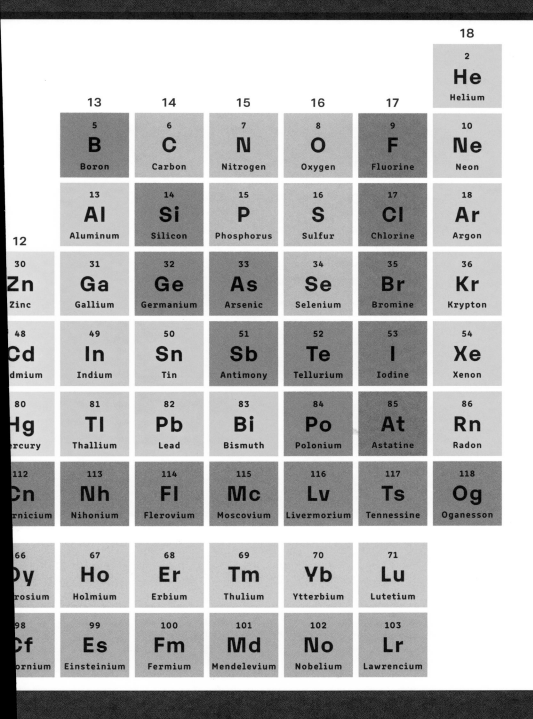

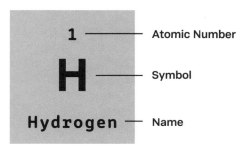

Atomic Number

Symbol

Name

Each element has a unique symbol as well as a name. It also shows their atomic number (the number of protons in atoms of that element).

CATEGORIES

- Alkali Metals
- Alkaline Earth Metals
- Transition Metals
- Post-Transition Metals
- Metalloids
- Non-Metals
- Halogens
- Noble Gases
- Lanthanides
- Actinides
- Superheavy Elements

WHERE DID ALL THESE ELEMENTS COME FROM?

The universe began billions of years ago with the Big Bang. This created the simplest atoms of all—atoms of the elements hydrogen, helium, and lithium. Atoms of most other elements we find on Earth were formed inside burning, collapsing, or merging stars and thrown out across space by giant explosions. A handful of others were made in the space between stars, when fast-moving particles smashed into one another. The periodic table also lists a few actinides and superheavy elements that we never find naturally on Earth. These have been created by humans, by smashing other atoms together at high speeds.

EXPLORING THE ELEMENTS

Chemistry is the scientific study of all the different substances we find around us, including the elements. When chemists come across a substance, they ask:

- What is it made of?
- What are its properties?
- How does it behave around other substances, and why?

For 150 years, the periodic table has helped chemists to look for answers. It guided the hunt for new elements and helped us discover the relationships between them. It helped us to better understand what atoms are, and how they combine to build everything in the universe. Chemists have also used their understanding of the elements to build new substances that aren't found in nature. These include thousands of chemicals and materials we take for granted today, from plastics, fuels, and fertilizers to food additives and medicines, from the **magnetic alloys** needed to generate electricity to the **semiconductors** needed to make computer chips.

The periodic table is still an important map, telling chemists and other scientists where to look when they are trying to answer a question, invent a new material, or solve a problem.

BUILDING WITH THE ELEMENTS

The periodic table helps us understand how the atoms of 92 different elements combine to build everything in the universe. A few substances—such as air and some alloys—are mixtures of elements. But most chemicals and materials aren't just mixtures. They are **compounds**, made from two or more elements that have combined to form a completely new substance.

In a compound, the atoms of elements form **molecules**, held together by **bonds** that are hard to break. Compounds often have completely different properties to the elements they are made of. For example, atoms of hydrogen and oxygen—both reactive gases at room temperature—combine to form molecules of water, a compound that is liquid at room temperature. Atoms of the reactive metal sodium and the toxic gas chlorine combine to form of molecules of sodium chloride, the **salt** that we sprinkle on our food! Turn to page 211 to find out more.

ELEMENTS OF EARTH

Many of the elements we use are found in the form of **minerals** in the Earth's crust. Sodium chloride, or rock salt, is an example of a mineral. Minerals are solid compounds that are found in nature, and each one is made from a particular set of elements. Inside a mineral, these elements are arranged in a very orderly way to form crystals. Most elements form at least one mineral, and some elements form hundreds of different minerals! Rocks are made of one or more minerals, mixed together.

Water is a compound made from two elements: hydrogen and oxygen. It's a liquid at 59°F, the average temperature on Earth's surface. This is why most of Earth's water is found as a liquid, in ponds, lakes, rivers, and oceans. Water is very good at dissolving other compounds, so we rarely find pure water. It usually has many other things dissolved in it.

Air is a mixture of different gases. They include pure elements, such as nitrogen and oxygen, as well as compounds, such as carbon dioxide and water vapor.

WHERE ELEMENTS OF EARTH ARE FOUND

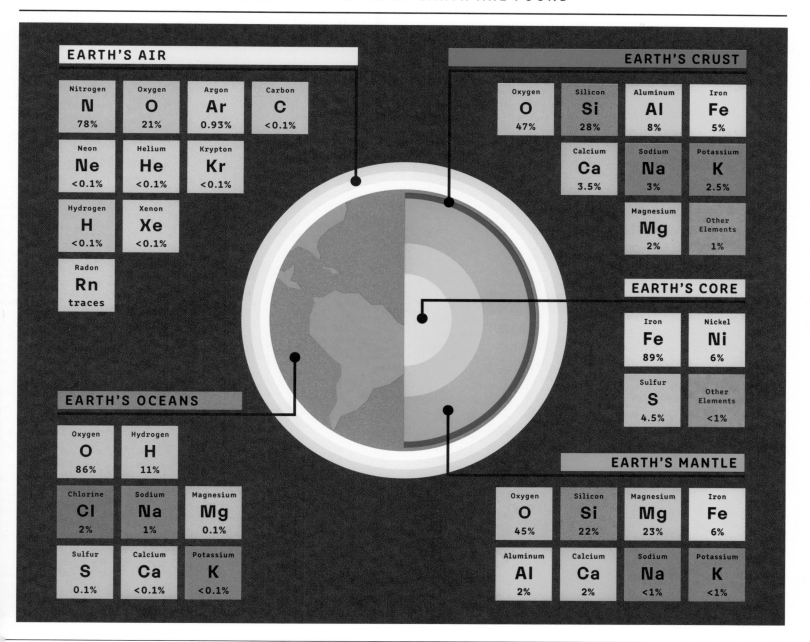

EARTH'S AIR

Nitrogen	Oxygen	Argon	Carbon
N	**O**	**Ar**	**C**
78%	21%	0.93%	<0.1%

Neon	Helium	Krypton
Ne	**He**	**Kr**
<0.1%	<0.1%	<0.1%

Hydrogen	Xenon
H	**Xe**
<0.1%	<0.1%

Radon
Rn
traces

EARTH'S CRUST

Oxygen	Silicon	Aluminum	Iron
O	**Si**	**Al**	**Fe**
47%	28%	8%	5%

Calcium	Sodium	Potassium
Ca	**Na**	**K**
3.5%	3%	2.5%

Magnesium	Other Elements
Mg	
2%	1%

EARTH'S CORE

Iron	Nickel
Fe	**Ni**
89%	6%

Sulfur	Other Elements
S	
4.5%	<1%

EARTH'S OCEANS

Oxygen	Hydrogen
O	**H**
86%	11%

Chlorine	Sodium	Magnesium
Cl	**Na**	**Mg**
2%	1%	0.1%

Sulfur	Calcium	Potassium
S	**Ca**	**K**
0.1%	<0.1%	<0.1%

EARTH'S MANTLE

Oxygen	Silicon	Magnesium	Iron
O	**Si**	**Mg**	**Fe**
45%	22%	23%	6%

Aluminum	Calcium	Sodium	Potassium
Al	**Ca**	**Na**	**K**
2%	2%	<1%	<1%

ELEMENTS OF LIFE

Oxygen, carbon, hydrogen, and nitrogen are the main building blocks of EVERY living thing, including humans. In fact, our bodies are mostly made up of just 11 elements, plus tiny traces of boron, chromium, cobalt, copper, fluorine, iodine, iron, manganese, molybdenum, selenium, silicon, nickel, bromine, vanadium, and zinc. It sounds incredible that something as complex as a human can be built from just 26 types of building blocks, but remember that these elements aren't plonked together in a jumble.

Inside our bodies, a few types of atom combine in thousands of different ways to form simple compounds, which are themselves the building blocks of bigger, more complicated molecules. These molecules—big and small—are the building blocks of different types of **cells**. And these cells are the building blocks of our moving, breathing, talking, thinking bodies.

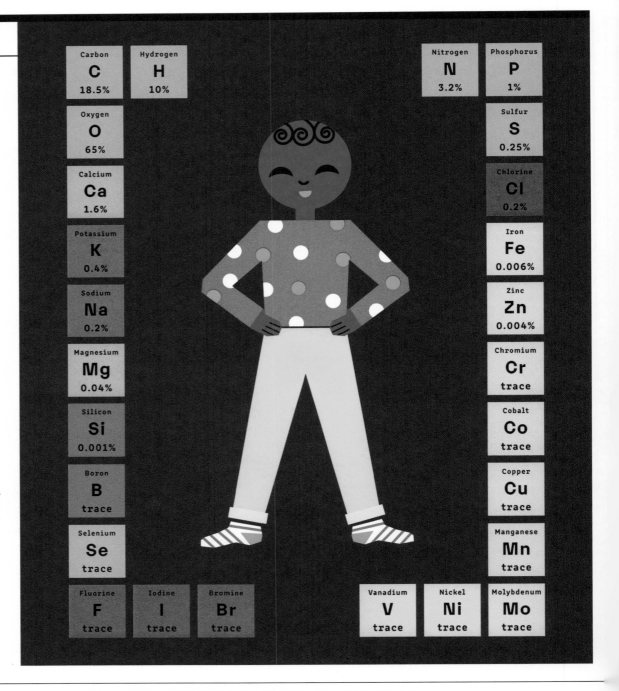

| Magnesium | Lithium | Potassium | | Arsenic | Antimony | Silicon |
| Mg | Li | K | | As | Sb | Si |

| Silver | | | | | | Carbon |
| Ag | | | | | | C |

| Gold | | | | | | Oxygen |
| Au | | | | | | O |

| Cobalt | | | | | | Phosphorus |
| Co | | | | | | P |

| Copper | | | | | | Bromine |
| Cu | | | | | | Br |

| Nickel | | | | | | Dysprosium |
| Ni | | | | | | Dy |

| Tantalum | | | | | | Europium |
| Ta | | | | | | Eu |

| Yttrium | | | | | | Gadolinium |
| Y | | | | | | Gd |

| Aluminum | Gallium | | | | | Lanthanum |
| Al | Ga | | | | | La |

| Indium | Lead | Tin | | Terbium | Praseodymium | Neodymium |
| In | Pb | Sn | | Tb | Pr | Nd |

ELEMENTS OF TECHNOLOGY

Strangely, it takes more elements to build a smartphone than it does to build a human! Over thousands of years, humans have become good at combining elements in new and ingenious ways to give us "superpowers" such as the ability to fly thousands of miles in a few hours, the ability to turn the energy stored inside fossil fuels or moving wind into electricity, and the ability to talk to anyone, anywhere on the planet, simply by dialing a number. However, humans are not very good at mimicking the natural cycles of nature, which recycle the elements inside rocks, minerals, and living things to be used over and over again. Many of the elements used to make smartphones and other devices are quickly running out. Mining and using what is left is putting tremendous pressure on our planet.

26

Fe

Iron
(EYE-URN)

WE LIVE ON AN "IRON PLANET" WITH A CORE OF SOLID AND LIQUID IRON. HUMANS HAVE USED THIS ELEMENT TO BUILD TODAY'S INDUSTRIAL, IRON AGE WORLD.

TRANSITION METAL

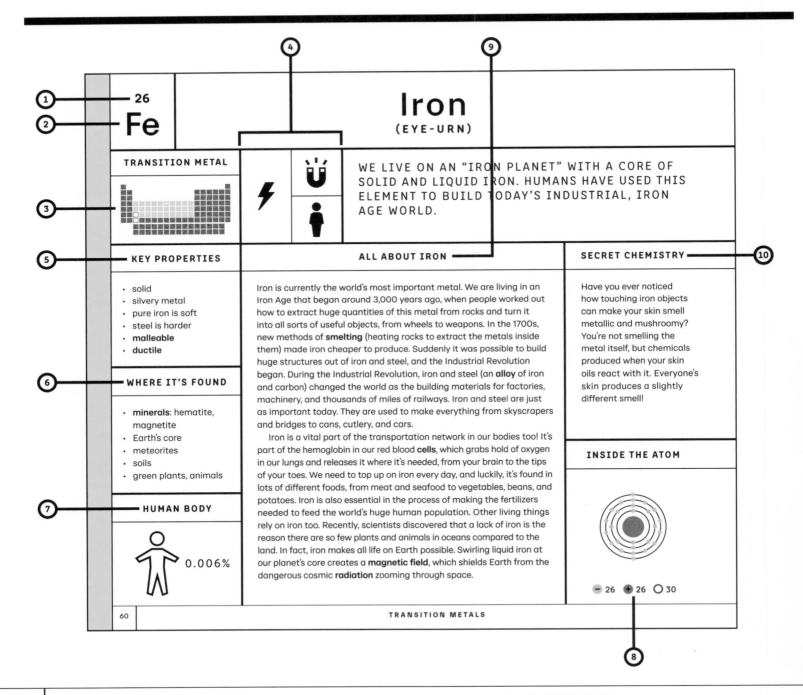

KEY PROPERTIES

- solid
- silvery metal
- pure iron is soft
- steel is harder
- **malleable**
- **ductile**

WHERE IT'S FOUND

- **minerals**: hematite, magnetite
- Earth's core
- meteorites
- soils
- green plants, animals

HUMAN BODY

0.006%

ALL ABOUT IRON

Iron is currently the world's most important metal. We are living in an Iron Age that began around 3,000 years ago, when people worked out how to extract huge quantities of this metal from rocks and turn it into all sorts of useful objects, from wheels to weapons. In the 1700s, new methods of **smelting** (heating rocks to extract the metals inside them) made iron cheaper to produce. Suddenly it was possible to build huge structures out of iron and steel, and the Industrial Revolution began. During the Industrial Revolution, iron and steel (an **alloy** of iron and carbon) changed the world as the building materials for factories, machinery, and thousands of miles of railways. Iron and steel are just as important today. They are used to make everything from skyscrapers and bridges to cans, cutlery, and cars.

Iron is a vital part of the transportation network in our bodies too! It's part of the hemoglobin in our red blood **cells**, which grabs hold of oxygen in our lungs and releases it where it's needed, from your brain to the tips of your toes. We need to top up on iron every day, and luckily, it's found in lots of different foods, from meat and seafood to vegetables, beans, and potatoes. Iron is also essential in the process of making the fertilizers needed to feed the world's huge human population. Other living things rely on iron too. Recently, scientists discovered that a lack of iron is the reason there are so few plants and animals in oceans compared to the land. In fact, iron makes all life on Earth possible. Swirling liquid iron at our planet's core creates a **magnetic field**, which shields Earth from the dangerous cosmic **radiation** zooming through space.

SECRET CHEMISTRY

Have you ever noticed how touching iron objects can make your skin smell metallic and mushroomy? You're not smelling the metal itself, but chemicals produced when your skin oils react with it. Everyone's skin produces a slightly different smell!

INSIDE THE ATOM

● 26 ⊕ 26 ○ 30

TRANSITION METALS

INTRODUCTION: THE BUILDING BLOCKS OF EVERYTHING

This book uses the periodic table as a starting point for exploring the elements—what they are made of, what they look like, where they are found, and how they behave when they get near one another. Each chapter includes a collection of elements that have certain things in common. Some of these categories align with groups of the periodic table. Others include elements from different groups.

HOW TO READ EACH ENTRY

1 The element's atomic number (the number of protons in atoms of that element).
2 The element's chemical symbol.
3 The element's position in the periodic table.
4 Key facts at a glance (see key to the right).
5 Other important properties, including the element's state at room temperature (whether it is a solid, liquid, or gas at 68°F)
6 The main places the element can be found in nature.
7 Whether the element is found in the human body, and what proportion of a person's weight it makes up.
8 A model of how the electrons are arranged in the element's atoms—to help you see the patterns that explain how the elements behave. In these models, the nucleus of each atom is shown as a single large circle, rather than showing all the protons and neutrons separately. As the number of neutrons in atoms of an element can vary, the number of neutrons in the most abundant **isotope** is given (see page 209).
9 The unique story of the element, and its significance to humans and the living world, past, present, and future.
10 The secret chemistry and secret physics boxes delve into the reasons *why* each element behaves as it does.

Each entry also includes a gallery of illustrations and captions, highlighting some of the most important, weird, or wonderful uses of that element.

LOOK OUT FOR THESE SYMBOLS, WHICH SHOW YOU SOME KEY FACTS AT A GLANCE:

Toxic: Most elements are dangerous in large doses, but elements with this symbol are considered particularly toxic for humans.

Conductor: These elements conduct electricity—an **electric current** will flow through them.

Semiconductor: These elements are semi-conductors—an electric current will flow through them under certain conditions but not others.

Human body: These elements are a vital part of the human body—we can't live without them.

Radioactive: Radioactive forms of most elements exist (or can be created) but *all* forms of elements with this symbol are radioactive (see page 210).

Ferromagnetic: These elements are strongly attracted by magnets, and can form permanent magnets themselves.

Paramagnetic: These elements are weakly attracted to magnets, but don't form permanent magnets in their pure form.

Non-metal: These elements don't share the chemical and physical properties of metals, for example they don't conduct heat or electricity easily.

1	
H	

Hydrogen
(HIGH-DRUH-GIN)

NON-METAL		
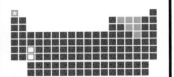		WE BEGIN WITH HYDROGEN—A VERY SPECIAL ELEMENT BECAUSE IT'S EVERYWHERE! IN SPACE, IT FUELS STARS IN WHICH MANY OTHER ELEMENTS ARE CREATED. ON EARTH, IT FORMS WATER, A SUBSTANCE NEEDED BY EVERY LIVING THING. IT'S THE SIMPLEST AND MOST ABUNDANT ELEMENT IN THE UNIVERSE!

KEY PROPERTIES

- gas
- transparent
- colorless
- invisible
- odorless

WHERE IT'S FOUND

- water
- animals
- plants
- air/atmosphere
- fossil fuels

HUMAN BODY

 10%

ALL ABOUT HYDROGEN

Hydrogen is the most common element in the universe. If you counted every atom in every galaxy, at least three quarters would be atoms of hydrogen! Most of hydrogen is found inside stars, including our sun. At the center of the Sun, hydrogen atoms are smashed and squashed together to make bigger atoms of helium. This releases enough energy to light and heat our entire solar system! On Earth, hydrogen is far less fiery. Most of the hydrogen on our planet is part of water, sloshing around in rivers, seas, and oceans. Living things contain lots of hydrogen too, including humans! It's one of the most important building blocks of life.

It's hard to find pure hydrogen on Earth, but we can produce it by splitting apart water or natural gas. This takes a lot of energy but it's worth it because pure hydrogen is very useful. We rely on it to feed the world! All plants need nitrogen to grow, but they can't get it from the air. They have to soak it up from the soil. Farmers add nitrogen fertilizers to the soil to help crops grow better, and hydrogen gas is vital for making these fertilizers. It's used to grab nitrogen from the air and trap it in a form that plants can use.

When hydrogen reacts with oxygen, the elements combine to form water. This **reaction** releases lots of energy. So much energy, that an exploding mixture of hydrogen and oxygen can even blast a rocket into space! Liquid hydrogen can also be burned in engines or used in fuel cells to power cars, buses, and trains. The only waste product is clean water, so if we can find an energy-efficient way to make and store pure hydrogen, it could be the fuel of the future.

SECRET CHEMISTRY

Hydrogen atoms are the smallest and simplest atoms of all—each one is just a **proton**, orbited by an **electron**. These atoms like to cling together in pairs, so hydrogen gas is not very reactive at room temperature—only when heated!

INSIDE THE ATOM

— 1   ⊕ 1   ◯ 0

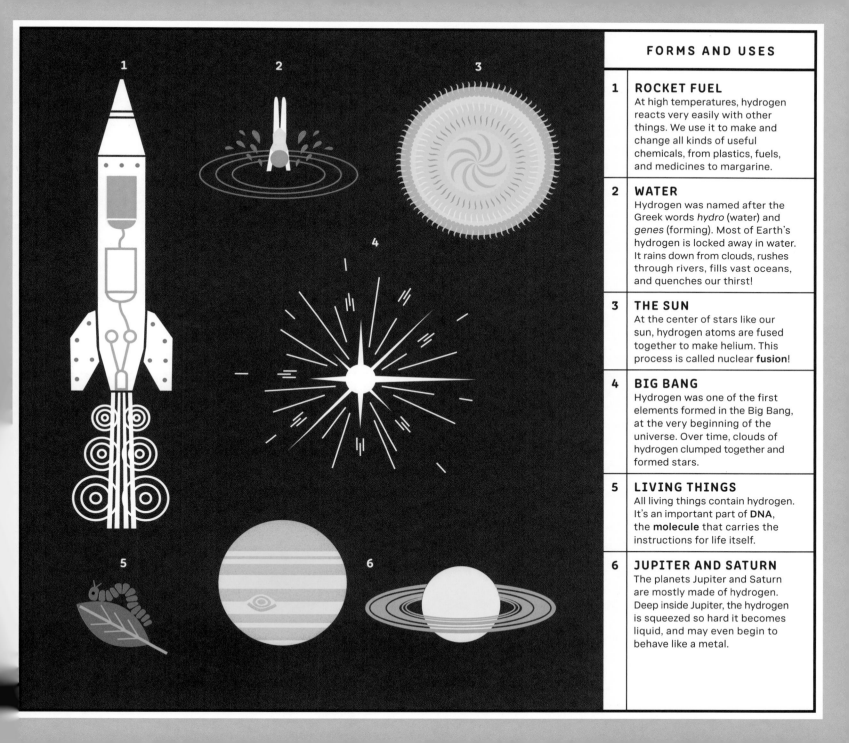

FORMS AND USES

1 ROCKET FUEL
At high temperatures, hydrogen reacts very easily with other things. We use it to make and change all kinds of useful chemicals, from plastics, fuels, and medicines to margarine.

2 WATER
Hydrogen was named after the Greek words *hydro* (water) and *genes* (forming). Most of Earth's hydrogen is locked away in water. It rains down from clouds, rushes through rivers, fills vast oceans, and quenches our thirst!

3 THE SUN
At the center of stars like our sun, hydrogen atoms are fused together to make helium. This process is called nuclear **fusion**!

4 BIG BANG
Hydrogen was one of the first elements formed in the Big Bang, at the very beginning of the universe. Over time, clouds of hydrogen clumped together and formed stars.

5 LIVING THINGS
All living things contain hydrogen. It's an important part of **DNA**, the **molecule** that carries the instructions for life itself.

6 JUPITER AND SATURN
The planets Jupiter and Saturn are mostly made of hydrogen. Deep inside Jupiter, the hydrogen is squeezed so hard it becomes liquid, and may even begin to behave like a metal.

  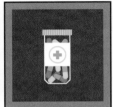

			3		
			Li		
			Lithium		

 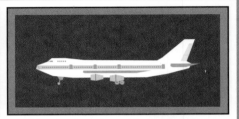

 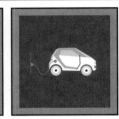

			11		
			Na		
			Sodium		

 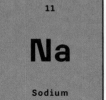 

			19		
			K		
			Potassium		

			37		
			Rb		
			Rubidium		

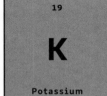 

 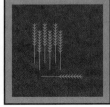 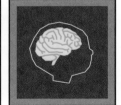

			55		
			Cs		
			Cesium		

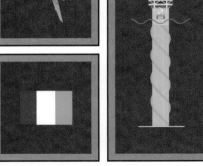 

			87		
			Fr		
			Francium		

  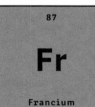

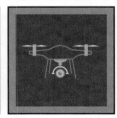  

Alkali Metals

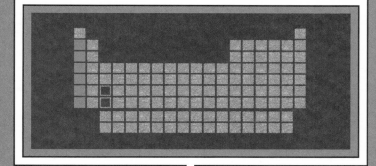

THE **ALKALI** METALS ARE ALL HIGHLY REACTIVE. ALTHOUGH THEIR REACTIVITY MEANS WE RARELY SEE THEM AS PURE METALS, TWO OF THE ALKALI METALS ARE VITAL BUILDING BLOCKS OF OUR BODIES.

The metals that form group 1 of the periodic table are known as the alkali metals. Each alkali metal has atoms with just one outer **electron**, which means they react very easily with all kinds of other substances. A single drop of water is enough to make most of the alkali metals explode into flames! Each one burns with flames of a different color.

This reactivity means that we never find pure alkali metals in nature. Instead, they're most often joined with non-metals, as part of **compounds** called **salts**. The best-known salt is the sodium chloride we sprinkle on food, but there are dozens of others. When these salts are dissolved in water, the liquid becomes **alkaline** (the opposite of **acidic**). This is how the alkali metals got their name.

Because the alkali metals are so reactive, they were only discovered quite recently. The chemist Humphry Davy discovered potassium and sodium in 1807, by passing **electricity** through salts to separate the metal from the non-metal. This is called electrolysis. Lithium was first discovered in 1817, but it clung so tightly to other substances that it took decades before anyone managed to separate the pure metal from its salts. Cesium and rubidium were discovered in 1860 and 1861, using a totally different method. When Dmitri Mendeleev made his first periodic table in 1869, he predicted that there must be a sixth alkali metal. This gap was finally filled in 1939, when Marguerite Perey discovered francium.

Potassium and sodium are needed by almost every living thing. Plants soak these elements up from the soil, and animals have to eat them. Humans have found hundreds of other uses for the alkali metals too.

Lithium
(LITH-EE-UM)

3
Li

ALKALI METAL

LITHIUM IS THE LIGHTEST METAL. IT IS A KEY INGREDIENT IN MANY OF THE WORLD'S BATTERY-POWERED GADGETS, FROM SMARTPHONES TO ELECTRIC CARS.

KEY PROPERTIES

- solid
- silvery-white metal
- very soft
- floats on water

WHERE IT'S FOUND

- **minerals**: spodumene, petalite, lepidolite
- natural spring waters, **salt** lakes, seawater
- seaweed
- vegetables such as potatoes

HUMAN BODY

TRACE

ALL ABOUT LITHIUM

Lithium is the lightest solid element on Earth. A lump of lithium would feel as light as a piece of cork in your hands. But you'd have to wear protective gloves! Lithium reacts quickly and easily with water, including the water in your skin. This **reaction** releases lots of heat, so just holding lithium can cause burns.

Happily, we have found lots of ways to use lithium safely, in ways that have changed the world! The first cell phones used large, heavy batteries made with nickel, which took hours to charge and were about the height and weight of a large pineapple! When lithium-**ion** batteries were developed in the 1990s and 2000s, they changed everything. Rechargeable lithium-ion batteries are superthin and superlight, making it possible to design digital devices that can fit in a pocket.

Large lithium-ion batteries are also the driving force behind electric vehicles. At least 2 million electric cars are sold every year and they are becoming more popular as people try to use fewer fossil fuels. By 2040, it is estimated that more than 500 million electric vehicles will be zooming around the world's roads. Almost 40% of the lithium produced each year is already used to make batteries, and demand is increasing all the time.

SECRET CHEMISTRY

The **alkali** metals are special because their atoms only have one **electron** in their outermost **shell**. These outer electrons can easily break free, making lithium a good **conductor**. **Electricity** is just electrons breaking free from their atoms and flowing from place to place.

INSIDE THE ATOM

● 3 ● 3 ○ 4

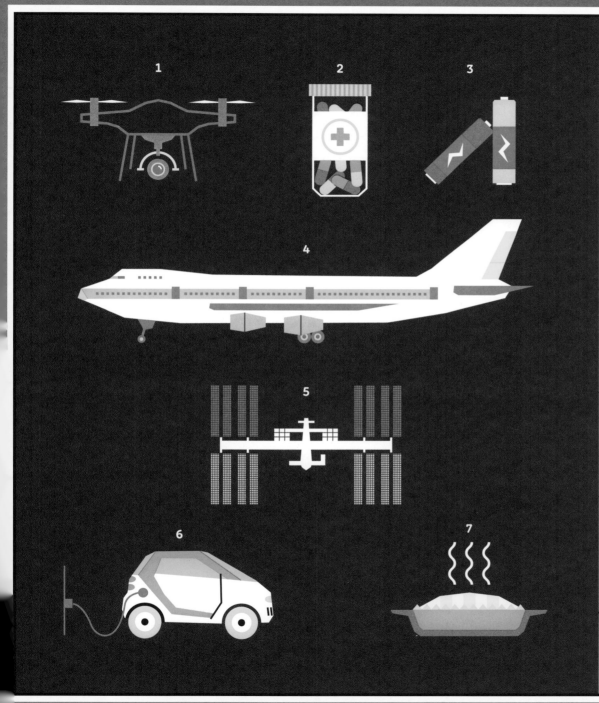

FORMS AND USES

1 LIGHTWEIGHT BATTERY
Lithium is the lightest metal in the universe. Lithium-ion batteries are used in all kinds of devices that need to be light, from cell phones and laptops to drones.

2 MAKING MEDICINES
Lithium carbonate is an important medicine for treating bipolar disorder. This mental health illness affects 1 in every 100 people.

3 PORTABLE POWER
The regular AA and AAA batteries in toys and gadgets also use lithium metal.

4 FLYING GIANTS
Adding a small amount of lithium to aluminum creates an **alloy** that's stronger and lighter than pure aluminum. It's used to make jumbo jets, which need to be as light as possible to use less fuel.

5 SPACE STATION
Lithium hydroxide is carried on board the International Space Station. It reacts with the carbon dioxide breathed out by astronauts, soaking it up to keep the air fresh and safe.

6 ELECTRIC CARS
Even a small electric car battery contains about 9 pounds of lithium. Most lithium is extracted from salty lakes. Scientists are finding out how to extract it from seawater—around 220 billion tons of lithium are dissolved in the world's oceans.

7 TOUGH GLASS
Lithium is also added to glass ceramics to make them less likely to crack when they are heated or cooled.

Sodium

(SO-DEE-UM)

11
Na

ALKALI METAL

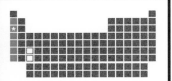

WE NEED TO EAT OR DRINK SODIUM TO SURVIVE, BUT SUBSTANCES CONTAINING SODIUM CAN ALSO BE VERY DANGEROUS!

KEY PROPERTIES

- solid
- silvery-white metal
- very soft
- floats on oil
- compounds taste salty

WHERE IT'S FOUND

- **minerals**: rock **salt**
- seawater (about 1.05%)
- meteorites
- living things
- table salt

HUMAN BODY

0.2%

ALL ABOUT SODIUM

Sodium is the sixth most common element on Earth, and there's more of it in Earth's crust than all the other **alkali** metals put together! But because it's so reactive, we don't see the pure metal in nature. Sodium is most often found combined with non-metals, in **compounds** called salts. The best-known is sodium chloride (NaCl)—the salt that we add to food. It's also the main type of salt dissolved in the world's seas and oceans. The sodium in seawater comes from rocks on land. It dissolves in water that flows across the rocks on its way to the ocean.

Sodium plays a vital role in our muscles, and in sending electrical and chemical signals zipping around our bodies. We need to eat or drink a little salt every day, to top up the sodium we lose through our sweat and urine. However, too much salt can be dangerous because it raises our blood pressure, making our heart have to work harder. We've found lots of other ways to use sodium salts too. The Ancient Egyptians collected crystals of sodium carbonate, a compound often referred to as "washing soda," that were left behind when floodwater in the Natron Valley dried up. They used this salt for cleaning, as well as for mummifying important people and animals! The Ancient Romans called soda "natrium," which is where sodium's symbol, Na, comes from. Sodium salts are still used for making soaps and detergents, and a host of other everyday things, such as glass, paper, and fabrics.

SECRET CHEMISTRY

Pure sodium metal reacts very easily with oxygen and other non-metals. It will even grab hold of non-metal atoms that are *already* joined to a less reactive metal (such as silicon or titanium). This means sodium can be used to separate these metals from the rocks they are found in.

INSIDE THE ATOM

● 11 ⊕ 11 ○ 12

FORMS AND USES

1 **PAPER MAKING**
Sodium hydroxide is used to help clean ink off used paper so it can be recycled back into new paper.

2 **KEY INGREDIENT**
We can thank sodium for many of our favorite treats, from salty popcorn to the sodium bicarbonate used to make cakes rise and to put the fizz in fizzy drinks!

3 **ESSENTIAL ELEMENT**
All animals need sodium to survive. In the Amazon in Peru, hundreds of macaws gather on cliffs to eat the salty clay, to top up the sodium in their diet.

4 **IN DEMAND**
Around 275 million tons of sodium chloride salt is produced every year, including sea salt, made by evaporating sea water, and rock salt from minerals. About a fifth is used in food making, but it's in demand from other industries too, especially for making chemicals.

5 **CAUSTIC CHEMICALS**
Sodium hydroxide, or "caustic soda," is a very useful substance. It's used to make the strong cleaning products that can unblock drains. Sodium hydroxide breaks up proteins, so it's very dangerous.

6 **KEEPING CLEAN**
Sodium carbonate is still one of the main ingredients in soaps and detergents. It's also used to treat dirty water.

Potassium
(POH-TASS-EE-UM)

ALKALI METAL

PLANTS AND PEOPLE NEED POTASSIUM TO LIVE. BUT TOO MUCH OF IT CAN STOP MUSCLES FROM WORKING—WHICH IS HOW A SCORPION'S POTASSIUM-RICH VENOM WORKS!

KEY PROPERTIES

- solid
- silvery-white metal
- very soft
- floats on water
- potassium chloride tastes salty and bitter

WHERE IT'S FOUND

- **minerals**: sylvite, carnallite, alunite
- shale
- seawater (especially the Dead Sea)
- plants and animals

HUMAN BODY

0.4%

ALL ABOUT POTASSIUM

Thousands of years ago, people began using a mineral **salt** called potash for all sorts of things, including making soap, glass, fertilizers, and even gunpowder. They got hold of potash by burning wood and soaking the ashes in a pot of water. However, no one knew what potash was actually made of until the early 1800s, when a chemist named Humphry Davy passed an **electric current** through potash and saw tiny blobs of metal appear. He called the new metal potassium, after potash.

Potash forms when wood burns because there is lots of potassium in plants. In fact, plants can't grow properly without it. Animals need potassium too. It does lots of different jobs in our bodies, working alongside sodium to control water levels and carry electrical signals through our nerves and muscles. But we can't store potassium. As with sodium, it's constantly leaving our bodies in our sweat and urine. This means we have to eat potassium every day, in foods such as bananas, dried fruits, tomato puree, potatoes, and lentils. However, too much potassium can be **toxic**. While eating several grams of sodium chloride at once might make a person sick, a similar-sized dose of potassium salts could stop muscles working and cause a heart attack. This is exactly how some animal venoms work.

SECRET CHEMISTRY

When potassium is dropped into water, it scoots around the surface, burning with a pale purple flame! Like all **alkali** metals, potassium reacts easily with the oxygen in water, setting the hydrogen free. This **reaction** releases heat, so the escaping hydrogen immediately catches fire.

INSIDE THE ATOM

● 19 ⊕ 19 ○ 20

FORMS AND USES

1 BREATHING APPARATUS
Potassium superoxide can release lots of oxygen in one go. It's carried in submarines, mines, and spacecraft for emergencies.

2 CLOUD-SEEDING
When potassium iodide is sprayed into clouds by rockets, drones, or aircraft, it freezes into ice crystals, which grow into water droplets and trigger rain or snow. "Cloud-seeding" has been used in droughts, and to make rain fall ahead of sporting events.

3 SCORPION VENOM
Scorpion venom contains potassium salts and a protein that stops potassium moving in and out of our **cells**. The effect is the same as eating too much potassium—it paralyzes muscles, including the heart.

4 BACKGROUND RADIATION
All potassium includes a tiny amount (0.012%) of **radioactive** potassium-40, so bananas (like all plants and animals) are a little bit radioactive!

5 FERTILIZING CROPS
When plants die and **decay**, the potassium inside returns to the soil so it can be used by new plants. Modern farming stops this from happening (because we take the crops away from the field). Most of the potassium produced each year is used to make fertilizers, to replace the lost potassium.

6 CLEANING PRODUCTS
Potassium salts are still used to make liquid soaps and detergents.

Rubidium
(ROO-BID-EE-UM)

ALKALI METAL

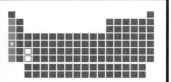

RUBIDIUM IS A SOFT METAL THAT MELTS AS EASILY AS CHOCOLATE. THERE'S MORE OF IT ON EARTH THAN COPPER OR LEAD, BUT IT'S RARELY USED.

KEY PROPERTIES

- solid
- silvery-white metal
- very soft

WHERE IT'S FOUND

- **minerals**: lepidolite, pollucite, carnallite
- seawater
- soils
- soya beans
- grass

HUMAN BODY

TRACE

ALL ABOUT RUBIDIUM

As scientists raced to fill gaps in the periodic table, mineral water was a good place to hunt for missing elements. Mineral water is rain that has trickled through underground rocks, dissolving minerals as it goes. Robert Bunsen and Gustav Kirchhoff boiled tens of thousands of gallons of mineral water from Germany. The water evaporated and the dissolved minerals were left behind. To find out what elements these minerals contained, Bunsen and Kirchhoff used flame **spectroscopy**. A year earlier, they had discovered that every element burns with a different-colored flame. By burning minerals and analyzing the light from the flames, they could work out exactly which elements were present. They spotted two lines of deep red light, which they had never seen before. This told them that there was a brand-new element in the mix. They named this new element rubidium after *rubidus*, the Latin word meaning ruby red.

A tiny amount of rubidium is produced each year, but it's hard to find ways to use it. It can be used to make atomic clocks, but cesium atomic clocks are more accurate (see page 30). However, rubidium finally hit the headlines when it was used in the coldest chemical **reaction** ever. A team of scientists cooled potassium-rubidium gas down almost to absolute zero (the temperature when atoms simply stop). At this temperature, **particles** move slowly instead of whizzing around. This made it possible for the scientists to watch a chemical reaction in slow motion. Rubidium was a good choice because its large atoms are easy to push around and herd into the right place using lasers!

SECRET CHEMISTRY

Rubidium has to be kept in grease or oil, because it bursts into flames as soon as it touches air. If there is any water around, the reaction is even more violent!

INSIDE THE ATOM

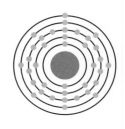

● 37   ⊕ 37   ○ 48

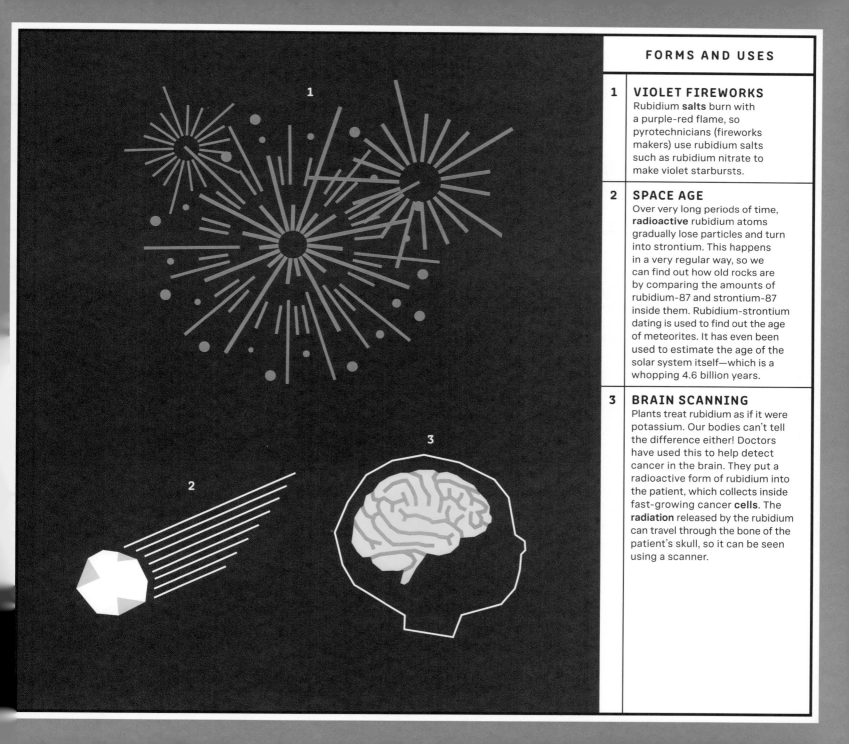

FORMS AND USES

1 VIOLET FIREWORKS
Rubidium **salts** burn with a purple-red flame, so pyrotechnicians (fireworks makers) use rubidium salts such as rubidium nitrate to make violet starbursts.

2 SPACE AGE
Over very long periods of time, **radioactive** rubidium atoms gradually lose particles and turn into strontium. This happens in a very regular way, so we can find out how old rocks are by comparing the amounts of rubidium-87 and strontium-87 inside them. Rubidium-strontium dating is used to find out the age of meteorites. It has even been used to estimate the age of the solar system itself—which is a whopping 4.6 billion years.

3 BRAIN SCANNING
Plants treat rubidium as if it were potassium. Our bodies can't tell the difference either! Doctors have used this to help detect cancer in the brain. They put a radioactive form of rubidium into the patient, which collects inside fast-growing cancer **cells**. The **radiation** released by the rubidium can travel through the bone of the patient's skull, so it can be seen using a scanner.

55

Cs

Cesium
(SEE-ZEE-UM)

ALKALI METAL

CESIUM METAL IS AS SOFT AS WAX, BUT ITS HEAVY, UNSHAKEABLE ATOMS HELP TO KEEP THE WORLD RUNNING ON TIME.

KEY PROPERTIES

- solid
- silvery-gold metal
- softest solid element
- melts in a warm room

WHERE IT'S FOUND

- **minerals**: pollucite, lepidolite
- **rocks**: traces in granite and **sedimentary rocks**

HUMAN BODY

TRACE

ALL ABOUT CESIUM

When cesium is burned, the colored light it gives out can be split into a rainbow, which includes two bright blue lines. This is why cesium was named after the Latin word for sky blue. Not much cesium is mined each year, but it's famous for making the world's most accurate clocks. All clocks work by counting something that moves in a regular way, such as a swinging pendulum. Atomic clocks count the natural vibrations of cesium atoms. These atoms vibrate exactly 9,192,631,770 times in one second. The atomic clock uses this fact to measure time. Cesium atomic clocks are so accurate that if they had been set when the first dinosaurs were alive, they would still be telling the right time now, hundreds of millions of years later!

All atoms vibrate, but cesium atoms are very heavy and stable, so their wobble is not affected by any nearby **electricity** or **magnets**. In fact, cesium atoms are so stable, scientists hope that they might one day help to solve a big mystery. So far, we have only been able to detect about 5% of all the energy and matter in the universe. The rest is known as "dark" energy and matter because we can't see it! The vibration of cesium atoms isn't affected by any of the types of energy or matter we know about, so any unexpected "wobbles" could be a clue about what dark energy is and does.

SECRET CHEMISTRY

A lump of cesium would react with oxygen in the air to form CsO_2 (cesium superoxide), which is dangerously explosive. To stop this from happening, cesium is stored in a gas or liquid that doesn't react easily, such as nitrogen.

INSIDE THE ATOM

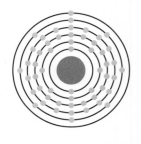

● 55 ⊕ 55 ○ 78

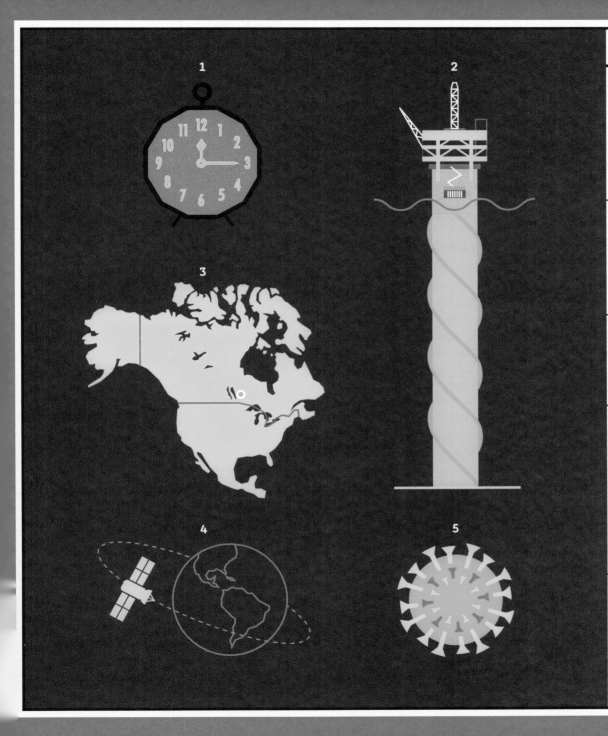

FORMS AND USES

1 SETTING THE TIME
Cesium atomic clocks are used to set Coordinated Universal Time (UTC), which is used to sync the internet, electricity supply, GPS systems, and communication around the world. We can't keep atomic clocks in our homes, but we set our own clocks by them.

2 DRILLING FOR OIL
When cesium formate is dissolved in water, it makes a gloopy liquid. This is used to help wash drilled rock out of the way when drilling huge holes in the earth. Most of the cesium produced each year is used to make drilling fluids like this.

3 RARE ELEMENT
Cesium is expensive because it's very rare. Most of the world's cesium comes from one pollucite mine in the rock beneath a lake in Canada.

4 STEERING SATELLITES
Some satellites have cesium "**ion** engines." Instead of using a blast of exhaust gases to change direction, these tiny thrusters use a jet of cesium atoms. Ion engines are also used to propel space probes on long journeys. The force of the atoms is small, but over long periods of time and with no friction in space, they can get a spacecraft traveling at more than 200,000 miles per hour!

5 STUDYING VIRUSES
When scientists want to separate a mixture of incredibly tiny things, they use a process called centrifugation. Cesium chloride can be used in a type of centrifugation that can separate viruses from **cells** in order to study them.

87

Fr

Francium
(FRAN-SEE-UM)

ALKALI METAL

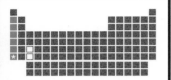

FRANCIUM IS THE SECOND RAREST ELEMENT. IF YOU COLLECTED ALL THE FRANCIUM ON THE PLANET RIGHT NOW, IT WOULD WEIGH ABOUT AS MUCH AS A SMALL BAG OF POTATO CHIPS!

KEY PROPERTIES

- solid
- most other properties unknown

WHERE IT'S FOUND

- a few atoms of francium are found in **minerals** that contain uranium, such as pitchblende

HUMAN BODY

NONE

ALL ABOUT FRANCIUM

When Dmitri Mendeleev made the first periodic table, he left gaps for elements yet to be discovered. Scientists raced to find them and one by one, most gaps were filled. But after 60 years had passed, there was still no trace of the mystery element 87, the last **alkali** metal of group 1. Every time a scientist claimed to find element 87, it turned out to be a false alarm.

In 1939, a lab assistant named Marguerite Perey made a sample of what she thought was pure actinium (see page 186) and noticed something strange. The sample was much more **radioactive** than actinium should be. Marguerite carried out careful tests to show the extra **radiation** must be coming from a second, even more radioactive element. She proved that this element must be element 87.

It was impossible for Marguerite to collect pure francium in a bottle or test tube. Atoms of francium are only made when a tiny **particle** of two **protons** and two **neutrons** breaks away from an actinium atom. This only happens to one in every 100 actinium atoms! Even when a francium atom is made it keeps on losing particles, quickly changing into different elements. This is why Earth's crust always contains less than 25 grams—about the weight of a small bag of potato chips— of francium at a time. It's impossible to collect francium from rocks, so scientists have to create it in a lab— usually by smashing smaller atoms together. They have to trap the francium atoms and study them quickly—in just a few minutes, they will disappear.

SECRET CHEMISTRY

We don't know much about francium, but we can get clues by looking at other alkali metals in the same group of the periodic table. This tells us that francium would probably react so quickly with water or air that it would explode!

INSIDE THE ATOM

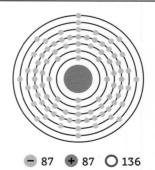

− 87   + 87   ○ 136

1 MAKING FRANCIUM

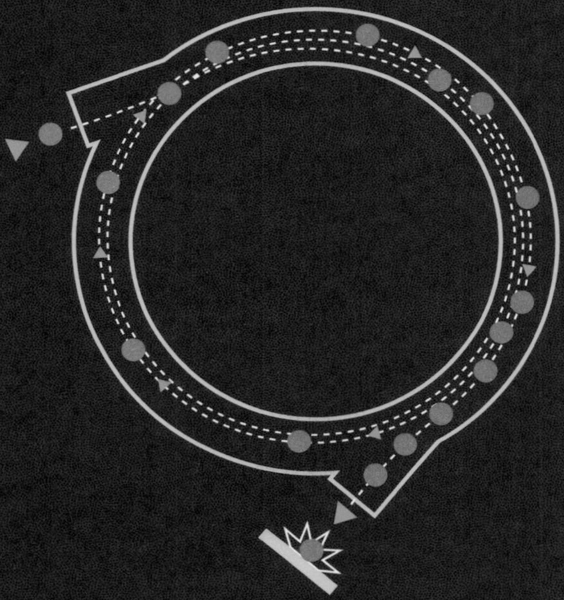

Today, francium is produced using **particle accelerators**—huge scientific instruments that use strong electrical currents and **magnetic fields** to get tiny particles traveling at very high speeds. The high-speed particles can be aimed at a target of other particles. When they collide, new substances may be formed. One team of scientists has collected several thousand francium atoms in the same place for long enough to notice that they glow with **radioactivity**. They hope that studying francium will help them to understand radioactive atoms better.

2 BREAKING APART

The type of francium that Marguerite found is called francium-223. It **decays** so quickly that after 22 minutes, half of it has changed into radium or astatine. We say that the **half-life** of francium-223 is 22 minutes. Other types of francium disappear even more quickly than this!

3 NAMED AFTER FRANCE

Marguerite Perey named the alkali metal she discovered francium, after France.

4 DANGEROUS ELEMENT

Marguerite was trained by Marie Curie (see page 46) and like Marie, she died of cancer caused by working so closely with radioactive elements.

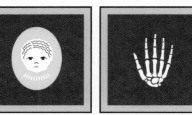

4

Be

Beryllium

12

Mg

Magnesium

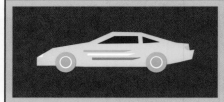

20

Ca

Calcium

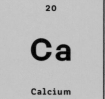

38

Sr

Strontium

56

Ba

Barium

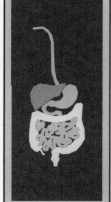

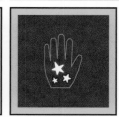

88

Ra

Radium

Alkaline Earth Metals

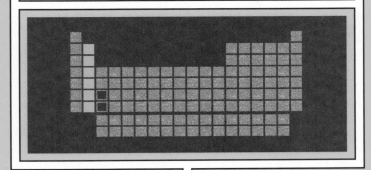

THE ALKALINE EARTH METALS ARE VERY IMPORTANT IN MEDICINE. THEY INCLUDE TWO OF THE MOST IMPORTANT ELEMENTS IN THE HUMAN BODY, AS WELL AS TWO ELEMENTS USED TO DIAGNOSE DISEASE AND SAVE THOUSANDS OF LIVES EVERY YEAR.

The elements in group 2 of the periodic table are known as the alkaline earth metals. Their atoms each have two outer **electrons**, which they're quite happy to give up. This means these metals react easily with other elements, but a little less violently than the **alkali** metals of group 1. All of the alkaline earth metals are found in the natural world, but never as pure metals. When alkaline earth metals react with non-metal elements they form **compounds** called **salts**, which can be more useful than the pure metals themselves. These salts dissolve in water to form alkaline liquids, which is how the alkaline earth metals got their name.

Although they react with other elements in a similar way, each element in this group is unique and useful to humans in different ways. Beryllium is rare and **toxic**, but magnesium and calcium are some of the most common elements on the planet and a major part of almost every living thing. Strontium is rare and hard to find, but can be made in **nuclear power** plants, and is used for treating certain types of cancer. Barium compounds are an important part of a doctor's toolkit, used to help diagnose digestive diseases. Radium was added to the group after it was discovered by Marie and Pierre Curie in 1898. This discovery helped scientists to understand **radioactivity** and atoms better, leading to the science of nuclear physics that has changed the world in ways both good and bad.

Beryllium
(BUH-RIL-EE-UM)

4

Be

ALKALINE EARTH METAL

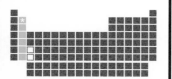

MOST BERYLLIUM IS USED TO MAKE **ALLOYS** OF BERYLLIUM AND COPPER, WHICH HAVE HUNDREDS OF DIFFERENT USES.

KEY PROPERTIES

- solid
- silvery-white metal
- sweet-tasting but **toxic salts**

WHERE IT'S FOUND

- **minerals:** beryl, bertrandite
- gemstones: emerald, aquamarine
- dust in air
- water
- soil

HUMAN BODY

TRACE

ALL ABOUT BERYLLIUM

Unlike most elements, beryllium isn't produced in burning or dying stars. Instead, most beryllium is made in the space between stars, when cosmic rays (tiny **particles** traveling at tremendous speeds) collide with atoms of other elements. Earth has a strong **magnetic field** that acts as a shield against cosmic rays. This means beryllium is rare on Earth. Sometimes the magnetic field becomes weaker for a while, and a little more beryllium gets made as cosmic rays collide with particles in Earth's atmosphere. By measuring how much beryllium is trapped in ancient ice, scientists can tell how strong Earth's magnetic field was in the past!

Beryllium has a very low **density**—its atoms are not packed very closely together, and many types of **radiation** zoom straight through the metal as if it wasn't there. Although beryllium is the fourth-lightest element, it's also very strong. It has to get incredibly hot before it melts or begins reacting with air or water. These properties are very useful, but many beryllium **compounds** are highly toxic to humans, and it can cause bad allergic reactions. Today beryllium is mainly used where there are no alternatives, or in space, where there are no people around! For example, the giant mirror of the James Webb Space Telescope is made from beryllium—not only because the metal is strong and light, but because it doesn't change shape when it gets very cold. The huge mirror allows the telescope to peer at the most distant galaxies we can see from Earth.

SECRET CHEMISTRY

James Chadwick discovered that when beryllium was put near a **radioactive** element that bombarded it with radiation, it released a type of particle not seen before. He had discovered **neutrons**, one of the building blocks of atoms. Beryllium is still used to produce a supply of neutrons for scientific research.

INSIDE THE ATOM

– 4   + 4   ○ 5

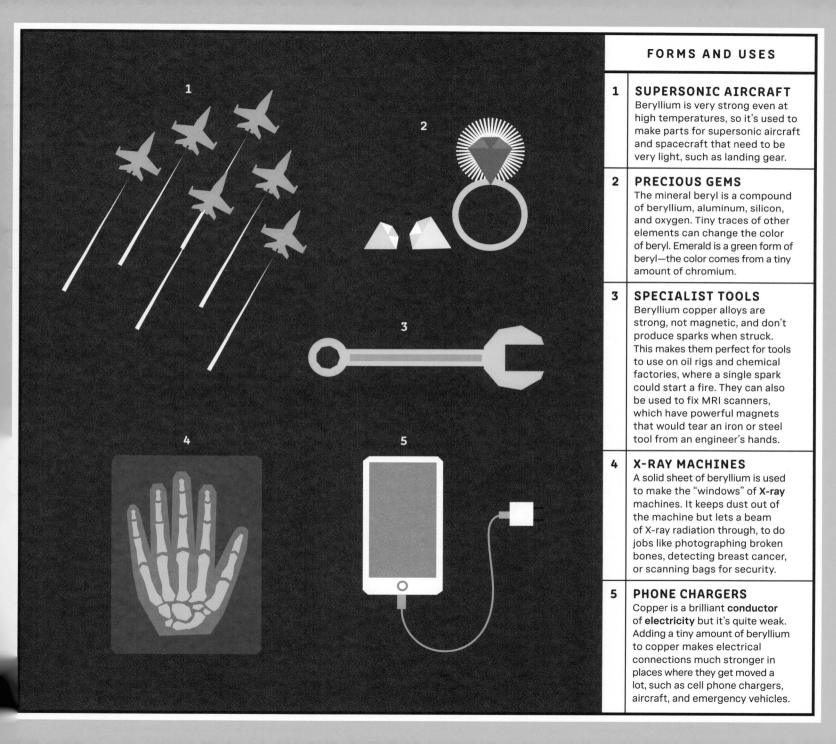

FORMS AND USES

1 SUPERSONIC AIRCRAFT
Beryllium is very strong even at high temperatures, so it's used to make parts for supersonic aircraft and spacecraft that need to be very light, such as landing gear.

2 PRECIOUS GEMS
The mineral beryl is a compound of beryllium, aluminum, silicon, and oxygen. Tiny traces of other elements can change the color of beryl. Emerald is a green form of beryl—the color comes from a tiny amount of chromium.

3 SPECIALIST TOOLS
Beryllium copper alloys are strong, not magnetic, and don't produce sparks when struck. This makes them perfect for tools to use on oil rigs and chemical factories, where a single spark could start a fire. They can also be used to fix MRI scanners, which have powerful magnets that would tear an iron or steel tool from an engineer's hands.

4 X-RAY MACHINES
A solid sheet of beryllium is used to make the "windows" of **X-ray** machines. It keeps dust out of the machine but lets a beam of X-ray radiation through, to do jobs like photographing broken bones, detecting breast cancer, or scanning bags for security.

5 PHONE CHARGERS
Copper is a brilliant **conductor** of **electricity** but it's quite weak. Adding a tiny amount of beryllium to copper makes electrical connections much stronger in places where they get moved a lot, such as cell phone chargers, aircraft, and emergency vehicles.

Magnesium

(MAG-NEE-ZEE-UM)

12

Mg

ALKALINE EARTH METAL

FROM THE SMALLEST **MICROBE** TO THE BIGGEST BLUE WHALE, ALMOST EVERY LIVING THING RELIES ON MAGNESIUM.

KEY PROPERTIES

- solid
- silvery-white metal
- fairly soft, lightweight
- **ductile, malleable**
- forms bitter-tasting **salts**

WHERE IT'S FOUND

- **minerals**: magnesite, magnesia, dolomite
- soil
- plants and animals
- seawater
- meteorites

HUMAN BODY

 0.04%

ALL ABOUT MAGNESIUM

Without magnesium, there would be no food on Earth. This element is a vital part of **chlorophyll**, a substance in plants and algae that uses sunlight energy to turn carbon dioxide and water into food. This process is called **photosynthesis**. Plants make food so they can use it for energy themselves, but it's also passed on to animals, including humans. All the energy in our food ultimately comes from photosynthesis. We also need to eat a little magnesium itself for our bodies to work properly. The element does more than 300 different jobs in our bodies, including controlling the amount of calcium in our bones to keep them strong. If we don't get enough magnesium in our diet we can become very ill. Luckily it's in lots of foods, from chocolate to spinach!

Outside our bodies, magnesium **compounds** are used to make heat-resistant bricks, fertilizers, cattle feed, plastics, and all kinds of other chemicals. Pure magnesium is very useful too. It's a strong and light metal, which isn't **toxic** like beryllium or as reactive as the **alkali** metals. It's also affordable, because there is so much magnesium in rocks and seawater. Magnesium is used in **alloys** with aluminum, to make the bodies of vehicles that need to be both strong and light such as race cars, aircraft, and electric vehicles. Magnesium is also being investigated as a metal for making the batteries of the future. It's cheaper than lithium (see page 22) and easy to recycle, and magnesium batteries may be able to store more power, more safely.

SECRET CHEMISTRY

Although a lump of magnesium is not too reactive, small pieces of the metal can react very quickly with oxygen in the air, burning with a bright white light. If the oxygen is taken away it will begin reacting with nitrogen in the air instead!

INSIDE THE ATOM

– 12 + 12 ○ 12

FORMS AND USES

1 GETTING A GRIP
Gymnasts, weightlifters, and rock climbers rub magnesium carbonate powder on their hands to help them grip. It soaks up sweat and stays dry because it doesn't dissolve in water.

2 ESSENTIAL ELEMENT
Plants get magnesium from the soil through their roots. If they don't get enough, their leaves start to yellow. Magnesium is added to soils in fertilizer.

3 GREEN VEGETABLES
We need to eat around 200 milligrams of magnesium a day. Leafy vegetables are a good source.

4 EVERYDAY METAL
Strong and light, magnesium is used to make many everyday things, including laptops, cameras, and tools. It's also the metal of school pencil sharpeners.

5 SPORTS CARS
Magnesium aluminum alloys are used to make lighter vehicles, which travel farther for every tank of fuel or battery charge.

6 SPARKLERS
Magnesium is the element that makes a sparkler burn brightly. It's also used to make trick candles that relight themselves.

7 SALT LICK
Magnesium is vital for other animals too. A dairy cow needs to eat 30 grams every day to stay healthy. It's hard to get enough grass, so magnesium salts, such as Epsom salts, are added to feed or provided in a block for cows to lick.

20
Ca

Calcium
(CAL-SEE-UM)

ALKALINE EARTH METAL

SUPER-STRONG, METALLIC SKELETONS DON'T ONLY EXIST IN SCI-FI STORIES. THE METAL CALCIUM IS ONE OF THE MAIN BUILDING BLOCKS OF BONES AND TEETH!

KEY PROPERTIES

- solid
- silvery-gray metal
- fairly soft
- **ductile, malleable**
- unique taste

WHERE IT'S FOUND

- **minerals:** calcite, limestone, gypsum
- coral and seashells
- water
- chalky soils
- plants
- stalactites/stalagmites

HUMAN BODY

 1.6%

ALL ABOUT CALCIUM

Calcium is needed by almost every living thing on Earth. Most of the hard, structural parts of animals—skeletons, teeth, seashells, coral, and even the spiky parts of many plants—are built from calcium **compounds**. We use calcium-based materials in all kinds of human-made structures too. A good example of this is limestone, a **sedimentary rock** formed from the calcium carbonate of shells, coral, and other parts of sea creatures. Limestone is one of the most useful rocks in the world. It's used in all kinds of construction work—cut into blocks, crushed into stones, or ground into a powder. Limestone can also be heated to produce lime (calcium oxide). Along with gypsum—another calcium-rich mineral—lime is used to make cement, which in turn is used to make concrete.

Cement and concrete have been seen as wonder-materials ever since the Ancient Romans used them to build their empire. It's so long-lasting and strong under pressure that some of these buildings are still standing, 2,000 years after they were built! The name calcium even comes from *calx*, the Latin word for lime. From roads, bridges, and tunnels to skyscrapers and sewers, concrete has reshaped our planet. However, concrete has a giant carbon footprint, most of which comes from heating limestone to make lime. We also use lime for cleaning water in water treatment plants, making soils less **acidic** so they are better for growing crops, and for making steel. Although pure calcium metal isn't as useful as lime, it is used in some **alloys**, and to help extract other, rarer elements from rocks.

SECRET CHEMISTRY

Calcium may be one of the basic tastes, along with salty, sweet, bitter, sour, and savory. A small amount of calcium may make other flavors taste better!

INSIDE THE ATOM

● 20 ✚ 20 ○ 20

FORMS AND USES

1 STRONG SHELLS
Sea creatures use calcium carbonate to make shells and corals. By touching an empty shell with its antenna, a hermit crab can detect the amount of calcium in it. This tells the crab if the shell is a good choice.

2 ESSENTIAL ELEMENT
We need to eat at least 700 milligrams of calcium every day (children, pregnant women, and older people need more). Dairy foods, leafy greens, red kidney beans, and sardines are all rich in calcium.

3 CONSTRUCTION HERO
Concrete-type materials have been used in buildings since ancient times, including the 1,500-year-old Mayan city of Chichén Itzá. As concrete sets, tiny crystals of a calcium compound form in the gaps, binding the gravel and sand together.

4 BUILDING BONES
Calcium **salts** (such as calcium phosphate) don't dissolve in water very easily. This makes them great for building the bones of living things, which are constantly in contact with water.

5 STINGING NETTLES
Plants can't run away from hungry animals, so many build defenses. More than 200 types of plants use calcium oxalate crystals to form spikes and needles, like the tiny, stinging hairs on nettles.

6 PLASTER CASTS
If we don't eat enough calcium, our bones become weaker and break more easily. Calcium sulfate is used to make casts that set rock hard.

Strontium

38
Sr

(STRON-CHEE-UM)

ALKALINE EARTH METAL

STRONTIUM IS THE SECRET BEHIND COSMIC FIREWORKS AND GLOWING STARS, BOTH IN SPACE AND DOWN HERE ON EARTH!

KEY PROPERTIES

- solid
- silvery-gray metal
- fairly soft
- **malleable**
- **ductile**

WHERE IT'S FOUND

- **minerals**: celestite, strontianite
- plants
- seashells and corals
- seawater
- forest and desert soils

HUMAN BODY

TRACE

ALL ABOUT STRONTIUM

The **alkaline** earth metals are reactive metals, happily combining with all sorts of different elements to form **compounds**. This means that most alkaline earth metals are found in lots of different rocks and minerals. Strontium is different. It's mainly found in just two minerals—celestite and strontianite, a mineral named after the Scottish town of Strontian, where it was first discovered. Some deep-sea creatures and corals need strontium to make the hard parts of their bodies, so it's often added to aquarium water. Humans don't need strontium, but it's found in plants so we end up eating quite a bit. High levels of strontium in the skeletons of Roman gladiators even give us a clue about their diets, telling us that they ate mainly vegetables!

Normal strontium isn't harmful, but a **radioactive** form called strontium-90 is very dangerous. It's made when uranium atoms are split apart to release energy in a **nuclear power** plant. In the past it has been released into the atmosphere when nuclear weapons were tested or by accidents at nuclear power plants. The **radiation** that it gives out is very harmful, stopping our **cells** from working properly. However, strontium-90 can also be used to help humans. Doctors use a tiny amount to kill cancer cells that have spread into a patient's bones. The energy released by strontium-90 can also be used as a source of power in remote places with no access to an **electricity** source, such as weather stations, lighthouses, and spacecraft.

SECRET CHEMISTRY

Our bodies treat strontium as if it were calcium. This is what makes radioactive strontium-90 so dangerous. It's used as a building block for bones and stays inside a person for years, all the while releasing harmful radiation.

INSIDE THE ATOM

— 38 + 38 O 50

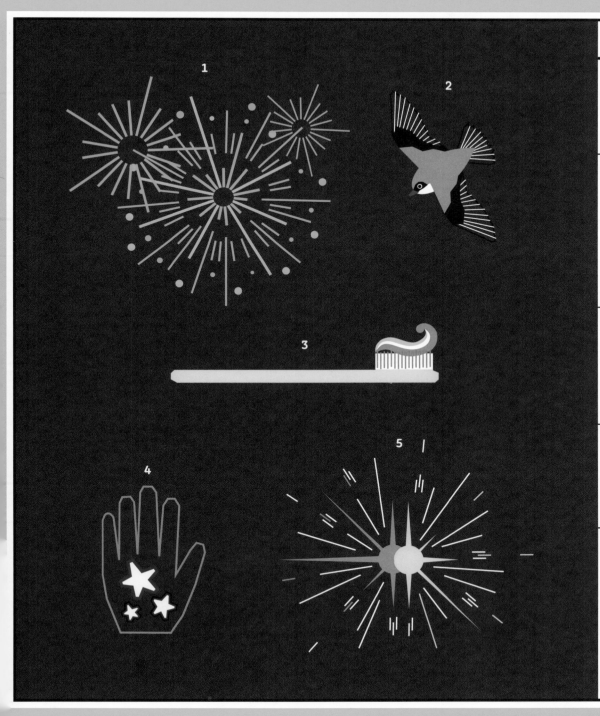

FORMS AND USES

1 GLOWING SKIES
Strontium **salts** (strontium combined with a non-metal, such as strontium nitrate) burn with a red glow. This is used in fireworks and flares.

2 FEATHERY CLUES
A different mix of strontium **isotopes** is found in different places. By looking at the mix of strontium isotopes in a bird's feathers, scientists can tell exactly where that bird has migrated from. Collecting feathers is much easier than trying to tag and track birds as they fly around the planet.

3 CALMING TEETH
Toothpastes for sensitive teeth sometimes contain a version of strontium chloride. It forms a barrier over tiny holes in teeth, stopping hot or cold food and drinks from activating nerves inside the teeth.

4 GLOW-IN-THE-DARK
Glow-in-the-dark paint and stickers can be made from powdered strontium aluminate. It absorbs **UV** light energy and releases it as soft, green light over several hours.

5 STAR ORIGINS
Astronomers recently spotted that strontium was created when two super-dense stars smashed into each other, in a galaxy far away. This is exciting because it helps to explain how certain elements are formed that were not made during the Big Bang or inside burning stars.

56
Ba

Barium
(BEAR-EE-UM)

ALKALINE EARTH METAL

SOME BARIUM **SALTS** ARE SO **TOXIC** THEY COULD KILL A PERSON IN MINUTES. OTHERS ARE SAFE TO EAT, AND HELP DOCTORS TO DIAGNOSE THOUSANDS OF PATIENTS EVERY DAY.

KEY PROPERTIES

- solid, fairly **malleable**
- silvery-gray metal
- barium sulfate tastes chalky and nasty

WHERE IT'S FOUND

- **minerals**: barite, witherite
- seaweed
- plants (and their ash)
- Brazil nuts
- soils
- seawater
- ocean floor sediments

HUMAN BODY

TRACE

ALL ABOUT BARIUM

An adult's body contains about 24 milligrams of barium (the weight of six sesame seeds), and although we don't need it, it does no harm. However, salts of this element that dissolve in water can be very toxic—they are even used to make rat poison. Barium salts that don't dissolve in water can be eaten safely. Because they don't dissolve, they will travel straight through the body and out the other end! This property is used by doctors to help take **X-rays** of a patient's digestive system. X-rays usually pass straight through the squidgy bits of our bodies, so the patient is given a dose of safe barium salts to eat or drink. While they're inside the digestive system, the dense salts block the path of X-rays just like bones do.

Although minerals that contain barium seem dense—the element is named after *barys*, the Greek word for heavy—the pure metal itself is strangely light. In your hand, a lump of barium would weigh half as much as a lump of iron the same size. However, there are not many uses for the pure metal. Barium salts (barium combined with one or more non-metals) are far more useful. Barium carbonate and barium fluoride are used to make useful chemicals, and special types of glass and ceramics. Barium sulfate is used to make paints, pigments, and coatings. A coating of barium sulfate is even used to help protect very old fresco paintings on walls. The barium sulfate forms a tough, see-through coating over the painting that refuses to dissolve in water. It protects the paints underneath from water in the air.

SECRET CHEMISTRY

Barium can help us to get copper out of the rocks it's found in. The barium reacts with any oxygen atoms, wrestling them away from copper atoms, leaving pure copper behind.

INSIDE THE ATOM

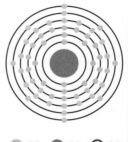

— 56 + 56 ○ 82

FORMS AND USES

1 GREEN FIREWORKS
Barium salts such as barium nitrate are used to give a green glow to fireworks and flares. However, barium nitrate is toxic to humans and other wildlife, so fireworks makers are searching for alternatives.

2 WHITE PAINT
Barium sulfate reflects light very well, so it has been used to make pure white paints and coatings for hundreds of years. It feels very smooth to the touch, so it's also used in some cosmetics to disguise spots and wrinkles.

3 MEDICAL HERO
A "barium meal" or "barium swallow" helps doctors to take a picture of any blockages in a patient's intestines.

4 GREEN ALGAE
Although barium is toxic to most living things, tiny freshwater algae called desmids need it to grow! They absorb barium from water and store crystals of barium sulfate inside their beautiful, symmetrical bodies. If you have a chance to look at water from a pond, river, or lake under a microscope, you might spot some.

5 SMOOTH SURFACES
A thin layer of barium sulfate is used to coat certain types of paper, to make it smooth and glossy. When these papers are burned, white powdery barium sulfate is left behind.

88
Ra

Radium
(RAY-DEE-UM)

ALKALINE EARTH METAL

THE DISCOVERY OF RADIUM CHANGED THE WORLD FOR GOOD AND FOR BAD, BY HELPING SCIENTISTS TO UNLOCK THE SECRETS OF RADIOACTIVITY.

KEY PROPERTIES

- solid
- silvery-white metal
- no smell or taste

WHERE IT'S FOUND

- plants
- soils
- some groundwater
- **ores** of uranium and phosphates

HUMAN BODY

 TRACE

ALL ABOUT RADIUM

Radioactive elements have unstable atoms, which tend to break apart over time. When an unstable atom breaks apart, some of the energy that was holding the atom together is released in the form of invisible rays and **particles**, known as **radiation**. The radiation can be harmful to living things, including humans, but it can also be useful. The story of radium's discovery is famous because it shows these two sides of radioactivity. It began when the scientists Marie and Pierre Curie noticed that a **mineral** called pitchblende was still giving out invisible radiation, even once the radioactive elements uranium and polonium had been extracted from it. This told them that there must be another highly radioactive, undiscovered element in the pitchblende! They announced their discovery in 1898, and named the new element radium, meaning "ray." Marie decided to try to extract pure radium metal from the pitchblende. It took three years, but from 11 tons of rock they managed to extract 1 milligram of radium—the weight of two grains of sugar.

Radium proved very useful because the strong radiation it gave out could destroy diseased **cells**. Doctors quickly began using tiny needles of radium to destroy cancer cells. This "Curietherapy" was the first step toward today's "radiotherapy" treatments, which save thousands of lives every year. The invisible rays released by radium were also used to kill bacteria on hospital equipment. Scientists could also use radium as a source of radiation, leading to hundreds of other discoveries that changed the world, such as **nuclear power**. The Curies could have become very rich if they had charged people to use their method of extracting radium. Instead, they shared their knowledge for free.

SECRET CHEMISTRY

A piece of radium gives out radiation because its atoms are constantly breaking apart, to make other elements including the gas radon (see page 170). Radium metal has to be stored in containers that won't pop open as radon gas builds up.

INSIDE THE ATOM

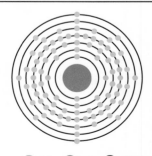

$-$ 88 $+$ 88 $\bigcirc$ 138

FORMS AND USES

1 DEADLY ELEMENT
It took Marie and Pierre Curie years to extract pure radium from the rocks it is found in. As they worked, the Curies often felt sick and exhausted. They had no idea that radiation was dangerous. Pierre was killed in an accident, but Marie died of a bone disease caused by working so closely with radioactive elements.

2 A NEW ERA
Although radium is very dangerous, its discovery led to several new types of science that save lives. They include radiotherapy and radioactive tracers that help doctors to find out what is happening inside a patient's body without cutting it open.

3 RELEASING RADIUM
Most radium in Earth's crust is safely locked away in rocks underground, including coal. When we dig up and burn coal, we increase the amount of radium hanging around on Earth's surface.

4 GLOWING PAINT
About 100 years ago, radium was used in glow-in-the-dark paints for clocks and watches, toys, and dozens of other products. The radiation from the radium made the paint glow. When factory workers who used the paints became very ill and died, the world realized how dangerous radium was.

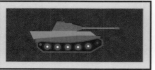

21 Sc Scandium	22 Ti Titanium	23 V Vanadium	24 Cr Chromium	25 Mn Manganese	26 Fe Iron	27 Co Cobalt	28 Ni Nickel	29 Cu Copper	30 Zn Zinc
39 Y Yttrium	40 Zr Zirconium	41 Nb Niobium	42 Mo Molybdenum	43 Tc Technetium	44 Ru Ruthenium	45 Rh Rhodium	46 Pd Palladium	47 Ag Silver	48 Cd Cadmium
	72 Hf Hafnium	73 Ta Tantalum	74 W Tungsten	75 Re Rhenium	76 Os Osmium	77 Ir Iridium	78 Pt Platinum	79 Au Gold	80 Hg Mercury

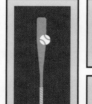

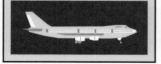

Transition Metals

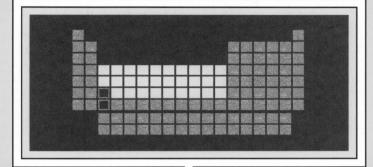

THE TRANSITION METALS HAVE SHAPED HUMAN CULTURE, HISTORY, AND TECHNOLOGY MORE THAN ANY OTHER CATEGORY OF ELEMENTS.

Most elements are metals, and most metals are transition metals, from everyday metals, such as iron, nickel, and copper, to rare, precious metals such as platinum and gold. Pure transition metals are usually shiny or **lustrous** and **conduct electricity** and heat well. Copper and silver are the best **conductors**, and are found inside every electronic gadget and device in our homes. Most transition metals are strong, but also **malleable** (they can be hammered or beaten into shape without cracking) and **ductile** (they can be drawn into thin wires without breaking). Some of these metals have been so important in human history that entire periods—the Bronze Age and the Iron Age—are named after them!

Three transition metals are **ferromagnetic**, which means they are strongly attracted to **magnets** and can form permanent magnets themselves. The most famous of these is iron, which gives Earth its **magnetic field**, and makes life on our planet possible. Many other transition metals are **paramagnetic**, meaning that they are weakly attracted to a magnetic field. Magnetism is very important for generating electricity and is another way that transition metals have shaped our world.

The chemistry of transition metals—the way they react or behave around other substances—is also unique. They can be mixed together to form **alloys**, including materials with amazing properties. Many transition metals can act as **catalysts**—substances that start or speed up a chemical **reaction**, without getting used up or changed themselves—and are the key to making most of the chemicals and materials we take for granted, from fuels and plastics to fertilizers. Last but not least, several transition metals play vital roles in living things, including the iron that carries oxygen around our bodies, and the molybdenum that limits how far and fast a forest can grow.

21
Sc

Scandium
(SCAN-DEE-UM)

TRANSITION METAL

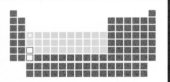

ALTHOUGH SCANDIUM IS FOUND IN HUNDREDS OF DIFFERENT **MINERALS**, IT'S DIFFICULT TO GET IT OUT OF THESE ROCKS. THIS MAKES IT ONE OF THE MOST EXPENSIVE ELEMENTS.

KEY PROPERTIES

- solid
- silvery-white metal
- fairly soft
- scandium **salts** taste sour

WHERE IT'S FOUND

- hundreds of minerals such as thortveitite
- lanthanide **ores**
- transition metal ores
- seawater

HUMAN BODY

NONE

ALL ABOUT SCANDIUM

Scientists aren't quite sure whether scandium belongs with the transition metals or the lanthanides. Scandium is often found in the same rocks as lanthanides and, like these "rare earth metals," it is difficult and expensive to extract from the rocks. However, it also shares properties with transition metals, such as a high **melting point**. Scandium is found in lots of different rocks and minerals, but only a little in each one. This means it's not worth mining rock *just* to get scandium. Instead, it's mainly collected from the "waste" rocks that are left over from when metals such as uranium, aluminum, and titanium are extracted.

Scandium has a special set of properties. Its low **density** makes it very light, but it doesn't melt until it reaches 2806°F—more than 800°F hotter than lava! Adding a tiny amount of scandium to a cheaper metal, such as aluminum, makes **alloys** that are light but stay strong at very hot temperatures. Scandium-aluminum alloys are useful for making lots of things, from ceramics to electronic equipment and lasers. They are also used to make aircraft parts that have to cope with tremendous heat and forces—such as the turbine blades in a jet engine. These blades are cast from molten metal. As metal cools down and becomes solid, millions of tiny crystals usually form. These can make a metal weak if they get too big. If scandium is in an alloy, it stops these crystal grains from growing too large. Scandium is also used to make fuel cells. These are devices that produce **electricity** directly from a fuel, without having to burn it to make steam to turn a turbine in an electricity generator. Fuel cells are becoming more important as people look for ways to produce cleaner energy.

SECRET CHEMISTRY

Scandium reacts slowly with oxygen in the air to form a yellowish or pinkish coating— a thin layer of a **compound** called scandium oxide. Scandium will also react with the oxygen in water, breaking its H_2O **molecules** apart. The hydrogen bubbles off as a gas.

INSIDE THE ATOM

− 21   + 21   ○ 24

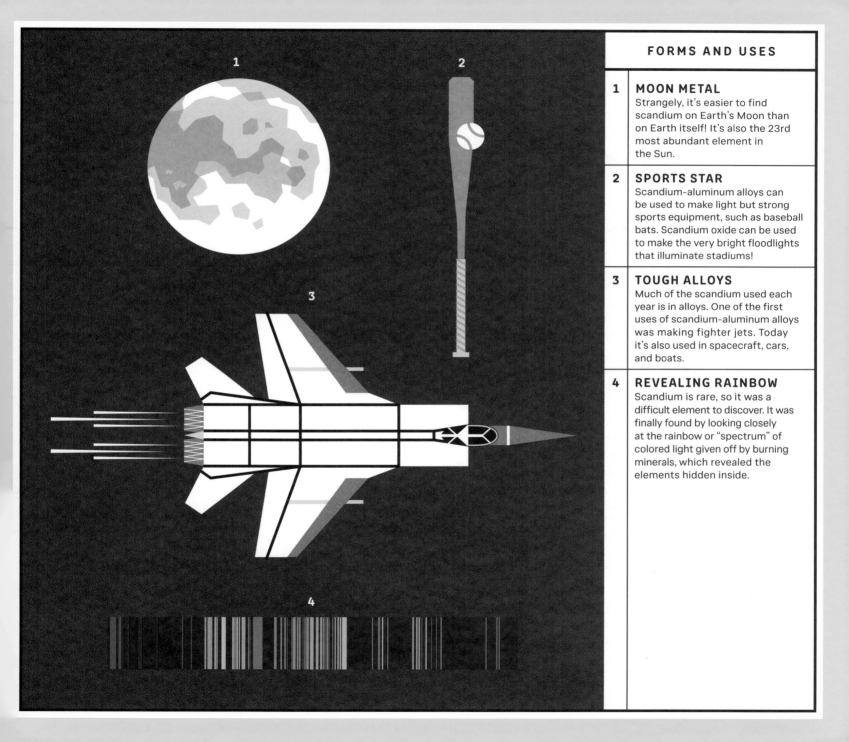

FORMS AND USES

1 MOON METAL
Strangely, it's easier to find scandium on Earth's Moon than on Earth itself! It's also the 23rd most abundant element in the Sun.

2 SPORTS STAR
Scandium-aluminum alloys can be used to make light but strong sports equipment, such as baseball bats. Scandium oxide can be used to make the very bright floodlights that illuminate stadiums!

3 TOUGH ALLOYS
Much of the scandium used each year is in alloys. One of the first uses of scandium-aluminum alloys was making fighter jets. Today it's also used in spacecraft, cars, and boats.

4 REVEALING RAINBOW
Scandium is rare, so it was a difficult element to discover. It was finally found by looking closely at the rainbow or "spectrum" of colored light given off by burning minerals, which revealed the elements hidden inside.

22
Ti

Titanium
(TIE-TAY-NEE-UM)

TRANSITION METAL

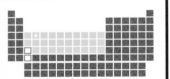

TITANIUM'S RARE COMBINATION OF SUPER STRENGTH AND LIGHTNESS IS IN DEMAND FOR BUILDING TOUGH OBJECTS SUCH AS AIRCRAFT PARTS. IN EVERYDAY LIFE, IT'S PART OF SOME SUNSCREENS AND PAINTS.

KEY PROPERTIES

- solid
- silvery-gray metal
- very hard
- brittle when cold
- **malleable**, **ductile** when hot

WHERE IT'S FOUND

- **minerals**: ilmenite, rutile
- almost all rocks, sand, and soils
- meteorites
- plants and animals
- ocean sediments

HUMAN BODY

TRACE

ALL ABOUT TITANIUM

Titanium is hard to extract from rocks and minerals, but it's worth doing because its unique combination of lightness and strength make it very useful. Titanium is as strong as steel, but much lighter—a lump of titanium weighs half as much as a lump of iron the same size! So why don't we see titanium bridges, car, and skyscrapers all around us? The chemistry of titanium is to blame. It takes a lot of energy to separate titanium from the other elements it is mixed with in rocks and minerals. This makes it far more expensive than iron and steel, and is the reason it's used in combination with other, cheaper metals such as iron, aluminum, and copper.

Titanium refuses to rust like iron and steel do. Only the very outer atoms of titanium react with oxygen, forming a layer of oxide that protects the rest of the metal underneath. The Guggenheim Museum in Bilbao is covered with 33,000 very thin sheets of titanium, which are still as shiny as the day it was built in 1997. When titanium is mixed with other metals, it can make them more resistant to **corrosion** too. For example, ships and submarines with titanium **alloy** hulls can stay underwater for years without rusting. Titanium will react with different non-metals when it's heated. It will even burn in pure nitrogen, which few other elements do! Almost all the titanium used each year is used to make titanium dioxide—a **compound** of titanium and oxygen. Titanium dioxide reflects all colors in sunlight, so it looks very white. It's used to give everything from paint and paper to toothpaste and icing their bright white color. It's also used in **solar cells** and computer chips.

SECRET CHEMISTRY

"Noxer blocks" are concrete paving slabs with a thin coating of titanium dioxide. The special layer works as a **catalyst**, using the energy of sunlight to break apart nasty pollutants in vehicle exhaust fumes. They can help to keep city air cleaner.

INSIDE THE ATOM

● 22 ✚ 22 ○ 26

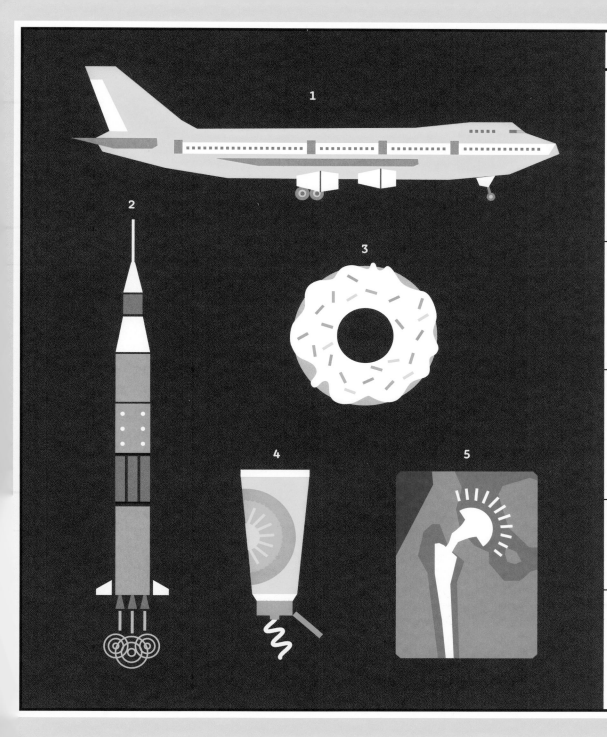

FORMS AND USES

1 EXPENSIVE ELEMENT
Titanium is very light, which makes it perfect for making aircraft, but it's also very expensive. The titanium used by one large aircraft manufacturer over ten years cost $4 billion! It's used where it's most needed—like the blades in jet engines, and the front edge of wings that reach very high temperatures as they push their way through the air!

2 3D-PRINTED PARTS
Light but tough elements like titanium are essential for making spacecraft. Excitingly, aircraft manufacturers are experimenting with 3D-printed titanium parts! This technique could one day mean that new titanium parts can be printed in space.

3 FOOD ADDITIVE
On food labels, titanium dioxide is often listed as the ingredient E171. Some studies have raised concerns that tiny **particles** of titanium dioxide are bad for people with certain digestive conditions. Some areas of the world are considering banning E171 from foods.

4 SUN PROTECTION
Titanium dioxide blocks **UV** light, a type of light that we can't see with our eyes, but which harms our skin. This makes titanium dioxide useful in sunscreens.

5 ARTIFICIAL BONES
Tough titanium is used to fix or replace broken or worn-out bones. It's light, and won't react with water in the body. Titanium nitride is even harder. It's used to coat hip implants and tools that might otherwise wear down.

23
V

Vanadium
(VUH-NAY-DEE-UM)

TRANSITION METAL

VANADIUM IS A HIDDEN HERO IN STEEL-MAKING, CHEMISTRY, HUMAN HEALTH—AND SEA CUCUMBERS!

KEY PROPERTIES

- solid
- silvery metal
- **ductile**
- high **melting point**

WHERE IT'S FOUND

- **minerals**: vanadinite, patronite, carnotite
- plants and animals
- toadstools
- soils
- seawater

HUMAN BODY

 TRACE

ALL ABOUT VANADIUM

Discovering a new element is very difficult, but it can be even harder to persuade other people you've done it! Spanish-Mexican mineralogist Andrés Manuel del Rio noticed that a substance he had extracted from lead **ore** formed unusual **salts**, in a rainbow of different colors. He was convinced he'd found a new element and suggested the names panchromium (meaning all colors) or erythronium (meaning red). However, scientists in Europe looked at it and decided it was actually just chromium, which had already been discovered and also forms multicolored salts. That was a huge mistake. Years later, a Swedish chemist began investigating a strange piece of cast iron, which was strong in some places but broke easily in others. He found a mystery element lurking in the iron, and called it vanadium, after Vanadis, the Scandinavian goddess of love and beauty. Other chemists put two and two together and worked out it was the same one Andrés had found 30 years earlier.

We don't really use vanadium metal on its own, but adding a small amount to steel makes the steel rustproof, and better able to stand up to shocks and vibrations. This is useful for all sorts of things, including jet engines, power tools, and armor. Many living things need vanadium, from tiny **microbes** to humans. We need to eat a small amount every day, but we don't yet know exactly how our bodies use it. It's found in lots of different foods, especially seafood, liver, and sunflowers.

SECRET CHEMISTRY

Vanadium **compounds** can be useful **catalysts** in chemical **reactions**. This means that they help different elements to react together, without getting used up themselves. For example, vanadium oxide is used to help make sulfuric **acid**, a very important chemical (see page 142).

INSIDE THE ATOM

● 23　＋ 23　○ 28

FORMS AND USES

1 SPORTING STRENGTH
Titanium **alloys** often contain a little vanadium. They are used to make things that need to be light but very strong, such as sports wheelchairs.

2 SEA CUCUMBERS
Blob-like sea cucumbers crawl slowly across the ocean floor, hoovering up poop, dead animals, and anything else that falls to the ocean floor. They have so much vanadium in their blood that people have actually used them as a source of this metal!

3 DAMASCUS STEEL
Long before vanadium was discovered, it was a part of the world's strongest steel weapons, simply because it happened to be in the iron used to make them. The vanadium made steel swords less likely to shatter when they struck hard objects, and "Damascus steel" became famous around the world.

4 TOADSTOOL
Some poisonous fungi soak up a lot of vanadium from the soil and store it in their fruiting bodies. Fly agaric toadstools can contain up to 400 times more vanadium than nearby plants!

5 VANADIUM STEEL
Today, lots of people have chromium-vanadium steel in their homes and garages. It is used to make the metal parts of tough tools, such as pliers.

6 PART OF THE FIRST CARS
The world's first mass-produced car, the Model T Ford, was made using vanadium steel, to make the different parts strong yet light.

Chromium

24
Cr

(CROW-MEE-UM)

TRANSITION METAL

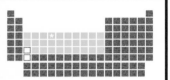

CHROMIUM IS THE SUPER-SHINY ELEMENT OF CAR BUMPERS AND STAINLESS STEEL KITCHEN UTENSILS.

KEY PROPERTIES

- solid
- silvery-blue metal
- hard

WHERE IT'S FOUND

- **minerals**: chromite
- living things
- rubies and emeralds
- soils
- oceans

HUMAN BODY

TRACE

ALL ABOUT CHROMIUM

Pure chromium metal famously becomes very shiny when it's polished. It also reacts with air to form a tough layer of chromium oxide, which stops the metal underneath from rusting or losing its shine. An extremely thin layer of chromium can be added to almost any metal object—and even some plastics—to make them shine like a mirror. This is called chrome plating. Chromium can also be mixed with other metals to make **alloys** with different properties to the pure metals. Stainless steel is the most famous of these alloys. It was discovered by an expert metal worker named Harry Brearley, who added different amounts of chromium to steel to try to make a type of steel that wore down less quickly. He noticed that the alloy containing the most chromium wasn't **corroded** by rainwater, or even by **acids**. This rustless or "stainless" steel is now used all around the world.

Chromium combines with other elements to form brightly colored red, green, yellow, and orange **compounds**. That's why it was named after *chroma*, the Greek word for color. These compounds can be very useful. For example, green chrome oxide is often used to make green paints, including the paints used on military vehicles.

Although our bodies contain a little chromium, some chromium compounds seem to be very dangerous. They may damage the **DNA** inside our **cells**, potentially causing cancer. This means it is worrying when chromium gets into water supplies. This can happen naturally, or when waste from processes, such as leather tanning, escape from factories or get dumped into the environment. This cancer-causing form of chromium is also found in tobacco smoke.

SECRET CHEMISTRY

Kilns and furnaces have to get hot enough to melt other elements, without melting themselves! The secret is chromite bricks (a compound of chromium, iron, and oxygen), which have a **melting point** of more than 3200°F— hot enough to boil lead!

INSIDE THE ATOM

● 24 ✛ 24 ○ 28

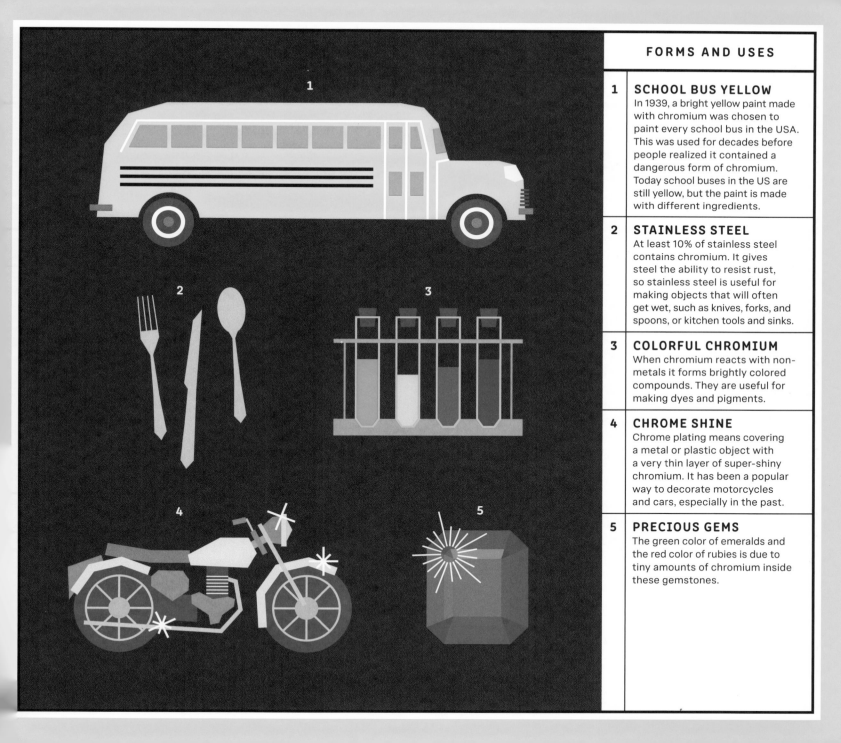

FORMS AND USES

1 SCHOOL BUS YELLOW
In 1939, a bright yellow paint made with chromium was chosen to paint every school bus in the USA. This was used for decades before people realized it contained a dangerous form of chromium. Today school buses in the US are still yellow, but the paint is made with different ingredients.

2 STAINLESS STEEL
At least 10% of stainless steel contains chromium. It gives steel the ability to resist rust, so stainless steel is useful for making objects that will often get wet, such as knives, forks, and spoons, or kitchen tools and sinks.

3 COLORFUL CHROMIUM
When chromium reacts with non-metals it forms brightly colored compounds. They are useful for making dyes and pigments.

4 CHROME SHINE
Chrome plating means covering a metal or plastic object with a very thin layer of super-shiny chromium. It has been a popular way to decorate motorcycles and cars, especially in the past.

5 PRECIOUS GEMS
The green color of emeralds and the red color of rubies is due to tiny amounts of chromium inside these gemstones.

25
Mn

Manganese
(MANG-GUH-NEES)

TRANSITION METAL

MANGANESE IS AN IMPORTANT BUILDING BLOCK OF BOTH OUR BODIES AND THE HUMAN-MADE WORLD. OUR BODIES CAN'T STORE IT, SO WE NEED TO EAT A LITTLE MANGANESE EVERY DAY TO STAY HEALTHY.

KEY PROPERTIES

- solid
- gray-white metal
- very hard
- very brittle
- makes water taste metallic and smell bad

WHERE IT'S FOUND

- **minerals**: pyrolusite
- soils
- plants and animals
- ocean floor

HUMAN BODY

TRACE

ALL ABOUT MANGANESE

All living things need manganese. In humans its many roles include helping our skin heal itself after a cut or scrape. Adults need about 2 milligrams a day, the amount you'd find in a handful of peanuts, half a cup of leafy vegetables such as spinach, plus a sweet potato. Lots of manganese is found in the rocks and soils of Earth's crust—it's one of the five most common metals on our planet, and cheap to produce. Long before anyone knew what elements were, the manganese mineral pyrolusite was ground up to make the black paint used in prehistoric cave paintings.

Manganese reacts fairly easily with many other elements. At the moment, most manganese use each year is in steel-making. It is used indirectly, to react with oxygen and sulfur atoms and remove them from the steel. It is also used directly, to make superstrong manganese steel **alloys**. Manganese also lends its strength to drink cans, making the thin aluminum stiffer and stronger (think of the difference between an aluminum can and aluminum foil). Because manganese is cheap and easy to find, scientists are looking for new ways to use it—such as replacing expensive metals like cobalt in batteries. Better and cheaper batteries will be very important as we move from fossil fuels to renewable energy sources such as wind and solar power. Batteries allow us to store the energy from renewable sources, to use when we need it—not just when the sun is out, or the wind is blowing.

SECRET CHEMISTRY

One group of manganese **compounds** may help us to tackle global warming. These compounds can convert carbon dioxide (a greenhouse gas) into carbon monoxide, as soon as it's produced. The carbon monoxide can then be converted into useful chemicals.

INSIDE THE ATOM

— 25   + 25   O 30

FORMS AND USES

1 STRONG STEEL
Manganese steel is very strong and resistant to damage caused by rubbing or grinding. It is used in cement mixers, rock crushers, and railway tracks.

2 ON THE SEABED
Small lumps or "nodules" of manganese are found scattered over the ocean floor in several parts of the world. They are formed over millions of years, as manganese that is dissolved in the ocean gathers around a shark's tooth or a small piece of seashell. The lump of manganese that forms can grow as big as a head of lettuce.

3 PURPLE AMETHYSTS
Manganese gives amethysts their beautiful purple color. It can be used to make glass purple too, and also to remove all traces of color from glass (so it doesn't have a greenish tint).

4 ATTENTION FUTURE SPIES!
Scientists have invented a manganese-based coating for paper that changes water into invisible ink! When you write on the paper with water, the words are invisible, except for under UV light. Heating the paper with a hair dryer erases the message... and the paper can be used again, up to 30 times!

5 TEA LEAVES
Black tea contains high levels of manganese.

6 BULLETPROOF BOXES
Barely any materials can saw, drill, or pierce manganese steel, so it's used to make safes and bullet-proof containers.

26
Fe

Iron
(EYE-URN)

TRANSITION METAL

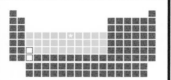

WE LIVE ON AN "IRON PLANET" WITH A CORE OF SOLID AND LIQUID IRON. HUMANS HAVE USED THIS ELEMENT TO BUILD TODAY'S INDUSTRIAL, IRON AGE WORLD.

KEY PROPERTIES

- solid
- silvery metal
- pure iron is soft
- steel is harder
- **malleable**
- **ductile**

WHERE IT'S FOUND

- **minerals**: hematite, magnetite
- Earth's core
- meteorites
- soils
- green plants, animals

HUMAN BODY

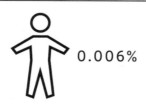 0.006%

ALL ABOUT IRON

Iron is currently the world's most important metal. We are living in an Iron Age that began around 3,000 years ago, when people worked out how to extract huge quantities of this metal from rocks and turn it into all sorts of useful objects, from wheels to weapons. In the 1700s, new methods of **smelting** (heating rocks to extract the metals inside them) made iron cheaper to produce. Suddenly it was possible to build huge structures out of iron and steel, and the Industrial Revolution began. During the Industrial Revolution, iron and steel (an **alloy** of iron and carbon) changed the world as the building materials for factories, machinery, and thousands of miles of railways. Iron and steel are just as important today. They are used to make everything from skyscrapers and bridges to cans, cutlery, and cars.

Iron is a vital part of the transportation network in our bodies too! It's part of the hemoglobin in our red blood **cells**, which grabs hold of oxygen in our lungs and releases it where it's needed, from your brain to the tips of your toes. We need to top up on iron every day, and luckily, it's found in lots of different foods, from meat and seafood to vegetables, beans, and potatoes. Iron is also essential in the process of making the fertilizers needed to feed the world's huge human population. Other living things rely on iron too. Recently, scientists discovered that a lack of iron is the reason there are so few plants and animals in oceans compared to the land. In fact, iron makes all life on Earth possible. Swirling liquid iron at our planet's core creates a **magnetic field**, which shields Earth from the dangerous cosmic **radiation** zooming through space.

SECRET CHEMISTRY

Have you ever noticed how touching iron objects can make your skin smell metallic and mushroomy? You're not smelling the metal itself, but chemicals produced when your skin oils react with it. Everyone's skin produces a slightly different smell!

INSIDE THE ATOM

● 26 ✚ 26 ○ 30

FORMS AND USES

1 IRONBRIDGE
The Iron Bridge in Ironbridge, England, was the first big bridge in the world to be made entirely out of metal.

2 ELECTRICITY
Iron's **magnetism** has always been important for generating **electricity**. Now scientists are finding exciting new ways to use iron to store electrical energy in the future.

3 CROP HERO
Green plants need iron just as much as we do. Without it, they can't make **chlorophyll**, the chemical that allows plants to make their own food.

4 IRON'S WEAKNESS
Iron reacts easily with the oxygen in air and water, to form iron oxide—aka rust—making strong iron objects crumbly and weak.

5 RED BLOODED
Human blood looks red because of the combination of iron and oxygen in our red blood cells. Creatures that use a different metal to carry oxygen have blue blood instead!

6 IRON PLANET
Earth's inner and outer cores are mainly iron.

7 ANIMAL NAVIGATION
Compasses make use of Earth's magnetic field to help us find our way around the planet. Some animals, such as Monarch butterflies, can sense Earth's magnetic field and carry out incredible journeys using their inner compass!

Cobalt
(CO-BAULT)

27 Co

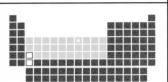

THIS "GOBLIN" METAL CAN HAVE A NASTY SIDE, BUT IT HAS ALSO BEEN HARNESSED TO HELP HUMANS IN MANY DIFFERENT WAYS.

KEY PROPERTIES

- solid
- silvery-blue metal
- hard
- brittle

WHERE IT'S FOUND

- **minerals:** cobaltite, linnaeite, erythrite, skutterudite
- meteorites
- vitamin B12
- Earth's core
- plants such as legumes

HUMAN BODY

TRACE

ALL ABOUT COBALT

Cobalt is a little rarer than its neighbors in the periodic table, and hard to get out of its **ores**. So instead of digging up these ores, most cobalt is extracted from the rock left over once iron, nickel, copper, or zinc have been extracted from their ores. Cobalt is a hard metal, so it's often combined with other metals to make strong **alloys** such as stainless steel. Cobalt alloys can be used to make permanent **magnets** that stay magnetic even when they get really hot. Cobalt is also used to give color to paints and ceramics, and as a **catalyst**—a substance that speeds up the chemical **reactions** needed to make all sorts of other substances. Cobalt is also used for making portable electronic devices such as smartphones. However, the United Nations has warned the world that thousands of people, including 40,000 children, are working in cobalt mines in terrible conditions to feed this demand.

Although natural cobalt is not **radioactive**, an artificial **isotope** called cobalt-60 is formed by the reactions that happen in **nuclear power** plants. If the waste from these power stations drains into the environment, cobalt-60 can end up in the sea or soil. Atoms of cobalt-60 are unstable and break apart or **decay** over time. As they do this, they release **radiation** that is very dangerous for living things. However, cobalt-60 can also be used to help humans—for example, to kill cancer **cells**, or to kill any disease-causing bacteria living on food (this does not make the food radioactive). Cobalt-60 is also used to help detect tiny cracks in pipes and machinery—leaks are detected with a machine that can sense radiation.

SECRET CHEMISTRY

A **compound** of cobalt and chlorine called cobaltous chloride changes from pink to blue, depending on how dry it is. In the past it was used to make an invisible ink that was pale pink on paper, but darkened to blue when it was warmed up!

INSIDE THE ATOM

 27 + 27 ◯ 32

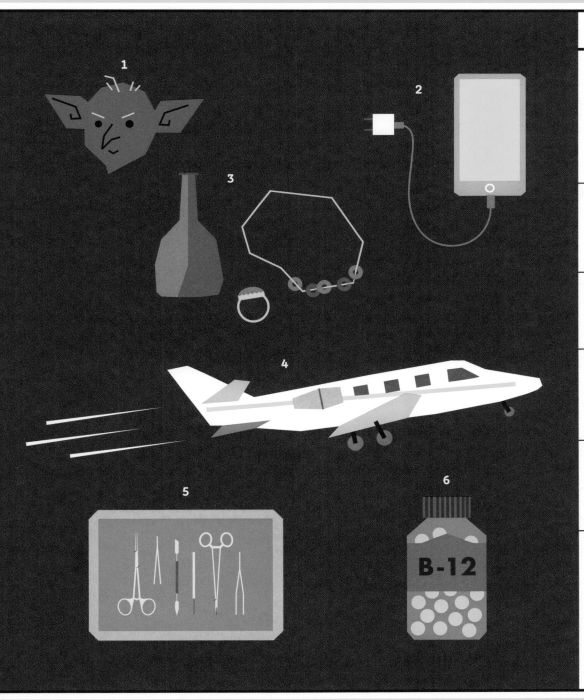

FORMS AND USES

1 GOBLIN METAL
In the 1500s, a group of miners tried to extract silver from rocks that they thought were silver **ore**. They failed and named the disappointing rocks *kobald*, meaning goblin. When cobalt was discovered in this rock 200 years later, it was named after *kobald* too.

2 PORTABLE POWER
Cobalt is so important for making the rechargeable batteries that power smartphones, electric cars, and other portable devices that it's known as "blue gold."

3 BLUE GLASS
Long before people knew what cobalt was, they used bluish cobalt minerals to give glass and ceramics a blue color.

4 JET AIRCRAFT
Cobalt is used to make **superalloys** that won't rust, and stay strong even when they get really, really hot. They are used in aircraft engines and rockets.

5 STERILIZING SCALPELS
The radiation released by the isotope cobalt-60 can be used to kill any germs left behind on medical equipment, so it can be safely used again.

6 VITAMIN B12
Cobalt atoms are an important building block of cobalamin, or vitamin B12. Our bodies need this vitamin to make red blood cells, build nerve cells, and release energy from our food. The friendly bacteria that live in our intestines make some of the vitamin B12 we need, and the rest comes directly from our food.

28
Ni

Nickel
(NICK-ULL)

TRANSITION METAL

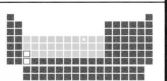

YOU WON'T OFTEN SEE PURE NICKEL, BUT IT'S BRILLIANT WHEN WORKING WITH OTHER ELEMENTS AS PART OF A TEAM.

KEY PROPERTIES

- solid
- silvery metal
- **malleable**
- **ductile**

WHERE IT'S FOUND

- **minerals**: millerite, pentlandite, limonite
- Earth's core
- meteorites
- some soils
- tea leaves

HUMAN BODY

TRACE

ALL ABOUT NICKEL

Pure nickel is very ductile, which means that it's easy to draw it into a wire. A single kilogram of nickel—a lump about as big as a hockey puck—could be stretched into a wire over 185 miles long! However, nickel is more commonly combined with other metals to make **alloys**. The stainless steel used to make cutlery, pans, and kitchen utensils is the best-known nickel alloy. The added nickel (and chromium) stops the steel from rusting, even at high temperatures. Nickel is also used in **superalloys** with extraordinary properties. They include Nichrome, which can get red hot without reacting with oxygen in the air. This alloy is used to make the glowing "elements" inside a toaster or electric heater. There are other nickel superalloys that refuse to rust and stay strong at high temperatures. Some even have metal memory, meaning they can be pushed or squished but spring back into their original shapes. These memory shape alloys are used to make objects such as glasses frames.

Nickel is an important part of rechargeable batteries, from small AA batteries used in toys and the lithium-**ion** batteries used in portable electronic devices, to large nickel-metal hydride (Ni-MH) batteries used in electric and hybrid cars. It's set to play an exciting role in the electronics of the future, because nickel is getting lots of attention from nanotech scientists and inventors who work with really, really small things.

SECRET CHEMISTRY

Nickel particularly likes reacting with sulfur. This can be a problem, because even a tiny amount of sulfur can make nickel more brittle. To avoid this, materials scientists make sure their metals and alloys are very pure before making things like turbine blades.

INSIDE THE ATOM

− 28   + 28   O 30

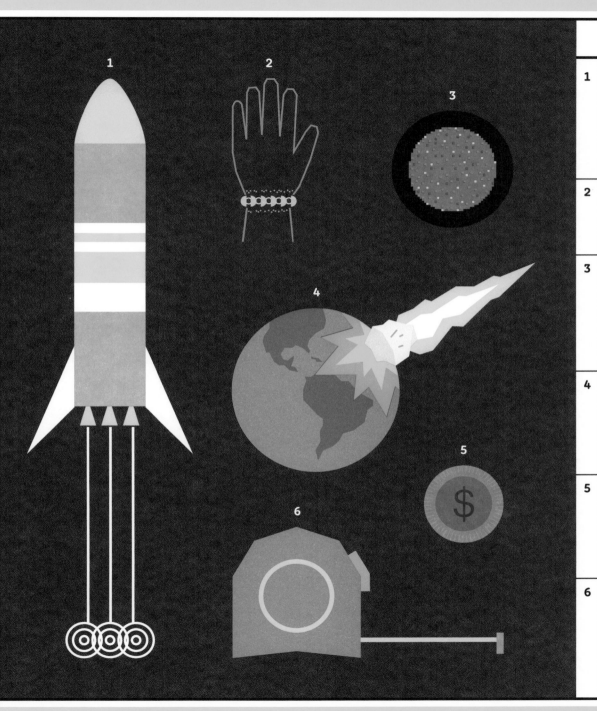

FORMS AND USES

1 BUILDING ROCKETS
Nickel superalloys are used to make the materials in the hottest parts of jet and rocket engines. Using such strong materials stops the engines from failing when a rocket or plane is thousands of miles above the Earth's surface.

2 WHITE GOLD
Some people are allergic to nickel. If they wear jewelry that contains nickel, such as white gold, they get itchy, sore skin.

3 TINY TECH
The words needed to understand 1,000 different languages have been scratched onto the surface of a tiny nickel disk less than an inch wide. The words on this "Rosetta disk" can only be read under a microscope.

4 SPACE ROCKS
Earth contains lots of nickel, but it's locked away deep inside its core. Most of the nickel we find on the surface actually comes from meteorites that landed on our planet long ago!

5 COINAGE METAL
Nickel is used to make coins, but names can be misleading! The "nickel" coins used in the USA are actually mostly copper, with only a quarter nickel, while the "copper" coins in the UK are mostly steel!

6 PRECISION INSTRUMENTS
Unlike most metals, the nickel alloy Invar doesn't get bigger when it's heated. It's important for making measuring devices that need to stay exactly the same size at all kinds of different temperatures.

29
Cu

Copper
(COP-PURR)

TRANSITION METAL

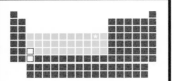

COPPER IS THE METAL THAT CARRIES **ELECTRICITY** THROUGH OUR HOMES, BUT ITS STARRING ROLE IN HUMAN HISTORY BEGAN ALL THE WAY BACK IN THE BRONZE AGE.

KEY PROPERTIES

- solid
- orangey-gold metal
- shiny
- soft
- **malleable**
- **ductile**

WHERE IT'S FOUND

- **minerals:** chalcopyrite, green malachite, cuprite
- soils
- living things
- vegetables

HUMAN BODY

TRACE

ALL ABOUT COPPER

It's possible to find lumps of pure copper in Earth's crust, so humans have been able to use it for at least 10,000 years. Around 5,000 years ago, people worked out how to separate "hidden" copper from other elements that it was combined with in rocks and minerals. Then they worked out how to make copper much harder and stronger, by combining it with tin. This copper-tin **alloy** was named bronze, and it was an alloy that changed the world. In North Africa and parts of Asia, people began using bronze to make everything: from stronger weapons and tools to musical instruments and giant statues. The Bronze Age lasted more than 2,000 years.

Today we rely on iron more than bronze, but copper is still the world's third most-used metal. About a fifth of the world's copper is mined not by workers in hard hats, but by tiny bacteria! Biomining uses bacteria that "eat" rocks for energy. As they feed away on the rocks, they release copper, which can be collected and turned into solid metal. Copper **conducts** heat and electricity very well. It's also easy to soften, **weld**, or bend into shape, so it's used to make the pipes that carry water through our homes. Copper from these pipes make up some of the copper we eat and drink. An adult needs just over a milligram of copper a day, from foods such as seafoods, liver, nuts, seeds, and leafy green vegetables. Many plants, including wheat, also need copper to stay healthy.

SECRET CHEMISTRY

Have you ever noticed that your skin smells strange after you touch a copper coin or pipe? It's not actually the metal you're smelling, but chemicals made when your skin oils react with copper. The exact smell produced is unique to you!

INSIDE THE ATOM

● 29 ✚ 29 ○ 34

FORMS AND USES

1 STATUE OF LIBERTY
As copper reacts with the oxygen in water and air, it forms a green substance. The copper Statue of Liberty in New York was shiny orange-gold when it was first made, but is now covered with a layer of green copper oxide.

2 SELF-STERILIZING
Some hospitals use copper to cover surfaces such as taps and sinks. Dangerous bacteria can't live for long on copper, so it helps to stop the spread of germs.

3 BRONZE ALLOYS
Bronze is mostly made of copper, with tin or other metals added to make it harder. Bronze swords were relatively soft, so people trained to fight with them in a special way.

4 PHAROAH'S PIPES
In Ancient Egypt, copper was still a rare and precious metal. But it was already being used to make water pipes for some of the most important temples. A protective coating of copper oxide allows these pipes to still carry water 5,000 years later!

5 BLUE BLOODED
Octopuses rely on a copper rather than iron to carry oxygen in their blood. This makes their blood blue rather than red!

6 ELECTRIC WIRING
It's a great **conductor** and easy to draw into wires, so copper is used to make electrical wiring. Engineers are finding out how to use copper to conduct electricity at smaller and smaller scales, in new types of electronics, sensors, and robots.

30
Zn
Zinc
(ZINK)

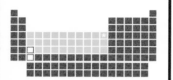

TRANSITION METAL

ALL LIVING THINGS NEED ZINC. IT'S JUST AS IMPORTANT TO YOU AS IT IS TO THE MICROSCOPIC DUST MITES THAT FEED ON FLAKES OF YOUR SKIN. IT'S ALSO NEEDED BY THE EVEN TINIER FUNGI THAT LIVE IN THOSE DUST MITES' DROPPINGS!

KEY PROPERTIES

- solid
- bluish-white metal
- brittle at 68°F
- **malleable** if heated

WHERE IT'S FOUND

- rocks/**minerals**: zinc blende, wurtzite, smithsonite
- soil
- **particles** in air
- living things

HUMAN BODY

 0.004%

ALL ABOUT ZINC

Zinc is a vital building block of proteins called **enzymes**, the **molecules** that get jobs done inside living things. An enzyme containing zinc is zooming around your body right now, inside every red blood **cell.** The zinc atoms inside it help to grab hold of the waste carbon dioxide produced by every cell in your body, removing it from your cells so it doesn't poison you. This is one of the fastest enzyme reactions in all of nature! Other living things, from trees to snails, can also become very ill if they don't get enough zinc. There is a fungus called aspergillus that lives in our homes, feeding on our dead skin, and it is one of the main causes of allergy and asthma when it gets into our lungs. Scientists have found that by blocking this fungus from soaking up the zinc in our bodies, we could stop it living in our lungs and causing allergic reactions.

Outside our bodies, zinc is the fourth most-used metal in the world. Long before people knew what elements were, the Ancient Greeks used zinc to produce brass, and the Ancient Romans used zinc oxide pastes to treat sore skin and eyes. In the Middle Ages in India, zinc was extracted from rocks on a huge scale, to make **alloys** such as brass and bronze. The metal is still used in this way today. Zinc oxide also has lots of uses, from making rubber last longer to coloring plastics, make-up, paper, and inks. Scientists have even found evidence that sucking zinc lozenges can make a viral infection such as a cold last for a shorter time. Perhaps one day this knowledge will even lead to a cure for the common cold!

SECRET CHEMISTRY

When zinc reacts with water and air, its surface turns dull gray. This layer protects the pure zinc underneath. Rubbing the zinc with a weak **acid** such as lemon juice makes the metal bright and shiny again.

INSIDE THE ATOM

⊖ 30   ⊕ 30   ◯ 34

FORMS AND USES

1 SKIN SOOTHER
Many diaper creams, used to soothe diaper rash, are made with zinc oxide. It protects and calms sore skin, stopping it from itching—though scientists still aren't sure why!

2 GALVANIZED STEEL
Most zinc produced each year is used to galvanize steel. This means coating steel with a very thin layer of zinc to stop the steel reacting with air and water and going rusty. All sorts of steel objects are galvanized, from nuts, bolts, and nails to huge lampposts and highway guardrails.

3 BRASS DOOR KNOCKER
Brass is an alloy of copper and zinc. It is hard, shiny, and golden.

4 BODY CLOCKS
Zinc does hundreds of jobs in our bodies, including regulating our natural body clocks so we sleep and wake at the right times. Our eyes contain a lot of zinc, and our brains also rely on zinc to process tastes and smells.

5 ESSENTIAL ELEMENT
We need to eat some zinc every day. It's found in red meat as well as in plant foods such as wheat and maple syrup—a perfect excuse to tuck into some pancakes!

6 SACRIFICED FOR STEEL
In seawater, a simple lump of zinc is often attached to steel objects such as pipes and ships' hulls and rudders to keep them from rusting. Air and water **corrode** the zinc first, so the steel stays intact.

Yttrium
(IT-TREE-UM)

39
Y

TRANSITION METAL

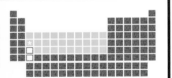

THERE IS 400 TIMES MORE YTTRIUM THAN SILVER IN EARTH'S CRUST, AND SCIENTISTS ARE FINDING EXCITING NEW WAYS TO USE IT.

KEY PROPERTIES

- solid
- silvery-white metal
- fairly soft
- **ductile**
- some yttrium **salts** taste sweet

WHERE IT'S FOUND

- rocks/**minerals**: monazite, bastnaesite, samarskite

HUMAN BODY

 TRACE

ALL ABOUT YTTRIUM

At the moment, most yttrium is used to light up the world, as a part of phosphors. These are substances that absorb different kinds of **radiation,** then glow as they release the energy as a form of radiation we can see—light! This is useful in hundreds of different ways, including the glowing displays of smartphone, computer, and tablet screens.

Pure yttrium metal is mixed into **alloys,** to boost the properties of metals such as magnesium, chromium, molybdenum, and iron. Some of these mixtures are tough **superalloys,** with extraordinary properties that make them useful in extreme environments such as jet engines, car engines, machines that pour and shape molten metal, and heating elements that need to become red hot without melting. Yttrium can even find its way into fake diamonds, when it's added to zirconium oxides to make them more stable (see page 72).

Compounds of yttrium and non-metals can also behave in surprising ways. A piece of glass coated in a thin layer of yttrium hydride behaves like a normal mirror. The metal reflects light. But if hydrogen gas is nearby, the yttrium hydride becomes yellowish and see-through! In the future this could be used to make mirrors that you can switch on and off, or sensors that can detect how much hydrogen gas is around.

SECRET CHEMISTRY

Although yttrium is physically like a transition metal, it reacts with other elements and chemicals in a similar way to the lanthanides. Even a chemist would find it hard to tell yttrium and the lanthanides dysprosium and holmium apart!

INSIDE THE ATOM

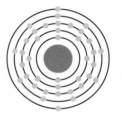

● 39   ✚ 39   ○ 50

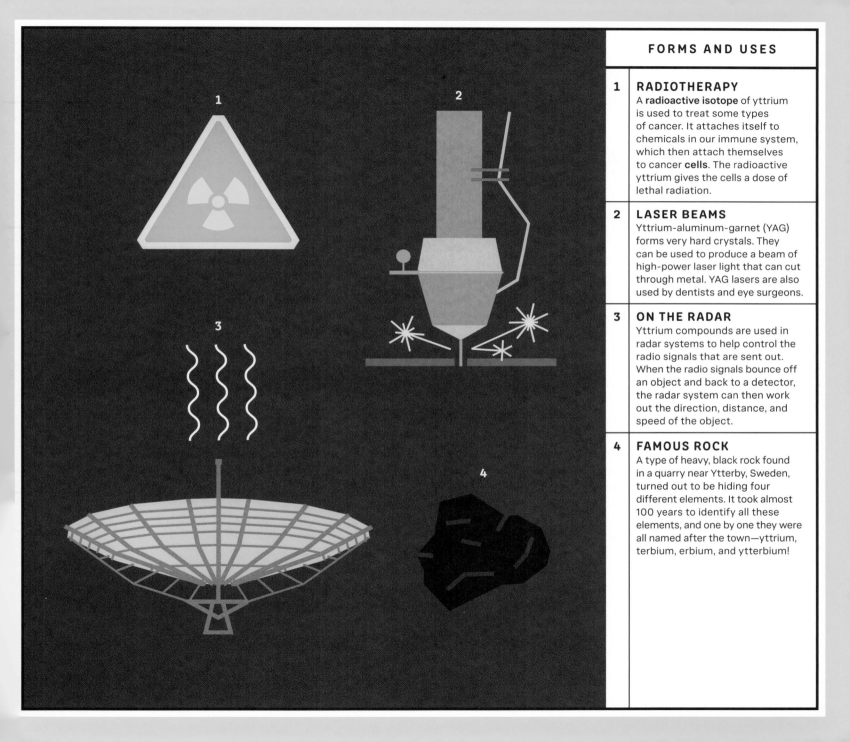

FORMS AND USES

1 RADIOTHERAPY
A **radioactive isotope** of yttrium is used to treat some types of cancer. It attaches itself to chemicals in our immune system, which then attach themselves to cancer **cells**. The radioactive yttrium gives the cells a dose of lethal radiation.

2 LASER BEAMS
Yttrium-aluminum-garnet (YAG) forms very hard crystals. They can be used to produce a beam of high-power laser light that can cut through metal. YAG lasers are also used by dentists and eye surgeons.

3 ON THE RADAR
Yttrium compounds are used in radar systems to help control the radio signals that are sent out. When the radio signals bounce off an object and back to a detector, the radar system can then work out the direction, distance, and speed of the object.

4 FAMOUS ROCK
A type of heavy, black rock found in a quarry near Ytterby, Sweden, turned out to be hiding four different elements. It took almost 100 years to identify all these elements, and one by one they were all named after the town—yttrium, terbium, erbium, and ytterbium!

40
Zr

Zirconium
(ZIR-CONE-EE-UM)

TRANSITION METAL

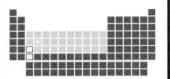

NON-**TOXIC**, EASY TO GET HOLD OF, AND INDESTRUCTIBLE—THIS WONDER METAL CAN HANDLE SOME OF THE WORLD'S TOUGHEST JOBS. BUT IT ALSO HAS A GLAMOROUS SIDE, LENDING SPARKLE TO COSMETICS AND FAKE DIAMONDS!

KEY PROPERTIES

- solid
- grayish-white metal
- flaky surface
- hard
- strong
- **malleable**
- **ductile**
- heat resistant

WHERE IT'S FOUND

- **minerals**: zircon, baddeleyite
- meteorites
- Moon rock

HUMAN BODY

TRACE

ALL ABOUT ZIRCONIUM

Is there any job that zirconium and its **alloys** and **compounds** can't handle? Let's start with zirconium silicate, which is found on many of the world's beaches, as sand! You've probably used it for building sandcastles, but engineers use it to make the lining of furnaces, which stay strong even as everything inside the furnace either melts or burns! Zirconium dioxide, or zirconia, is also super tough. It's used to make sandpapers that can smooth metal, and ceramics that are stronger than the very best steel! Zirconia doesn't melt until it gets hotter than 4,532°F, and also doesn't **conduct** heat very well. This makes it ideal for coating the metal blades of jet engines and turbines, to shield them from the superhigh temperatures and stresses inside an engine. It has even been used to coat space vehicles to protect them from the extreme heat generated by friction with air as they reenter the atmosphere.

Zirconia is equally useful down on the ground, and in our homes. It's used to make kitchen knives and glass. Some paper and cardboard food packaging even has a zirconium-based coating, because zirconium is not toxic. Large pieces of zirconia can also sit inside our bodies without doing any harm, so it's used to make "bioceramics" to replace worn-down joints. In the future, zirconia ceramics may be a good choice for replacing damaged or broken teeth. Zirconia could easily stand up to the **acids** released by bacteria in our mouths, and the wear and tear of chewing. It could even be 3D printed to exactly match a missing tooth!

SECRET CHEMISTRY

A piece of pure zirconium metal reacts with oxygen in the air immediately— but only for a short time. A very thin layer of super-tough zirconia forms on the surface. This protects the rest of the metal from almost anything, from strong acids to high temperatures.

INSIDE THE ATOM

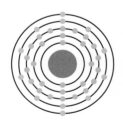

● 40 ⊕ 40 ○ 50

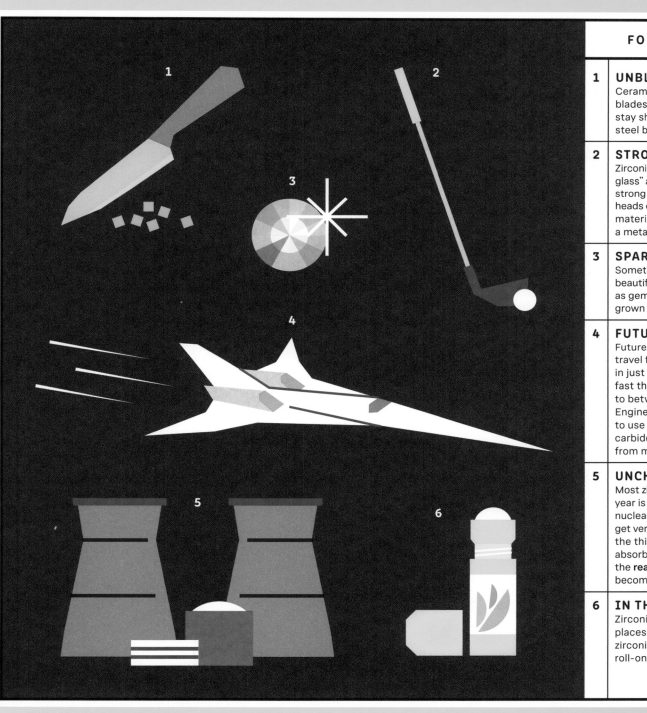

FORMS AND USES

1 UNBLUNTED BLADES
Ceramic knives and scissors have blades made from zirconia. They stay sharper for far longer than steel blades.

2 STRONG AND SPRINGY
Zirconium alloys known as "metallic glass" are used to make extremely strong and hard objects such as the heads of expensive golf clubs. The material is unusually springy for a metal alloy.

3 SPARKLING GEMS
Sometimes zirconia is found as beautiful crystals that can be used as gemstones. These can also be grown in a lab, as cubic zirconia.

4 FUTURE OF FLIGHT?
Future hypersonic planes could travel from London to Sydney in just 4 hours! Moving that fast through air heats objects to between 3,600 and 5,400°F! Engineers are working out how to use ceramics such as zirconium carbide to stop hypersonic planes from melting.

5 UNCHANGEABLE HERO
Most zirconium metal mined each year is used to build parts for nuclear reactors. Zirconium can get very hot without reacting with the things around it. It doesn't absorb **neutrons** (which would slow the **reaction** down), and it doesn't become **radioactive.**

6 IN THE BATHROOM
Zirconium pops up in surprising places in our homes, from tough zirconium silicate on nail files to roll-on deodorants!

41
Nb

Niobium
(NIGH-O-BEE-UM)

TRANSITION METAL

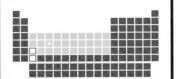

NIOBIUM CAN BE USED TO MAKE RAINBOW JEWELRY BUT IS EVEN MORE SPECTACULAR WHEN IT'S WORKING IN A TEAM WITH OTHER METALS.

KEY PROPERTIES

- solid
- gray-white metal
- shiny
- soft
- **ductile**

WHERE IT'S FOUND

- **minerals**: columbite, pyrochlore
- rocks that contain tin

HUMAN BODY

TRACE

ALL ABOUT NIOBIUM

Niobium is never found alone, but always found with its "twin," the transition metal tantalum. Even their names are closely linked. Niobium is named after Niobe, the Greek goddess of grief. In Greek myths she was the daughter of Tantalus, who tantalum is named after! Niobium sits just above tantalum in the periodic table. Elements in the same group typically have very similar chemical properties, but tantalum and niobium are practically identical! This makes them very hard to separate from each other, and as a result pure niobium is rare. It's worth tracking down because it's great at teaming up with other metals in **alloys**.

Adding niobium to stainless steel makes the steel stronger when it's **welded**, and adding it to zirconium stops this metal from being damaged by chemicals. Niobium alloys and **superalloys** have all sorts of other hi-tech applications, from cutting tools and electronics to equipment used to make chemicals. Niobium-titanium alloys lie at the heart of the world's most powerful **magnets** used by research scientists and doctors. Niobium also helps millions of people in everyday life. A coating of niobium oxide helps glass to bend light more, meaning that the glasses people wear to correct their vision can have thinner, lighter lenses.

SECRET CHEMISTRY

Niobium reacts with oxygen in the air to form a see-through layer of niobium oxide. It gives pure niobium a golden glow and protects the metal underneath from **corroding** or being attacked by **acids.**

INSIDE THE ATOM

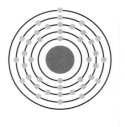

– 41 + 41 ○ 52

FORMS AND USES

1 NIOBIUM JEWELRY
If you spot metal jewelry shimmering in rainbow colors, it's probably niobium! Light bounces off the metal, but it also bounces off a thick, see-through layer of niobium oxide on the surface. The two sets of reflected light interfere with each other, like ripples from two different stones thrown into a pond. This changes the color of the reflected light that reaches our eyes!

2 ROCKET NOZZLES
Niobium added to an alloy can help other metals stand up better to heat. This is why niobium alloys are used to make the nozzles where superheated exhaust gases rush out of a rocket engine.

3 PACEMAKERS
Alloys of niobium are useful for making medical devices that sit inside a patient's body, such as pacemakers. The metal doesn't react with the body or cause an allergic reaction.

4 MEGA MAGNETS
The very powerful magnets inside MRI scanners and **particle accelerators** are made from coils of niobium alloy wire. When this alloy is very, very cold, it becomes a **superconductor**, capable of **conducting** enormous **electric currents**. When **electricity** flows through a coil of wire, it generates a **magnetic field** around the wire. The bigger the current, the stronger the magnetic field! The world's strongest superconducting magnets are 3,000 times stronger than a typical fridge magnet!

42
Mo

Molybdenum
(MUH-LIB-DEN-UM)

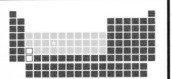

MOLYBDENUM IS ONE OF THE TOUGHEST TRANSITION METALS. IT'S THE SECRET BEHIND ARMORED TANKS AND STRONG STEEL STRUCTURES.

KEY PROPERTIES

- solid
- silvery-white metal
- fairly soft
- **malleable**
- **ductile**
- very heat resistant

WHERE IT'S FOUND

- **minerals**: molybdenite, wulfenite
- **ores** of other metals
- animals
- plants, especially legumes

HUMAN BODY

TRACE

ALL ABOUT MOLYBDENUM

Molybdenum has a history of causing confusion. In nature it's found as part of a soft, silvery-gray rock. At first, this rock was mistaken for lead ore, and named molybdenite (*molybdous* is a Greek word for lead ore). Then molybdenite itself was mistaken for graphite (a soft, gray form of carbon) and used to make pencil "lead" for more than a hundred years. Eventually, a chemist looked more closely at molybdenite, and realized that this mineral didn't actually contain graphite *or* lead, but a totally different element. The metal was extracted, and named molybdenum after its ore.

All plants and animals need a little molybdenum. It's so important for plants that the amount of molybdenum in the soil controls how quickly a tropical rainforest can grow. Molybdenum has one of the highest **melting points** of any element and is used to make some of the world's toughest steels. "Moly" steel is the secret to the strength of towering skyscrapers, enormous bridges, and impenetrable tanks. This **alloy** is the reason aircraft engines, drills, furnaces, and turbines stay strong when they reach temperatures that would melt some metals. Even a tiny amount of molybdenum makes steel less likely to rust and wear down, so it's used to make one of the most-used types of stainless steel. A **compound** of molybdenum and sulfur is used to coat the moving parts of machines. The tiny **particles** have layers that slide over each other easily, helping steel surfaces to slide over each other too. Molybdenum is an exciting element to research, and we're still learning what else this amazing metal can do.

SECRET CHEMISTRY

Molybdenum makes a good **catalyst**, and may one day help to split seawater into hydrogen and oxygen using only the energy of sunlight. This could help make hydrogen the fuel of the future (see page 18).

INSIDE THE ATOM

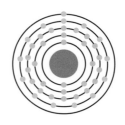

$-$ 42 $+$ 42 $\bigcirc$ 56

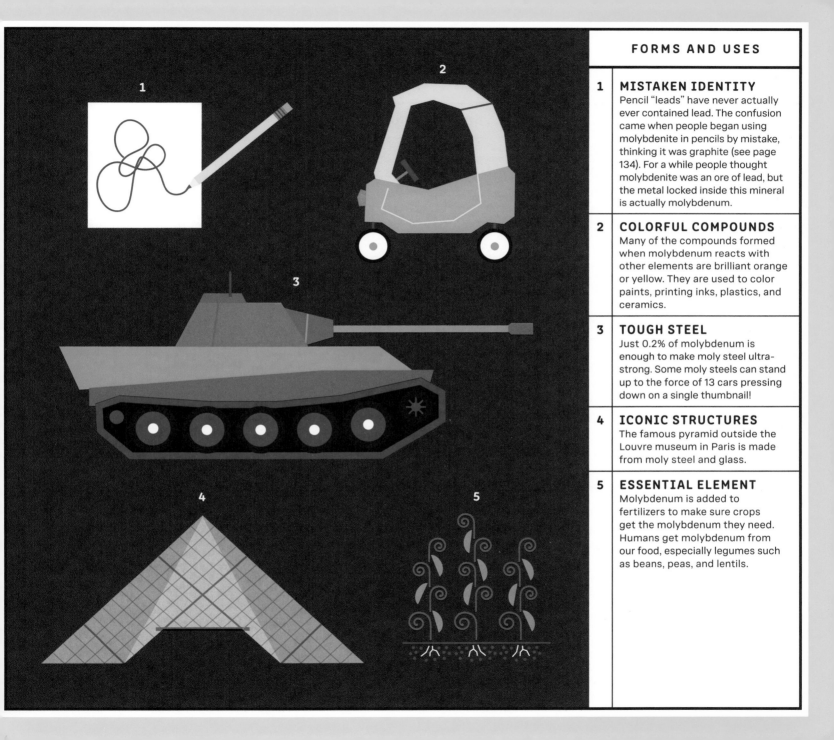

FORMS AND USES

1 MISTAKEN IDENTITY
Pencil "leads" have never actually ever contained lead. The confusion came when people began using molybdenite in pencils by mistake, thinking it was graphite (see page 134). For a while people thought molybdenite was an ore of lead, but the metal locked inside this mineral is actually molybdenum.

2 COLORFUL COMPOUNDS
Many of the compounds formed when molybdenum reacts with other elements are brilliant orange or yellow. They are used to color paints, printing inks, plastics, and ceramics.

3 TOUGH STEEL
Just 0.2% of molybdenum is enough to make moly steel ultra-strong. Some moly steels can stand up to the force of 13 cars pressing down on a single thumbnail!

4 ICONIC STRUCTURES
The famous pyramid outside the Louvre museum in Paris is made from moly steel and glass.

5 ESSENTIAL ELEMENT
Molybdenum is added to fertilizers to make sure crops get the molybdenum they need. Humans get molybdenum from our food, especially legumes such as beans, peas, and lentils.

43
Tc

Technetium
(TECK-NEE-SHEE-UM)

TRANSITION METAL

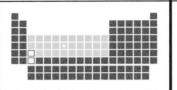

INSIDE THE ATOM

ALL ABOUT TECHNETIUM

This **radioactive** element breaks apart or **decays** very quickly compared to the life of a planet, so there is no natural technetium left on Earth. We have to make it by bombarding uranium with **neutrons**. This creates a radioactive form of molybdenum that gradually breaks apart to become technetium-99m. This form of technetium doesn't last long—half of the atoms break apart every six hours—but that's long enough for a special type of scan, which helps doctors spot diseases that would be hard to diagnose in any other way. Amazingly, technetium-99m is used in eight or nine out of every ten medical scans that use radioactivity. After a scan, the patient's body quickly gets rid of the technetium.

- − 43
- + 43
- ○ 55

45
Rh

Rhodium
(ROW-DEE-UM)

TRANSITION METAL

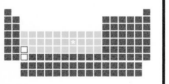

INSIDE THE ATOM

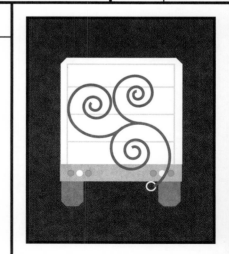

ALL ABOUT RHODIUM

Rhodium is very rare—the rarest metal that is not radioactive. Named after the Greek word for rose, it was discovered in the rose-red crystals left behind when a chemist had separated platinum and palladium from a lump of metal. Coincidentally, we now use rhodium to make air sweeter to breathe! It's an important metal in catalytic converters, the devices that sit inside the exhaust pipes of gasoline- and diesel-powered cars. The rhodium is a **catalyst** that helps to convert the **toxic** nitrogen oxides in exhaust fumes into harmless nitrogen gas (the main gas in normal air). Rhodium is also used as a catalyst to help make important chemicals, including nitric **acid**—the acid needed to make fertilizers, plastics, dyes, and medicines.

- − 45
- + 45
- ○ 58

TRANSITION METALS

Ruthenium

(ROO-THEE-NEE-UM)

44
Ru

ALL ABOUT RUTHENIUM

1 IN THE LAB
Scientists are finding ways to use ruthenium in new kinds of "dye-sensitized" **solar cells**, which mimic the process of **photosynthesis** in plants to produce **electricity**.

2 PEN NIBS
The nibs of expensive pens are tipped with hard metals such as ruthenium so they don't wear down.

Ruthenium metal is not very useful on its own. It's hard and brittle, so it breaks if you try to draw it into wire. But it's really good at protecting and improving other metals—for example, making titanium a hundred times more resistant to **corrosion**. Ruthenium **alloys** are used to make durable contacts inside electronic devices, and to coat the nibs of expensive fountain pens. Our bodies treat ruthenium atoms as if they were iron atoms, so researchers are looking at ways to use ruthenium in medicines to fight serious illnesses. Trial ruthenium medicines seem to be good at attaching themselves only to diseased **cells** and ignoring healthy cells. This could mean they have fewer side effects than medicines made with other metals in the platinum group.

TRANSITION METAL

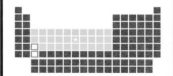

INSIDE THE ATOM

- 44
+ 44
○ 58

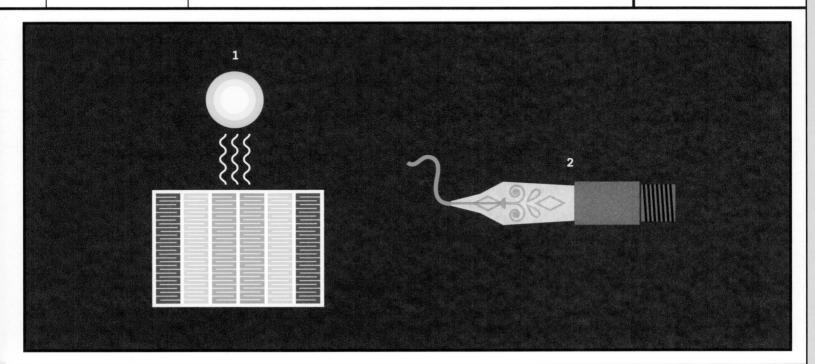

46
Pd

Palladium
(PUH-LAY-DEE-UM)

TRANSITION METAL

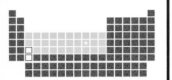

PALLADIUM IS THE MAIN METAL IN CATALYTIC CONVERTERS, THE DEVICES HIDDEN INSIDE MANY CARS AND TRUCKS TO KEEP THE AIR FRESHER.

KEY PROPERTIES

- solid
- silvery-white metal
- **malleable** when pure
- **ductile** when pure
- gets harder when worked

WHERE IT'S FOUND

- sulfide **ores:** braggite
- some rocks containing platinum, nickel, copper, and zinc
- some soils
- tree leaves

HUMAN BODY

NONE

ALL ABOUT PALLADIUM

Palladium was discovered more than 200 years ago, but at first it wasn't very popular. Its only useful property seemed to be that it didn't **corrode** (rust), so it was mainly used for making clocks and other instruments used to navigate at sea. Today, we know that palladium is a brilliant **catalyst**—a metal that can kick-start, change, or speed up chemical **reactions** without being used up itself. Palladium is used as a catalyst inside the catalytic converters hidden underneath most gasoline and diesel cars. In the future, palladium may also help us to purify hydrogen to allow us to use it as a fuel. Strangely, the metal can absorb hydrogen gas like a sponge. A piece of palladium the size of a die could soak up enough hydrogen to fill about two volleyballs! It ignores any other gases that are around, so palladium could be used to separate and purify hydrogen.

Plants and animals contain lots of complex "organic" **molecules**, with long chains of carbon atoms. To design chemicals that interact with living things—such as medicines and fertilizers—we had to figure out how to make new organic molecules in the lab. In the past, this was very difficult. Carbon atoms are so stable that it's hard to get them to link together in new ways. In 2010, a group of chemists won a Nobel Prize for discovering how to do this, using palladium as a catalyst. More than one carbon atom will attach to a palladium atom temporarily, which brings the carbon atoms close enough together to react with each other. This breakthrough has allowed chemists to build new organic molecules from scratch, to use in medicine, farming, and even in electronic devices!

SECRET CHEMISTRY

Palladium doesn't react easily with other elements, so it's good for making things like replacement teeth, which are constantly bathed in water and **acid**. This property also makes it popular in jewelry, because it stays shiny instead of reacting with the air to form **tarnish**.

INSIDE THE ATOM

 46   46 ◯ 60

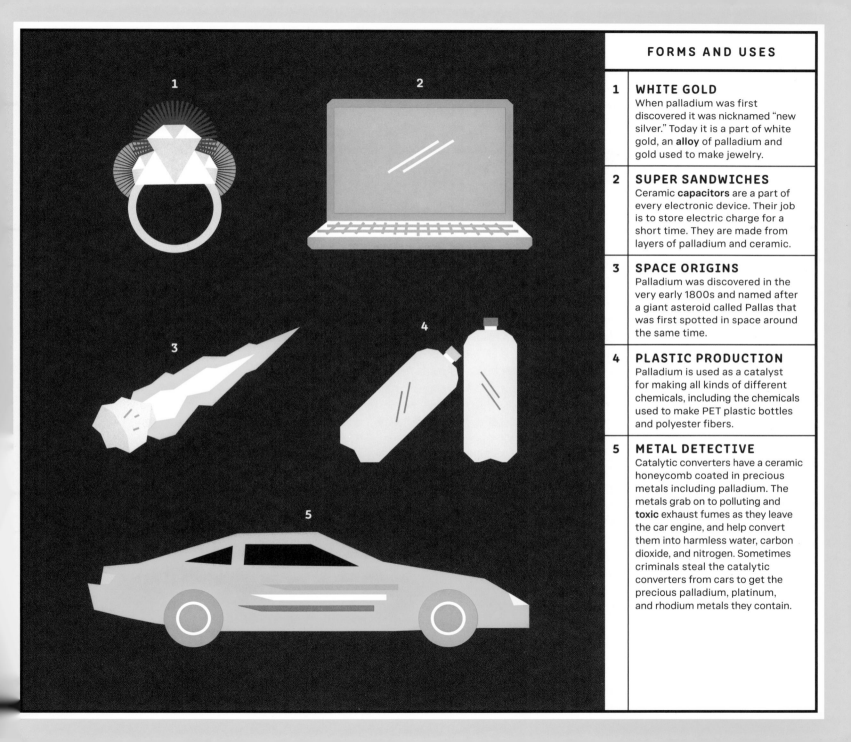

FORMS AND USES

1 WHITE GOLD
When palladium was first discovered it was nicknamed "new silver." Today it is a part of white gold, an **alloy** of palladium and gold used to make jewelry.

2 SUPER SANDWICHES
Ceramic **capacitors** are a part of every electronic device. Their job is to store electric charge for a short time. They are made from layers of palladium and ceramic.

3 SPACE ORIGINS
Palladium was discovered in the very early 1800s and named after a giant asteroid called Pallas that was first spotted in space around the same time.

4 PLASTIC PRODUCTION
Palladium is used as a catalyst for making all kinds of different chemicals, including the chemicals used to make PET plastic bottles and polyester fibers.

5 METAL DETECTIVE
Catalytic converters have a ceramic honeycomb coated in precious metals including palladium. The metals grab on to polluting and **toxic** exhaust fumes as they leave the car engine, and help convert them into harmless water, carbon dioxide, and nitrogen. Sometimes criminals steal the catalytic converters from cars to get the precious palladium, platinum, and rhodium metals they contain.

Silver

(SILL-VURR)

47

Ag

TRANSITION METAL

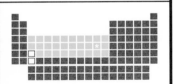

EVEN IF YOU DON'T HAVE ANY SILVER JEWELRY OR ORNAMENTS IN YOUR HOME, YOU'RE PROBABLY SURROUNDED BY SILVER! THIS METAL IS FOUND INSIDE ALMOST EVERY ELECTRICAL DEVICE, FROM CALCULATORS TO CARS.

KEY PROPERTIES

- solid
- silver metal
- very soft
- very **malleable**
- very **ductile**
- the best **conductor**

WHERE IT'S FOUND

- **minerals**: acanthite, stephanite
- as pure metal
- with gold as electrum
- **ores** of other metals
- some fungi, algae

HUMAN BODY

TRACE

ALL ABOUT SILVER

Silver was one of the first metals that people learned how to mine and separate from other elements. For more than 5,000 years it has been used to make shiny ornaments, jewelry, and tableware. Not many people eat from silver knives and forks today—pure silver reacts with certain foods and chemicals in a person's mouth, producing a metallic taste. But our homes are still full of hidden silver, quietly at work **conducting electricity**! No element does this better. As a result, almost every electronic device, television, battery-powered toy, car, and kitchen appliance contains some silver. It's particularly good for making switches, because it doesn't **corrode** or wear away easily. Silver-based switches can be used millions of times and keep working perfectly. Silver is also used to make **solar cells**, devices that convert sunlight into electricity. A thin layer of silver is painted onto a silicon wafer. The silicon releases **electrons** when sunlight hits it, and these electrons immediately begin flowing through the silver as an **electric current**.

Silver has very useful chemical properties too. Certain forms of silver kill bacteria. They are used to clean the water for our homes, swimming pools, and hospitals by stopping any bacteria and algae from growing. Silver is so good at this job, it has even been used to disinfect urine in space, so that astronauts can drink it again! Silver chloride in deodorants is the ingredient that stops stinky bacteria growing on skin, and silver **ions** in creams and bandages help to keep wounds clean. Some hospitals have also hidden silver inside stethoscopes, furniture, door handles, and even paper to stop dangerous bacteria from spreading.

SECRET CHEMISTRY

Silver reacts easily with sulfur to produce blackish silver sulfide, or **tarnish**. There is even some sulfur in the air in the form of hydrogen sulfide, one of the gases produced in our guts, which leaves our bodies as wind!

INSIDE THE ATOM

 ➖ 47 ➕ 47 ⚪ 60

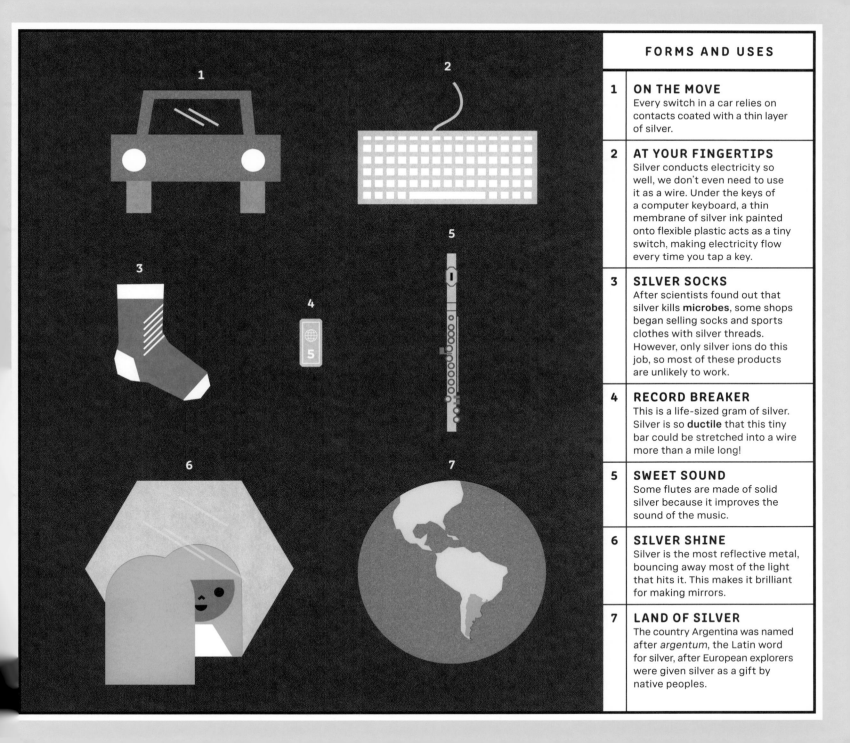

FORMS AND USES

1 ON THE MOVE
Every switch in a car relies on contacts coated with a thin layer of silver.

2 AT YOUR FINGERTIPS
Silver conducts electricity so well, we don't even need to use it as a wire. Under the keys of a computer keyboard, a thin membrane of silver ink painted onto flexible plastic acts as a tiny switch, making electricity flow every time you tap a key.

3 SILVER SOCKS
After scientists found out that silver kills **microbes**, some shops began selling socks and sports clothes with silver threads. However, only silver ions do this job, so most of these products are unlikely to work.

4 RECORD BREAKER
This is a life-sized gram of silver. Silver is so **ductile** that this tiny bar could be stretched into a wire more than a mile long!

5 SWEET SOUND
Some flutes are made of solid silver because it improves the sound of the music.

6 SILVER SHINE
Silver is the most reflective metal, bouncing away most of the light that hits it. This makes it brilliant for making mirrors.

7 LAND OF SILVER
The country Argentina was named after *argentum*, the Latin word for silver, after European explorers were given silver as a gift by native peoples.

Cadmium
(CAD-ME-UM)

48
Cd

TRANSITION METAL

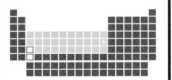

CADMIUM IS A VERY **TOXIC** HEAVY METAL. IT WAS RARE TO COME ACROSS IT IN NATURE ... UNTIL HUMAN ACTIVITIES BEGAN RELEASING CADMIUM INTO THE ENVIRONMENT FROM THE ROCKS WHERE IT HAD BEEN LOCKED AWAY.

KEY PROPERTIES

- solid
- silvery-blue metal
- very soft

WHERE IT'S FOUND

- **minerals**: greenockite, cadmoselite, otavite
- marine black shales
- rocks containing zinc
- polluted soils
- willow trees

HUMAN BODY

BUILDS UP WITH AGE

ALL ABOUT CADMIUM

Our bodies can't really tell the difference between cadmium and the metal zinc, which sits just above cadmium in the periodic table. We need zinc, so any cadmium we happen to breathe in or eat is welcomed in. Once it's inside us, our bodies can't get rid of cadmium. Its atoms cling tightly to **enzymes** in our body, and stay put for years. Before people knew how toxic cadmium was, it was often used to color plastics, rubbers, and inks bright red, orange, or yellow. Over time, lots of cadmium built up in some people's bodies, causing painful kidney and bone diseases. Today, we've almost stopped using cadmium as an everyday paint or dye, but humans are still digging up rocks that contain cadmium, and releasing this toxic element into Earth's air and soil.

We use cadmium to make rechargeable **batteries**, and to coat steel. A layer of cadmium that is about as thin as a human hair will react with chlorine in seawater to form a layer of tough cadmium chloride. This protects the steel of oil rigs and underwater pipes, so they can remain in ocean water for years. Phosphate rocks naturally contain a little cadmium, so crop fertilizers made from these rocks contain cadmium too. This toxic metal gets absorbed by plants and eaten by animals such as sheep. It's so widespread that it's hard to avoid eating a little in red meat, shellfish, rice, mushrooms, leafy plants such as spinach and cabbage, and root vegetables such as turnips. These tiny traces don't harm us, but it would be better to have no cadmium in the environment at all.

SECRET CHEMISTRY

Although cadmium isn't safe to use in everyday life, researchers are still uncovering its surprising secrets. For example, it may help scientists to design clocks so accurate, they could help us to redefine time itself!

INSIDE THE ATOM

 48   48 ◯ 66

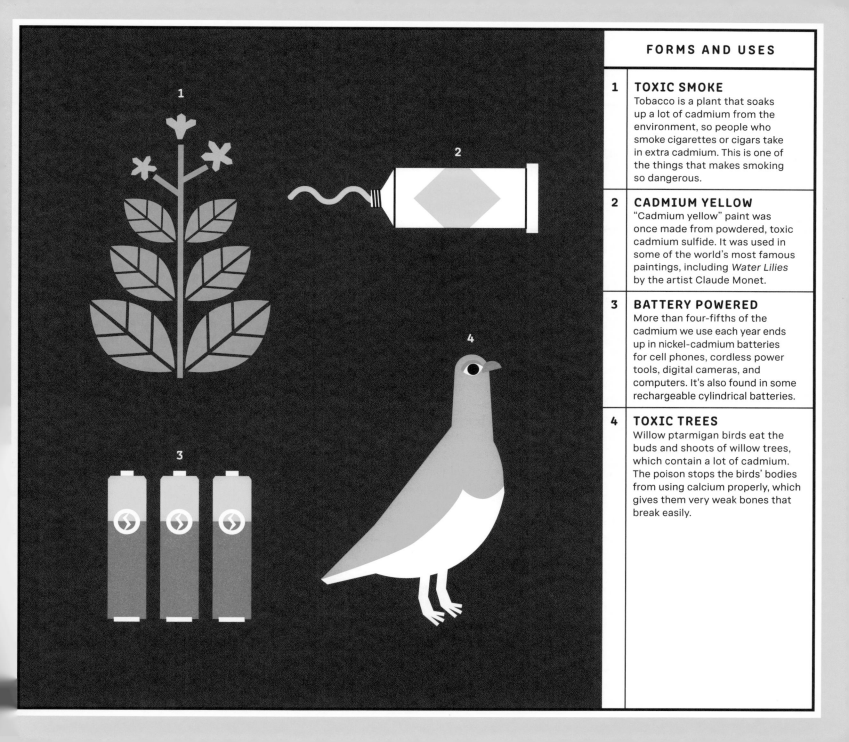

FORMS AND USES

1 TOXIC SMOKE
Tobacco is a plant that soaks up a lot of cadmium from the environment, so people who smoke cigarettes or cigars take in extra cadmium. This is one of the things that makes smoking so dangerous.

2 CADMIUM YELLOW
"Cadmium yellow" paint was once made from powdered, toxic cadmium sulfide. It was used in some of the world's most famous paintings, including *Water Lilies* by the artist Claude Monet.

3 BATTERY POWERED
More than four-fifths of the cadmium we use each year ends up in nickel-cadmium batteries for cell phones, cordless power tools, digital cameras, and computers. It's also found in some rechargeable cylindrical batteries.

4 TOXIC TREES
Willow ptarmigan birds eat the buds and shoots of willow trees, which contain a lot of cadmium. The poison stops the birds' bodies from using calcium properly, which gives them very weak bones that break easily.

72
Hf

Hafnium
(HAF-NEE-UM)

TRANSITION METAL

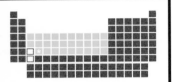

HAFNIUM HAS HELPED US WORK OUT HOW MANY BIRTHDAYS THE MOON HAS CELEBRATED! ON EARTH IT PLAYS AN IMPORTANT ROLE IN **NUCLEAR POWER** STATIONS.

KEY PROPERTIES

- solid
- silvery-gray metal
- **lustrous**
- very **ductile**
- very heat resistant

WHERE IT'S FOUND

- **minerals**: hafnon, alvite
- rocks containing zirconium

HUMAN BODY

NONE

ALL ABOUT HAFNIUM

Hafnium is always found in rocks that contain zirconium, the element just above hafnium on the period table. Finding it is easy. Separating out pure hafnium is far harder, because zirconium and hafnium react in such a similar way when they are around other elements. You can't simply add an element that will react with either zirconium or hafnium and leave the other one behind. Because it's hard to purify, hafnium is rare and expensive. Most of the hafnium that is produced ends up in **superalloys** and ceramics—wonder materials that stand up to incredible temperatures. For example, hafnium carbide (HfC) can get three times hotter than lava without melting! You won't find these materials in everyday life—they're reserved for rocket engines and turbines. However, a tiny amount of hafnium does find its way into homes, in the circuits of smartphones, laptops, and other hi-tech devices.

   Inside a nuclear reactor, small **particles** called **neutrons** zoom around, splitting apart heavy atoms of uranium and releasing even more neutrons. To keep this "chain **reaction**" under control, the number of neutrons zooming around has to be just right. Heavy hafnium happens to be great at soaking up neutrons *and* standing up to high temperatures, so it plays an important role in nuclear power stations. Some forms of hafnium are naturally **radioactive**, which means they change over time in a steady way that can be calculated and used as a natural clock! By comparing the hafnium in Moon rocks and Earth rocks, scientists were able to work out that the Moon was formed 4.51 billion years ago.

SECRET CHEMISTRY

Hafnium **catalysts** can break some of the toughest **bonds** in nature. This includes the bonds between pairs of nitrogen atoms in the air all around us. Only by breaking these atoms apart can we get them to react with other elements!

INSIDE THE ATOM

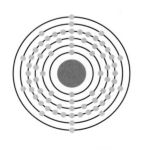

● 72 ✚ 72 ○ 108

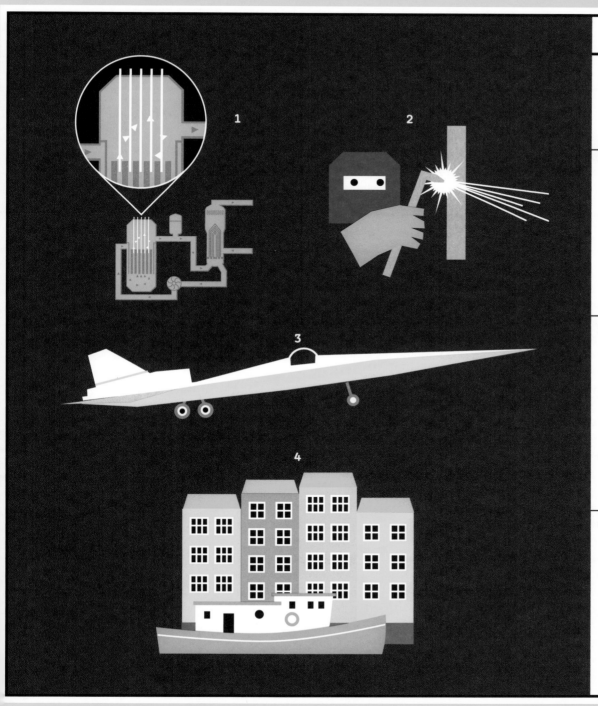

FORMS AND USES

1 CONTROLLING FISSION
Inside nuclear power stations, hafnium "control rods" are lowered into the fuel to slow down a **nuclear fission** reaction, or raised to speed it up.

2 WELDING METALS
Plasma **welding** torches use a spark of **electricity** to heat gas to such high temperatures that it will melt two pieces of metal and weld them together! The metal tips used to make the spark need to resist melting in order for the torch to work. Hafnium doesn't melt until it reaches 4051°F—twice as hot as flowing lava—so it's the perfect metal for the job.

3 HEAT RESISTANT
Hafnium **alloys** and ceramics are some of the most heat-resistant materials on Earth. One **compound** of tungsten, hafnium, and carbon can be heated to 7457°F without melting! Materials like this could one day be used to shield hypersonic planes from the heat generated by traveling at least five times faster than sound. At this speed, the trip from London to Washington, DC would take less than an hour!

4 COPENHAGEN
Hafnium was discovered inside rocks that contained zirconium, after many experiments. These were carried out in Copenhagen, Denmark, so hafnium was named after *Hafnia*, the Latin name for Copenhagen.

73
Ta

Tantalum
(TAN-TUH-LUM)

TRANSITION METAL

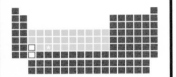

THE STORY OF TANTALUM HIGHLIGHTS THE HARM THAT CAN BE CAUSED TO PEOPLE, WILDLIFE, AND THE ENVIRONMENT IN MINING THE ELEMENTS WE USE TO MAKE ELECTRONIC DEVICES.

KEY PROPERTIES

- solid
- silvery metal
- shiny
- very hard
- **malleable** when pure
- **ductile** when pure
- high **melting point**

WHERE IT'S FOUND

- **minerals**: tantalite, samarskite, pyrochlore
- rocks containing tin

HUMAN BODY

TRACE

ALL ABOUT TANTALUM

Humans have found lots of different ways to use tantalum. **Alloys** and **compounds** of this hard metal can protect cheaper metals from heat, scratches, or chemicals. A layer of tantalum as thin as a piece of paper can be a formidable shield. Because tantalum doesn't react with chemicals that would eat holes in other metals, it's used to make tanks, pipes, valves, and other equipment needed to make and store **corrosive** chemicals. Tantalum doesn't react with the chemicals in our bodies either, so it's used to make replacement hip joints, bolts that hold broken bones together, and tubes that keep damaged blood vessels open. Dense tantalum also shows up well on **X-rays**, so it can also be used to help diagnose cancers that are really hard to spot in other ways.

Elements and their compounds may help humans in lots of different ways, but they can also have a terrible cost, especially to the people, wildlife, and environment in the areas where they are mined. Most of the tantalum the world uses is mined in Africa. Because tantalum is hard to get hold of, it is very expensive. This has led to fighting over who controls the few mines where rocks containing tantalum are found. The money made from selling tantalum has also been used to fund conflict. In some countries, this mining and conflict is harming the people and wildlife that lives around the mines—including endangered gorillas. Sadly, similar stories can be told for many other elements in the periodic table.

SECRET CHEMISTRY

Tantalum and niobium are always found together in the same rocks and minerals. They are very similar elements, which makes them hard and expensive to separate.

INSIDE THE ATOM

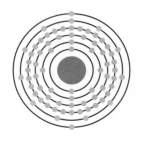

 — 73 + 73 ○ 108

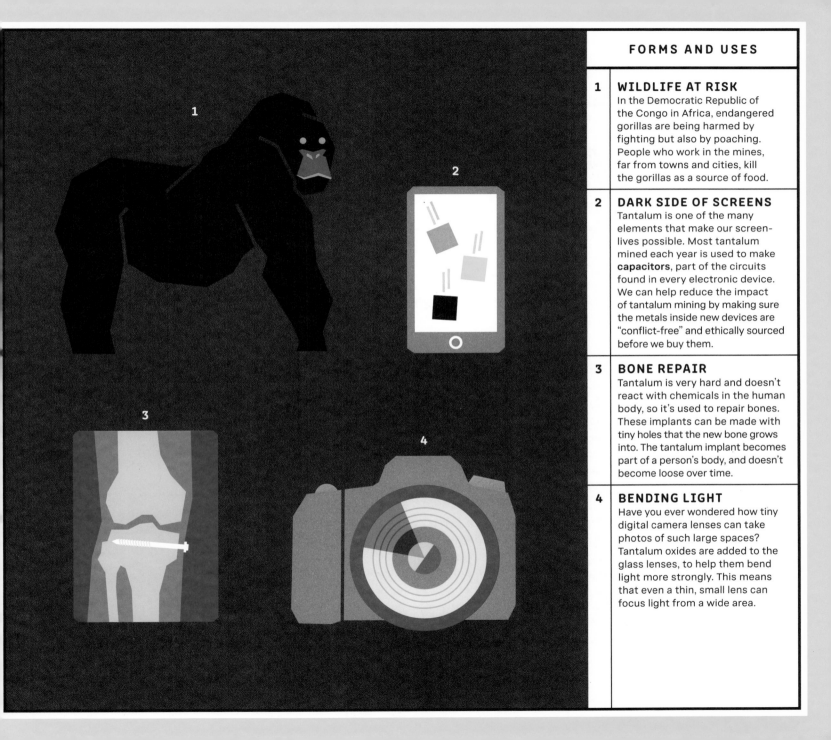

FORMS AND USES

1 WILDLIFE AT RISK
In the Democratic Republic of the Congo in Africa, endangered gorillas are being harmed by fighting but also by poaching. People who work in the mines, far from towns and cities, kill the gorillas as a source of food.

2 DARK SIDE OF SCREENS
Tantalum is one of the many elements that make our screen-lives possible. Most tantalum mined each year is used to make **capacitors**, part of the circuits found in every electronic device. We can help reduce the impact of tantalum mining by making sure the metals inside new devices are "conflict-free" and ethically sourced before we buy them.

3 BONE REPAIR
Tantalum is very hard and doesn't react with chemicals in the human body, so it's used to repair bones. These implants can be made with tiny holes that the new bone grows into. The tantalum implant becomes part of a person's body, and doesn't become loose over time.

4 BENDING LIGHT
Have you ever wondered how tiny digital camera lenses can take photos of such large spaces? Tantalum oxides are added to the glass lenses, to help them bend light more strongly. This means that even a thin, small lens can focus light from a wide area.

74
W

Tungsten
(TONGUE-STIN)

TRANSITION METAL

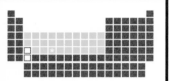

THIS INCREDIBLY TOUGH METAL LIES AT THE HEART OF THE WORLD'S STRONGEST **ALLOYS**, AND AT THE TIPS OF BALLPOINT PENS!

KEY PROPERTIES

- solid
- silvery-white metal
- **lustrous**
- very strong
- **malleable** when pure
- **ductile** when pure
- very high **melting point**

WHERE IT'S FOUND

- **minerals**: scheelite, wolframite, tungstenite
- **rocks**: granite

HUMAN BODY

TRACE

ALL ABOUT TUNGSTEN

Tungsten is almost three times as dense as iron, which means it's also three times as heavy. A lump of tungsten the shape and size of a tennis ball would weigh around 6.6 pounds—heavier than a typical house brick. Its **density** comes in handy in items like cell phones and clocks that have a vibrate mode. These often have a tiny but heavy lump of tungsten alloy inside. The lump is attached off-center to a tiny motor. This causes a strong vibration when the motor spins! Although pure tungsten is soft, it makes steel alloys superstrong. Tungsten steel was first used in the 1800s and 1900s to make weapons. Today it is still used to make bullets and armored tanks, but tungsten alloys and **compounds** are found in everyday objects too, from darts to drill bits. Because tungsten is so hard, these objects have to be shaped using the hardest substance of all—diamond!

Tungsten played an important role in the history of electric lighting as well. The very first lightbulbs changed electrical energy into light by passing **electricity** through a very thin wire, called a filament, that glowed when it got hot. All sorts of materials were tried out for the filaments, but tungsten proved to be the best. It glowed brightly and lasted the longest. Tungsten was also ideal because it stands up to heat better than any other metal—it has to be heated to 6177°F before it melts! Tungsten also expands less than other metals when it's heated and is less likely to evaporate (change into gas) when it gets hot.

SECRET CHEMISTRY

Almost half of the tungsten produced each year is used to make tungsten carbide, a material even stronger than tungsten steel. It can cut and drill through the world's hardest materials, from steel to tooth enamel!

INSIDE THE ATOM

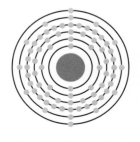

● 74　✚ 74　○ 110

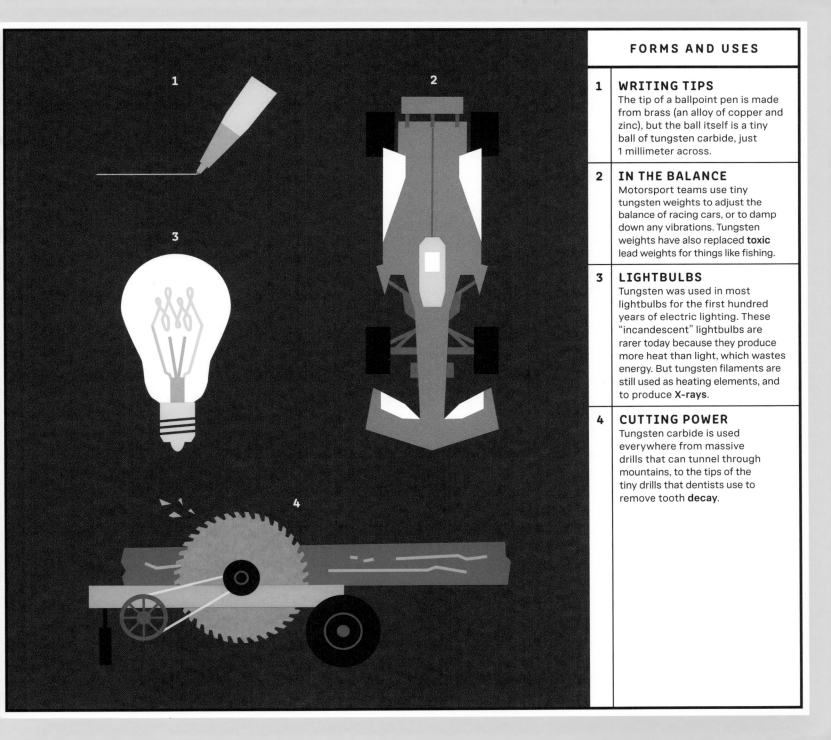

FORMS AND USES

1 WRITING TIPS
The tip of a ballpoint pen is made from brass (an alloy of copper and zinc), but the ball itself is a tiny ball of tungsten carbide, just 1 millimeter across.

2 IN THE BALANCE
Motorsport teams use tiny tungsten weights to adjust the balance of racing cars, or to damp down any vibrations. Tungsten weights have also replaced **toxic** lead weights for things like fishing.

3 LIGHTBULBS
Tungsten was used in most lightbulbs for the first hundred years of electric lighting. These "incandescent" lightbulbs are rarer today because they produce more heat than light, which wastes energy. But tungsten filaments are still used as heating elements, and to produce **X-rays**.

4 CUTTING POWER
Tungsten carbide is used everywhere from massive drills that can tunnel through mountains, to the tips of the tiny drills that dentists use to remove tooth **decay**.

75
Re

Rhenium
(REE-NEE-UM)

TRANSITION METAL

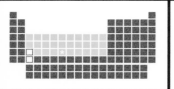

INSIDE THE ATOM

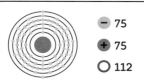

- − 75
- + 75
- ○ 112

ALL ABOUT RHENIUM

Rhenium has a very high **melting point**, so it is often used along with tungsten in **alloys** that have to stand up to very high temperatures, such as the elements that glow red hot in ovens and furnaces. These heat-resistant alloys are also used to produce the **X-rays** in hospital X-ray machines, and to make devices that can measure temperatures higher than 3600°F. The super-hard **compound** rhenium diboride is one of the only materials in the world that can scratch diamond. But there aren't many diamonds that need scratching, so rhenium's main use is in nickel alloys, to make the turbine and jet engine blades that can stand up to some of the toughest working conditions in the world (see page 64).

(see page 64)

76
Os

Osmium
(OZ-ME-UM)

TRANSITION METAL

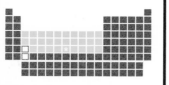

INSIDE THE ATOM

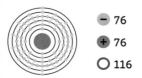

- − 76
- + 76
- ○ 116

ALL ABOUT OSMIUM

Osmium is rare, but it's not a metal you'd ever want to use as jewelry. It was named after the disgusting smell that it gives off as its metal surface reacts with oxygen in the air! The smell is caused by osmium tetroxide. Biologists use this **toxic** chemical to stain the **cells** of **microbes** so they are visible under powerful scanning **electron** microscopes. These microscopes capture images of electrons bouncing off objects, rather than light. Like its neighbors, osmium is very hard, dense, and resistant to **corrosion**. In the past it was used to make durable metal parts of pens, compasses, clocks, and the hard-tipped stylus of record players. But there are other metals that can do the same jobs, and which are easier to find (and less stinky!).

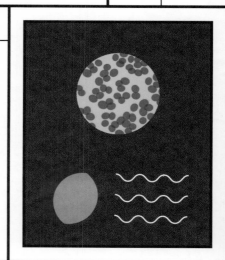

TRANSITION METALS

Iridium
(IH-RID-EE-UM)

77

Ir

ALL ABOUT IRIDIUM

1 ASTEROID STRIKE
The iridium dust from an asteroid strike would have been carried all the way around the world on the wind, eventually raining down on Earth, where it became part of soils and then rocks.

2 SPARK PLUGS
Iridium spark plugs last longer than copper spark plugs, because iridium is a much tougher metal.

Iridium is the rarest of all metals. Most iridium on Earth is found inside meteorites, or the ash thrown from active volcanoes. Only a little iridium is extracted each year, from the rock left over from nickel mining. It is a good metal for making objects that need to sit in difficult conditions without corroding, from the spark plugs that start gasoline or diesel cars, to underwater pipes. All around the world, rocks that are 66 million years old contain far more iridium than rocks from any other time in Earth's history. This is a clue to how dinosaurs—along with most Cretaceous plants and animals—became extinct. Space rocks contain more iridium than Earth rocks, suggesting that a huge meteorite or asteroid collided with Earth 66 million years ago and exploded into dust.

TRANSITION METAL

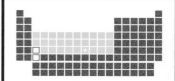

INSIDE THE ATOM

- – 77
- + 77
- O 116

78

Pt

Platinum

(PLA-TI-NUM)

TRANSITION METAL

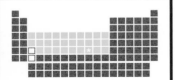

PLATINUM IS RARER AND MORE PRECIOUS THAN GOLD. IT'S ALSO MORE USEFUL, HELPING TO CURE CANCER, STORE INFORMATION ON COMPUTERS, AND CLEAN UP EXHAUST FUMES SO WE CAN BREATHE FRESH AIR.

KEY PROPERTIES

- solid
- silvery-white metal
- **lustrous**
- very soft
- **malleable**
- **ductile**

WHERE IT'S FOUND

- **minerals**: cooperite, sperrylite, braggite
- rocks containing copper and nickel

HUMAN BODY

CAN BUILD UP OVER TIME

ALL ABOUT PLATINUM

It's possible to find nuggets of pure platinum in Earth's crust, so like silver and gold, this metal has been used by different civilizations for thousands of years—long before people worked out how to separate metals from minerals and rocks. However, platinum melts at a much higher temperature than silver or gold, so for a long time the only way to use platinum was to hammer it into shape. It's a soft metal, so this wasn't as hard as it sounds. It can be hammered into a sheet of foil 100 times thinner than a sheet of paper! As people worked out how to generate the high temperatures needed to melt platinum, the number of ways we use this metal grew and grew. Today it has been estimated that this metal finds its way into as many as a fifth of all human-made products, from fuels and medicines, to computers and the fiber-optic cables that carry digital data around the world. Platinum is also a popular metal for making jewelry.

Platinum does not react easily with other elements, which makes it fairly safe to use inside a person's body—in pacemakers, replacement bones, or as part of medicines. Although platinum is not reactive itself, it's very good at speeding up **reactions** between other elements and chemicals, as a **catalyst**. Just holding a piece of platinum in a mixture of oxygen and hydrogen makes those gases react so quickly that they explode! Most platinum produced each year is used to make catalytic converters in cars and other vehicles. These devices convert harmful gases in vehicle exhaust fumes into non-**toxic** substances.

SECRET CHEMISTRY

The medicine cisplatin, which is used in chemotherapy, is a platinum **compound**. Cisplatin **molecules** can latch onto the **DNA** of a cancer **cell** and pull it out of shape, making it impossible for that cell to make copies of itself. This stops tumors growing and spreading.

INSIDE THE ATOM

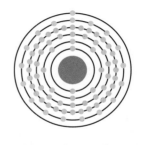

– 78   + 78   ○ 117

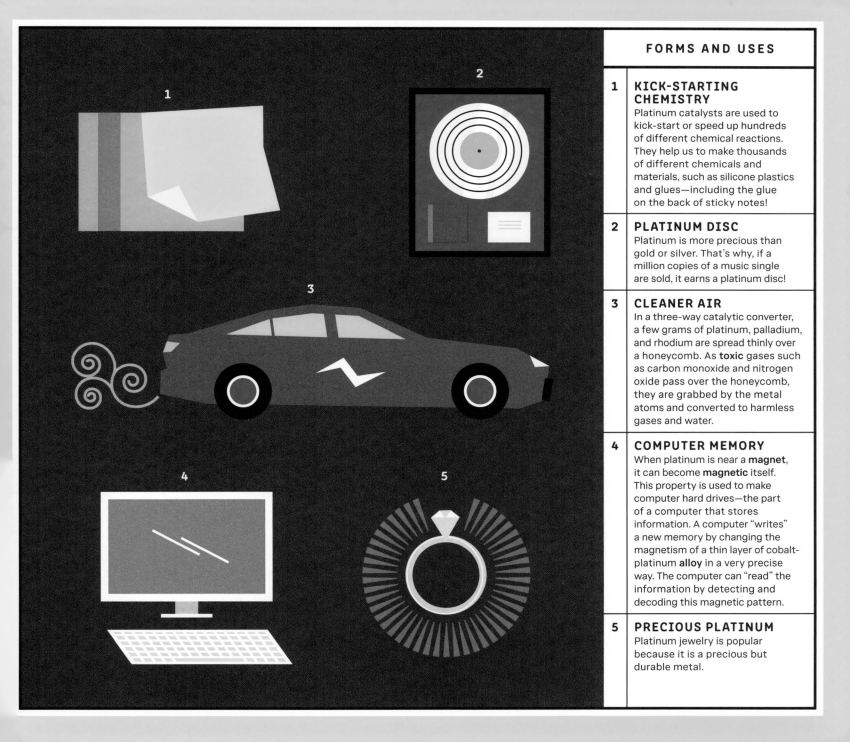

FORMS AND USES

1 KICK-STARTING CHEMISTRY
Platinum catalysts are used to kick-start or speed up hundreds of different chemical reactions. They help us to make thousands of different chemicals and materials, such as silicone plastics and glues—including the glue on the back of sticky notes!

2 PLATINUM DISC
Platinum is more precious than gold or silver. That's why, if a million copies of a music single are sold, it earns a platinum disc!

3 CLEANER AIR
In a three-way catalytic converter, a few grams of platinum, palladium, and rhodium are spread thinly over a honeycomb. As **toxic** gases such as carbon monoxide and nitrogen oxide pass over the honeycomb, they are grabbed by the metal atoms and converted to harmless gases and water.

4 COMPUTER MEMORY
When platinum is near a **magnet**, it can become **magnetic** itself. This property is used to make computer hard drives—the part of a computer that stores information. A computer "writes" a new memory by changing the magnetism of a thin layer of cobalt-platinum **alloy** in a very precise way. The computer can "read" the information by detecting and decoding this magnetic pattern.

5 PRECIOUS PLATINUM
Platinum jewelry is popular because it is a precious but durable metal.

Gold

79

Au

(GOLD)

TRANSITION METAL

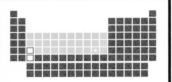

FOR THOUSANDS OF YEARS, PEOPLE HAVE SEARCHED, STOLEN, HOARDED, AND FOUGHT FOR GOLD. IT'S STILL ONE OF THE MOST PRECIOUS AND SOUGHT-AFTER METALS IN THE WORLD, DESPITE BEING FAR LESS USEFUL THAN MOST OTHER ELEMENTS.

KEY PROPERTIES

- solid
- shiny yellow metal
- very soft
- very **malleable**
- very **ductile**

WHERE IT'S FOUND

- **minerals**: quartz, pyrite, sylvanite
- rivers and streams
- inside some rocks
- Martian meteorites
- seawater
- some plants

HUMAN BODY

NONE

ALL ABOUT GOLD

Ever since the first nuggets of pure gold were discovered, gold has been considered one of the most beautiful metals. It doesn't react with gases in the air and it stays golden and shiny rather than **tarnishing** like silver. It's also easier to find than most other metals. Gold is very unreactive, so instead of combining with other elements to form minerals, grains, flakes, and lumps of gold are found lying around in and on Earth's crust. In some places, finding gold is as easy as sieving through the sand at the bottom of a stream. In every period of history, and almost every part of the world, people have worn gold jewelry, traded gold as money, decorated buildings, artwork, and important objects with gold, and awarded gold medals for great achievements. It still has great emotional, cultural, and financial value today.

Gold is too soft to make tools with, too unreactive to form useful chemicals, and too rare to be cheap—there is four million times more iron than gold in Earth's crust. For this reason, most of the gold mined and sold each year is still used to make jewelry. But humans have found some other uses for this unique metal. In medicines, gold can help to treat conditions ranging from arthritis to disease caused by parasites. Dentists use gold to make false teeth and fillings. Like platinum, gold's neighbor in the periodic table, gold is also a useful **catalyst**. It's especially good at persuading **molecules** of **toxic** carbon monoxide gas (CO) to combine with extra oxygen to form molecules of a safer gas, carbon dioxide (CO_2).

SECRET CHEMISTRY

Atoms on the surface of a lump of gold cling tightly to their outer **electron**, refusing to share it with other elements in a **reaction**. This is why gold can shine brightly for thousands of years, never reacting with the air around it.

INSIDE THE ATOM

● 79 ✚ 79 ○ 118

FORMS AND USES

1 MIXING METALS
Gold is so soft that it is often mixed with other metals for strength. Most gold we see in everyday life is not pure. For example, gold teeth and fillings are about three-quarters gold, **alloyed** with silver, palladium, and zinc.

2 SPACE SHIELD
A piece of gold the size of a grain of rice can be beaten into a sheet the size of a standard hula hoop! This gold leaf is so thin, you can see through it. A thin coating of gold on an astronaut's visor bounces away heat and other dangerous **radiation** from the sun.

3 ANCIENT ICON
The Ancient Egyptians found gold at the bottom of the Nile, and also mined it from inside rocks. They used it to make precious objects. This gold mask was found in the famous Egyptian pharaoh Tutankhamun's tomb, which contained more than 200 pounds of gold.

4 LOCKED AWAY
The Bank of England has around 400,000 bars of gold in its vaults, the second-largest collection in the world! Each one weighs 400 troy ounces (27 pounds). A troy ounce is a traditional measure of gold that has been used since the Middle Ages.

5 DAZZLING DOME
Gold leaf is used to cover domes, because solid gold would be far too heavy. The ultra-thin layer of pure gold covering the Dome of the Rock in Jerusalem, Israel, is just 2 micrometers thick— for comparison, a human hair is around 75 micrometers thick— but it weighs 176 pounds.

80
Hg

Mercury
(MERK-YOUR-EE)

TRANSITION METAL

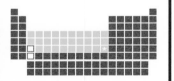

☠ ⚡

MERCURY IS THE ONLY METAL THAT IS LIQUID AT ROOM TEMPERATURE. FOR THOUSANDS OF YEARS IT WAS USED WIDELY BY HUMANS, BUT TODAY WE KNOW IT'S A **TOXIC** METAL THAT WE SHOULD TRY TO AVOID.

KEY PROPERTIES

- liquid
- silvery-white metal
- shiny
- high **surface tension**
- forms rounded drops

WHERE IT'S FOUND

- **minerals**: cinnabar, livingstonite
- soils
- air
- all living things

HUMAN BODY

VARIES

ALL ABOUT MERCURY

Mercury's **melting point** (−37.89°F) and **boiling point** (673.91°F) are far lower than those of most other metals. This made it easy for ancient peoples to extract pure mercury from rocks. All they had to do was crush and heat the bright red mineral cinnabar, and the mercury would evaporate. When this vapor was collected and cooled, it became a shiny, silver-colored liquid. The Ancient Chinese, Egyptians, Romans, Greeks, and Incas found all sorts of uses for this "liquid silver." Mercury was used as a medicine for almost 1,000 years, to treat everything from skin infections to sore gums. It was used in make-up, batteries, thermometers, electronic circuits, and to help make mirrors. Today we know that the things that make mercury good at killing disease-causing bacteria also make it toxic for humans. If it gets into our bodies through our nose or mouth, or a cut in our skin, it can damage our nervous system, or our liver and kidneys, where it collects as our body tries to get rid of it.

Most of the jobs that mercury used to do are now carried out by different, safer elements. But mercury is still found in our homes, in button batteries (which makes them incredibly dangerous for young children who might swallow them) and in some energy-efficient lightbulbs. Mercury is still allowed in these compact fluorescent lightbulbs because they are helping to reduce the amount of energy we use, but if they break or get dumped in the trash the mercury can escape into the environment. We also release mercury into the environment when we burn fossil fuels or throw old batteries into household trash that gets burned in an incinerator. You can help by making sure any bulbs and batteries used in your home are disposed of at a proper recycling center.

SECRET CHEMISTRY

Mercury is also known as quicksilver, because drops of the liquid metal move around so quickly when they are handled—almost as if the metal were alive. The metal is named after Mercury, the planet that moves most quickly around the Sun.

INSIDE THE ATOM

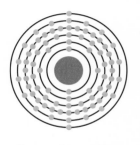

− 80   + 80   ◯ 122

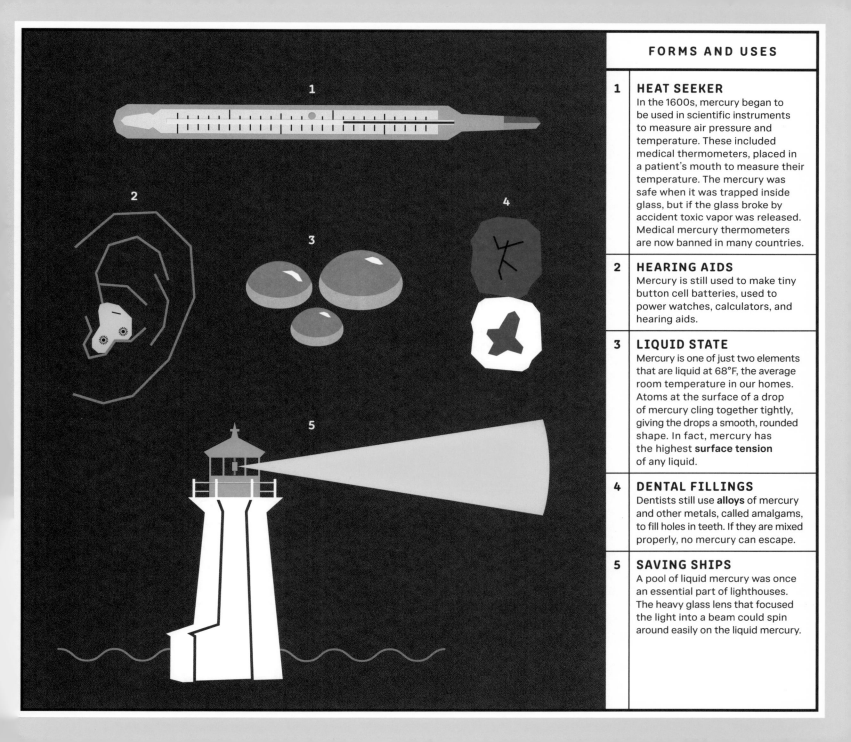

FORMS AND USES

1 **HEAT SEEKER**
In the 1600s, mercury began to be used in scientific instruments to measure air pressure and temperature. These included medical thermometers, placed in a patient's mouth to measure their temperature. The mercury was safe when it was trapped inside glass, but if the glass broke by accident toxic vapor was released. Medical mercury thermometers are now banned in many countries.

2 **HEARING AIDS**
Mercury is still used to make tiny button cell batteries, used to power watches, calculators, and hearing aids.

3 **LIQUID STATE**
Mercury is one of just two elements that are liquid at 68°F, the average room temperature in our homes. Atoms at the surface of a drop of mercury cling together tightly, giving the drops a smooth, rounded shape. In fact, mercury has the highest **surface tension** of any liquid.

4 **DENTAL FILLINGS**
Dentists still use **alloys** of mercury and other metals, called amalgams, to fill holes in teeth. If they are mixed properly, no mercury can escape.

5 **SAVING SHIPS**
A pool of liquid mercury was once an essential part of lighthouses. The heavy glass lens that focused the light into a beam could spin around easily on the liquid mercury.

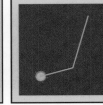

13

Al

Aluminum

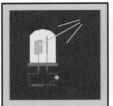

31

Ga

Gallium

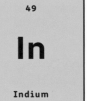

49

In

Indium

50

Sn

Tin

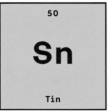

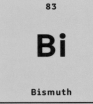

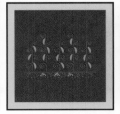

81

Tl

Thallium

82

Pb

Lead

83

Bi

Bismuth

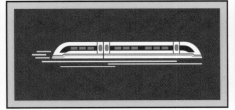

Post-Transition Metals

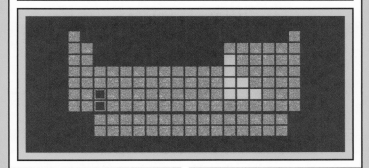

ALTHOUGH THESE ELEMENTS ARE NICKNAMED THE "POOR METALS," THE POST-TRANSITION METALS ARE INCREDIBLY USEFUL.

They include tin, which changed the world in the Bronze Age, and aluminum which is one of the most-used metals in the world today. You'll find them hard at work everywhere in your home, from your kitchen and car to electronic gadgets and medicines. They even include the element behind touch screens that respond to our fingertips. In power stations, hospitals, and labs, post-transition metals do jobs that no other element can.

In the periodic table, these metals are found between the transition metals and the metalloids. Their properties are quite "in between" as well. They are softer and weaker than transition metals, and don't **conduct electricity** as well. They also melt and boil at lower temperatures. However, the differences between the post-transition metals outweigh their similarities. They include one of the lightest metals in the world, as well as some of the heaviest and densest. They also include weird and wonderful gallium that melts in the palm of your hand, and bismuth that forms rainbow crystals so spectacular, they look like they belong in a storybook. The villain in this storybook would be thallium, a deadly poison.

13
Al

Aluminum
(AH-LOOM-IN-UM)

POST-TRANSITION METAL

ALUMINUM USED TO BE MORE PRECIOUS THAN GOLD. TODAY IT'S ONE OF THE LEAST EXPENSIVE AND MOST USEFUL METALS IN THE WORLD.

KEY PROPERTIES

- solid
- silvery-white metal
- soft when pure
- hard in **alloys**
- **malleable** and **ductile**
- very lightweight

WHERE IT'S FOUND

- hundreds of **minerals**, such as bauxite and gibbsite
- soils
- plants, especially grasses

HUMAN BODY

TRACE

ALL ABOUT ALUMINUM

The Earth's crust contains more aluminum than any other metal, but for most of human history no one knew it was there. Aluminum forms strong **bonds** with oxygen and silicon, so it was bound up inside rocks and minerals. Less than 200 years ago, a chemist managed to make the first pure sample of aluminum, and the world soon fell in love with its amazing properties. It is lightweight, shiny like silver, and strong under tension but soft enough to hammer into shape. It is also good at **conducting** heat and **electricity** and, like gold, it doesn't rust. Everyone wanted a piece of this "magic" metal. One French ruler even had aluminum plates, knives, and forks made to impress his most important guests!

Today, you're more likely to see aluminum knives and forks at a campsite than in a royal court. It's now so much easier and cheaper to extract aluminum from rocks that aluminum has become the second most-used metal in the world after iron. We can also recycle aluminum that has already been used over and over again! More than half of the aluminum made each year is from recycled scrap. It has hundreds of uses, from large car and aircraft bodies, electric power cables, and streetlamps, to the aluminum foil, cooking pans, and drink cans inside our homes. Aluminum **compound**s are even used to make deodorant, and to help purify water before it comes to our homes!

SECRET CHEMISTRY

Aluminum reacts with the air to form a layer of hard, transparent aluminum oxide, which protects the metal from **corrosion**. This makes it great for building things that spend many years outside in all weathers.

INSIDE THE ATOM

● 13 ⊕ 13 ○ 14

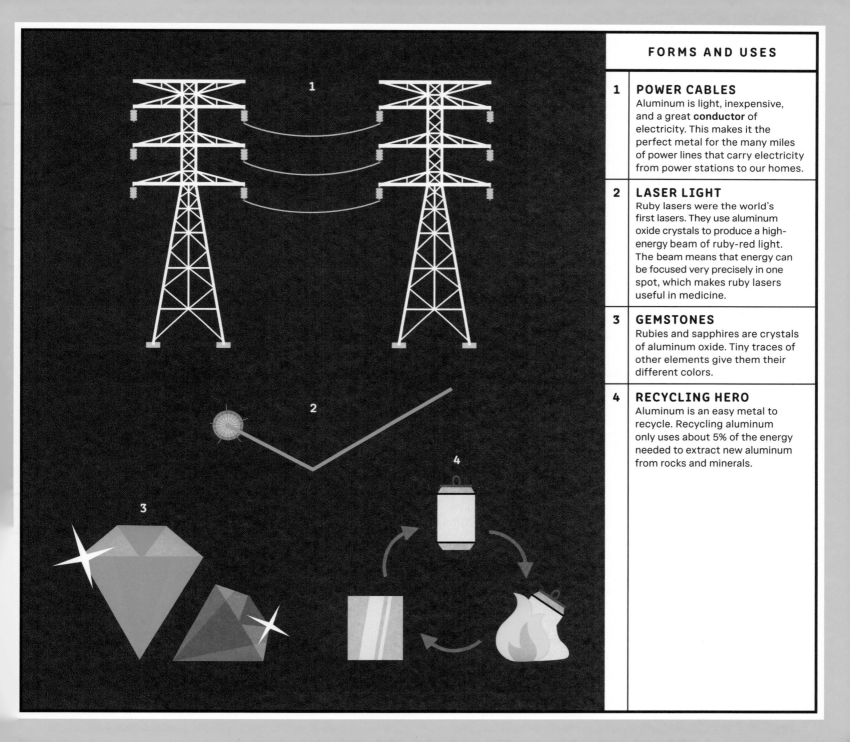

FORMS AND USES

1 POWER CABLES
Aluminum is light, inexpensive, and a great **conductor** of electricity. This makes it the perfect metal for the many miles of power lines that carry electricity from power stations to our homes.

2 LASER LIGHT
Ruby lasers were the world's first lasers. They use aluminum oxide crystals to produce a high-energy beam of ruby-red light. The beam means that energy can be focused very precisely in one spot, which makes ruby lasers useful in medicine.

3 GEMSTONES
Rubies and sapphires are crystals of aluminum oxide. Tiny traces of other elements give them their different colors.

4 RECYCLING HERO
Aluminum is an easy metal to recycle. Recycling aluminum only uses about 5% of the energy needed to extract new aluminum from rocks and minerals.

Gallium

31
Ga

(GAL-EE-UM)

POST-TRANSITION METAL

SCIENTISTS ARE STILL DISCOVERING THE STRANGE POWERS OF THIS METAL THAT MELTS IN YOUR HANDS.

KEY PROPERTIES

- solid
- silvery-blue metal
- glass-like
- very soft
- brittle
- melts in your hand

WHERE IT'S FOUND

- **minerals**: gallite
- rocks containing aluminum or zinc
- coal

HUMAN BODY

TRACE

ALL ABOUT GALLIUM

When Dmitri Mendeleev drew the first periodic table of the elements, he left gaps for elements that hadn't been discovered yet. Gallium was the first of these missing puzzle pieces to be found, and it was an exciting one! Gallium is a silvery metal that's soft enough to cut with a knife. Even more surprisingly, it's solid at room temperature but melts at just 85.58°F. This means that a piece of gallium will melt on a sunny day, or in the warmth of someone's hands. In the 1800s, scientists would play tricks on people by making teaspoons out of gallium. These people would be utterly baffled to see their metal spoons melt away into their tea!

Gallium is helping us to understand the universe better. Tons of liquid gallium are used to make special telescopes that can detect tiny **particles** (called neutrinos) deep inside the Sun! Gallium also mixes easily with other metals to form **alloys** that take advantage of gallium's low **melting point**. Some gallium **compounds**, such as gallium nitride and gallium arsenide, have an even more amazing property. When **electricity** flows through them, these materials glow with light. They are the key ingredient in LEDs (light-emitting diodes)—the tiny devices that light up the screens of laptops, cell phones, and some televisions and computer monitors. Because LEDs convert electrical energy to light but not heat, they don't waste energy like other types of lightbulbs. Scientists are excited about the ways that we might be able to use gallium nitride in the future. It will be able to do some of the jobs that silicon currently does, but better. This could lead to smaller electronics, better reception on cell phones, and space probes that can explore the hottest planets in the solar system.

SECRET CHEMISTRY

Gallium will melt in your hands but doesn't boil and turn into a gas until it reaches 4044°F, which is about 20 times the temperature of boiling water! This is one of the biggest gaps between melting and **boiling point** of any element.

INSIDE THE ATOM

− 31   + 31   ○ 38

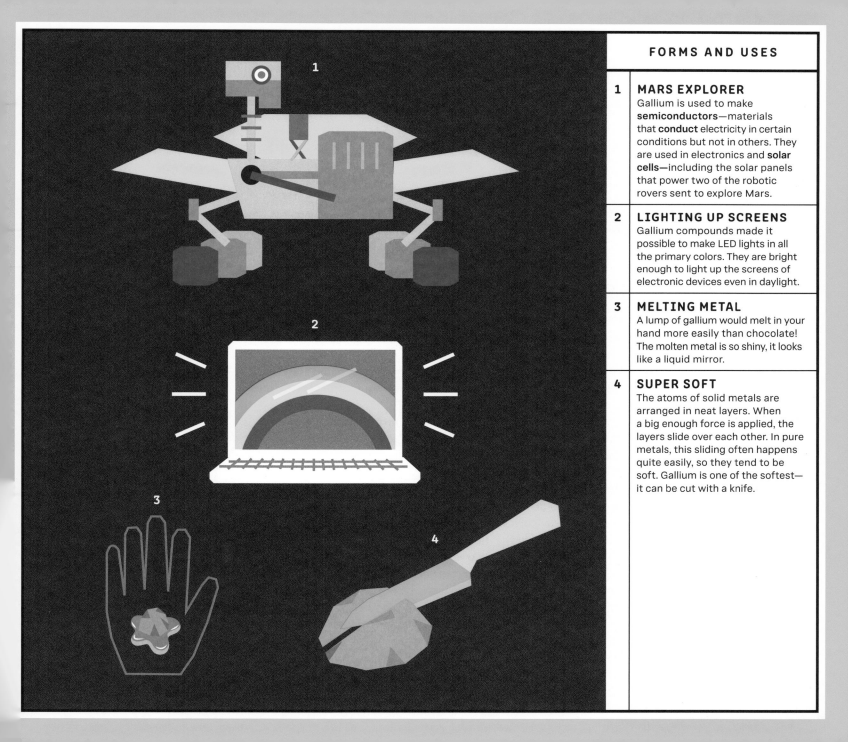

FORMS AND USES

1 MARS EXPLORER
Gallium is used to make **semiconductors**—materials that **conduct** electricity in certain conditions but not in others. They are used in electronics and **solar cells**—including the solar panels that power two of the robotic rovers sent to explore Mars.

2 LIGHTING UP SCREENS
Gallium compounds made it possible to make LED lights in all the primary colors. They are bright enough to light up the screens of electronic devices even in daylight.

3 MELTING METAL
A lump of gallium would melt in your hand more easily than chocolate! The molten metal is so shiny, it looks like a liquid mirror.

4 SUPER SOFT
The atoms of solid metals are arranged in neat layers. When a big enough force is applied, the layers slide over each other. In pure metals, this sliding often happens quite easily, so they tend to be soft. Gallium is one of the softest—it can be cut with a knife.

In

49

Indium
(IN-DEE-UM)

POST-TRANSITION METAL

INDIUM IS THE SPECIAL INGREDIENT THAT MAKES TOUCH SCREENS RESPOND TO OUR FINGERTIPS.

KEY PROPERTIES

- solid
- silvery-white metal
- **lustrous**
- soft
- **malleable**
- **ductile**

WHERE IT'S FOUND

- **minerals**: indite
- rocks containing zinc or tin or lead
- as pure metal (rare)

HUMAN BODY

TRACE

ALL ABOUT INDIUM

Indium was discovered by looking at the colorful light given off by the different elements hidden inside a mineral called sphalerite. A bright violet line that had never been seen before was the clue that a new element was waiting to be discovered. The new element was named indium, after the Latin word for violet or indigo. Indium is rare and expensive but is in demand for making **alloys** that melt at low temperatures, and **semiconductors** (materials needed to make computer chips and solar panels).

   Most indium goes into making indium tin oxide—a material with three very useful properties. It **bonds** to glass like glue, **conducts electricity** well, and is see-through. This makes it perfect for coating the touch screens of tablets, smartphones, and interactive display panels. When a finger touches the screen, it changes how the indium tin oxide layer conducts electricity in that spot. The device can detect this change, telling it which part of the screen we are touching. Indium is also used to coat the glass cladding of skyscrapers and other tall buildings, because it lets light through but bounces heat away— preventing the rooms inside from getting as hot as greenhouses! Indium will even cling to human white blood **cells**, so a **radioactive** form of indium can be used to tag white blood cells inside a patient's body. White blood cells are part of our immune system and rush to the site of an infection. Tracking indium-tagged cells can reveal where an infection is, so doctors can treat it.

SECRET PHYSICS

Molten indium clings to glass and other surfaces in a similar way to water, "wetting" the surfaces with the metal. This property makes indium useful for creating perfect seals through which nothing can leak—not even tiny atoms of helium gas!

INSIDE THE ATOM

● 49   ✚ 49   ○ 66

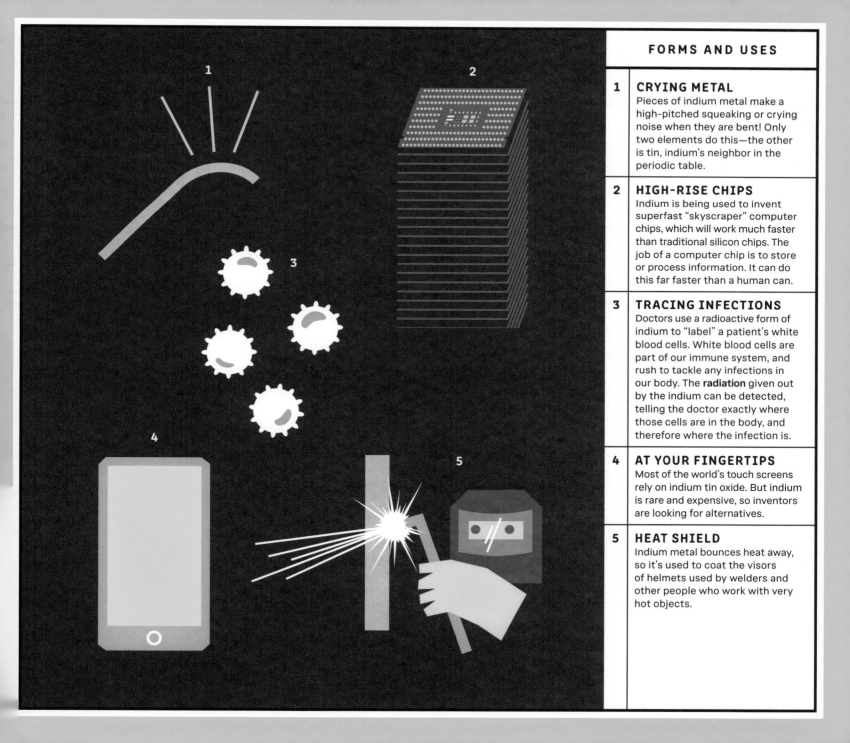

FORMS AND USES

1 CRYING METAL
Pieces of indium metal make a high-pitched squeaking or crying noise when they are bent! Only two elements do this—the other is tin, indium's neighbor in the periodic table.

2 HIGH-RISE CHIPS
Indium is being used to invent superfast "skyscraper" computer chips, which will work much faster than traditional silicon chips. The job of a computer chip is to store or process information. It can do this far faster than a human can.

3 TRACING INFECTIONS
Doctors use a radioactive form of indium to "label" a patient's white blood cells. White blood cells are part of our immune system, and rush to tackle any infections in our body. The **radiation** given out by the indium can be detected, telling the doctor exactly where those cells are in the body, and therefore where the infection is.

4 AT YOUR FINGERTIPS
Most of the world's touch screens rely on indium tin oxide. But indium is rare and expensive, so inventors are looking for alternatives.

5 HEAT SHIELD
Indium metal bounces heat away, so it's used to coat the visors of helmets used by welders and other people who work with very hot objects.

50
Sn

Tin
(TIN)

POST-TRANSITION METAL

TIN IS OFTEN THOUGHT OF AS AN UNREMARKABLE METAL, BUT IT HAS CHANGED THE WORLD—AND MORE THAN ONCE!

KEY PROPERTIES

- solid
- silvery-white metal
- four **allotropes**
- soft and bendy
- **malleable**
- **ductile**

WHERE IT'S FOUND

- **minerals**: cassiterite

HUMAN BODY

TRACE

ALL ABOUT TIN

The Bronze Age is a major part of human history. It began when people worked out how to combine copper and tin—two soft and bendy metals—to form an **alloy** called bronze, which melts at low temperatures but sets very hard. Bronze allowed people to make much harder metal objects, tools, and weapons. This changed the world, leading to new ways of building and farming, new forms of writing and art, and even the invention of the wheel. Bronze was the world's most important metal for about 2,000 years. When people found ways to use iron and steel, bronze became less important, but tin continued to play a supporting role. Tin doesn't react with air and water to rust like iron does. A thin layer was used to coat iron-based objects such as steel cans, making them safe for storing food. All that was needed was a layer of tin 15 micrometers thick—about a sixth of the width of a human hair!

Today a "tin can" is more likely to be made from aluminum, which is cheaper and lighter than tin and steel. But our modern world is still shaped by tin! This metal is the secret behind the perfectly flat and smooth glass used in windows, doors, cars, storefronts, mirrors, and oven doors. "Float glass" is made by floating molten glass on top of the perfectly flat and smooth surface of a pool of molten tin. A lot of the tin produced each year is used to make alloys called **solder**, which melt at low temperatures and are used to join other metals together—for example in plumbing and electronics. Scientists are busy finding new uses for tin in solar panels, batteries, and electronics, and it may change the world again in the future.

SECRET PHYSICS

You can tell if you have a piece of pure tin by listening carefully to hear whether it makes a squeaking sound (known as the "tin cry") when it's bent, rolled, or twisted. The sound is made by tiny crystals in the metal rubbing against one another.

INSIDE THE ATOM

⊖ 50 ⊕ 50 ◯ 70

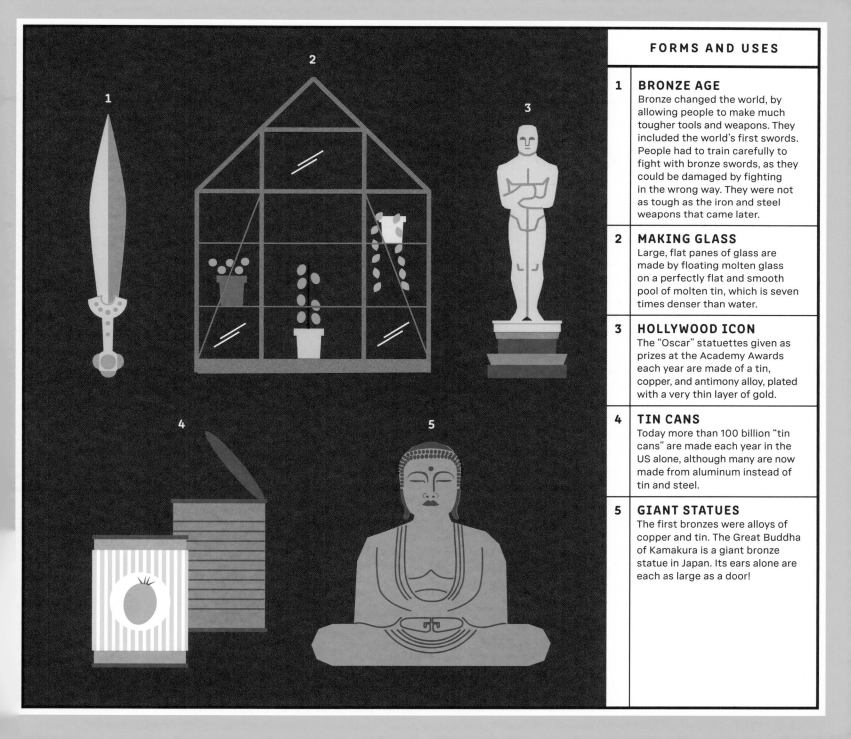

FORMS AND USES

1 BRONZE AGE
Bronze changed the world, by allowing people to make much tougher tools and weapons. They included the world's first swords. People had to train carefully to fight with bronze swords, as they could be damaged by fighting in the wrong way. They were not as tough as the iron and steel weapons that came later.

2 MAKING GLASS
Large, flat panes of glass are made by floating molten glass on a perfectly flat and smooth pool of molten tin, which is seven times denser than water.

3 HOLLYWOOD ICON
The "Oscar" statuettes given as prizes at the Academy Awards each year are made of a tin, copper, and antimony alloy, plated with a very thin layer of gold.

4 TIN CANS
Today more than 100 billion "tin cans" are made each year in the US alone, although many are now made from aluminum instead of tin and steel.

5 GIANT STATUES
The first bronzes were alloys of copper and tin. The Great Buddha of Kamakura is a giant bronze statue in Japan. Its ears alone are each as large as a door!

81
Tl

Thallium
(THAL-EE-UM)

POST-TRANSITION METAL

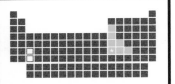

THALLIUM IS MOST FAMOUS FOR BEING A DEADLY POISON, BUT IT'S ALSO USED TO MAKE SPECIAL TYPES OF GLASS, IN WHICH THE ELEMENT IS SAFELY LOCKED AWAY.

KEY PROPERTIES

- solid
- silvery-blue metal
- very soft
- melts easily

WHERE IT'S FOUND

- **minerals**: sylvite, pyrite
- coal
- soil
- plants

HUMAN BODY

TRACE

ALL ABOUT THALLIUM

Thallium is very dangerous because our bodies mistake it for useful potassium (see page 26) and absorb it. Once **ions** of thallium are inside a person's body, they start taking the place of potassium ions found in every part of the body. However, they can't actually do the jobs potassium does in our bodies, so one by one the victim's organs stop working. Thallium has often been used as a poison, and has also poisoned people by accident. Luckily, in the 1970s, a German pharmacologist discovered a surprising antidote—blue ink! Prussian blue dye contains potassium, and once it's inside a patient, it swaps its potassium for any thallium it finds. The thallium is then carried out of the patient's body.

Thallium was once used mainly for its **toxic** properties—to make rat poisons and pesticides, hair-removal creams, and medicines to kill fungi that cause skin infections. Today these products are banned in most countries because thallium is just too toxic for humans. However, thallium can be used safely if it's trapped inside glass. Thallium is added to the glass used to make lenses for hi-tech equipment, and the glass used to make optical fibers—the thin glass tubes that carry information around the world and bring high-speed broadband to homes, schools, and offices. Although glass that contains thallium is safe to touch and use, thallium **compounds** can harm the workers who make these products, so they have to be used in very carefully controlled environments.

SECRET CHEMISTRY

Thallium sulfate is one of the most deadly thallium compounds. This substance has no smell, color, or taste, which makes it hard to detect. A typical 150-pound adult would be killed by eating just 700 milligrams—not even the weight of a jellybean.

INSIDE THE ATOM

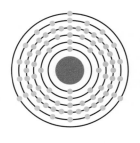

● 81 ✚ 81 ○ 124

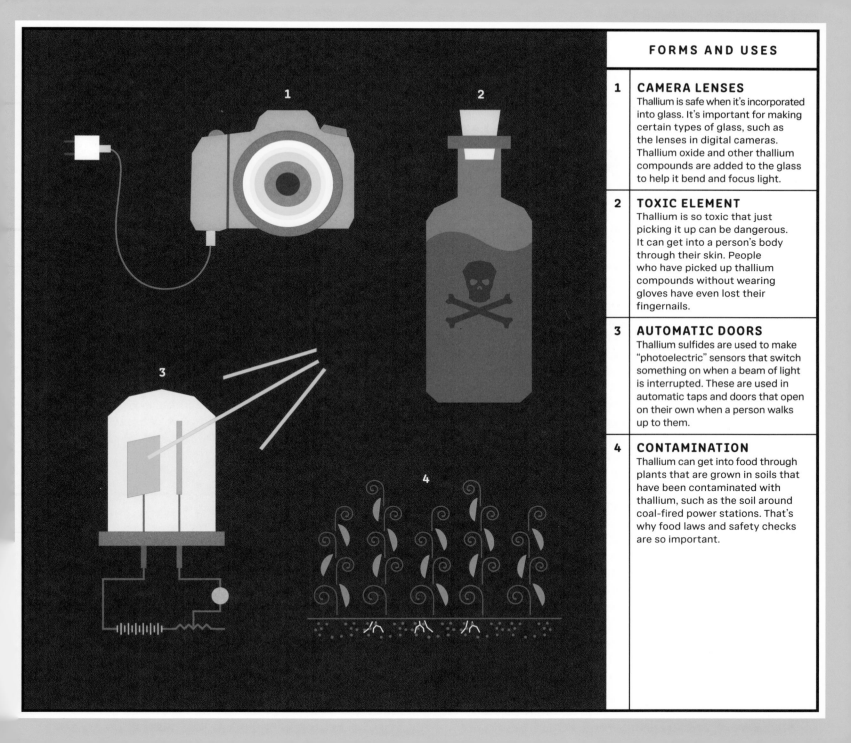

FORMS AND USES

1 CAMERA LENSES
Thallium is safe when it's incorporated into glass. It's important for making certain types of glass, such as the lenses in digital cameras. Thallium oxide and other thallium compounds are added to the glass to help it bend and focus light.

2 TOXIC ELEMENT
Thallium is so toxic that just picking it up can be dangerous. It can get into a person's body through their skin. People who have picked up thallium compounds without wearing gloves have even lost their fingernails.

3 AUTOMATIC DOORS
Thallium sulfides are used to make "photoelectric" sensors that switch something on when a beam of light is interrupted. These are used in automatic taps and doors that open on their own when a person walks up to them.

4 CONTAMINATION
Thallium can get into food through plants that are grown in soils that have been contaminated with thallium, such as the soil around coal-fired power stations. That's why food laws and safety checks are so important.

82
Pb

Lead
(LED)

POST-TRANSITION METAL

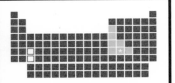

LEAD HAS BEEN VERY USEFUL IN THE PAST, BUT IT'S ALSO VERY **TOXIC**, SO TODAY WE TRY TO AVOID IT AS MUCH AS POSSIBLE.

KEY PROPERTIES

- solid
- dull bluish-gray metal
- soft
- weak
- **ductile**

WHERE IT'S FOUND

- **minerals**: galena, cerussite, anglesite
- soils near lead mines
- soils near industry

HUMAN BODY

CAN BUILD UP OVER TIME

ALL ABOUT LEAD

Lead is soft and easy to shape into different objects, so humans have been using it for more than 6,000 years. It's found in Ancient Egyptian objects, Ancient Greek paintings, and Ancient Roman water pipes, paints, plates, and coins. It has been used in leaded- and stained-glass windows for hundreds of years. A **salt**, lead acetate, was even once used instead of sugar in food because it tastes so sweet! Less than 50 years ago, lead was still common in paints, gasoline, batteries, plastic, and hair dyes. As the heaviest element that is not **radioactive**, it was used to make weights that are small but very heavy. It was even used to make the **solder** that plumbers use to join water pipes together. During the 20th century, scientists began to warn the world just how toxic lead is for humans. It doesn't poison someone in one go but collects in a person's body over time. If too much lead builds up, it stops the body from working properly.

Today many countries have banned lead from gasoline, paint, and everyday products, but it's still the best metal for certain jobs. Although many new types of battery have been invented, most of the world's car batteries are still lead-**acid** batteries. In hospitals, lead aprons and shields are used to protect patients and medics from **X-rays** and other scanners that use **radiation**. A layer of lead can absorb and block forms of radiation that are dangerous for the human body. Lead shields are also used in **particle accelerators** and **nuclear power** stations to stop dangerous radiation from escaping, and to make containers to transport dangerous radioactive substances.

SECRET CHEMISTRY

In nature, lead is usually found locked away in **compounds** that don't dissolve easily in water. However, over thousands of years humans have mined at least 385 million tons of lead, adding more of this toxic metal to the environment.

INSIDE THE ATOM

● 82   ✚ 82   ○ 126

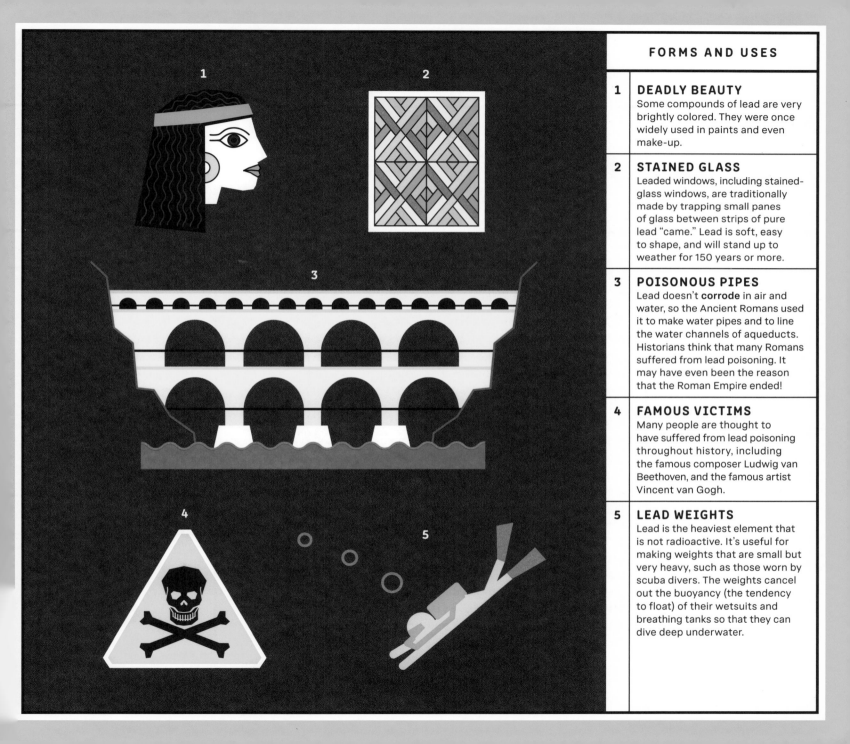

FORMS AND USES

1 DEADLY BEAUTY
Some compounds of lead are very brightly colored. They were once widely used in paints and even make-up.

2 STAINED GLASS
Leaded windows, including stained-glass windows, are traditionally made by trapping small panes of glass between strips of pure lead "came." Lead is soft, easy to shape, and will stand up to weather for 150 years or more.

3 POISONOUS PIPES
Lead doesn't **corrode** in air and water, so the Ancient Romans used it to make water pipes and to line the water channels of aqueducts. Historians think that many Romans suffered from lead poisoning. It may have even been the reason that the Roman Empire ended!

4 FAMOUS VICTIMS
Many people are thought to have suffered from lead poisoning throughout history, including the famous composer Ludwig van Beethoven, and the famous artist Vincent van Gogh.

5 LEAD WEIGHTS
Lead is the heaviest element that is not radioactive. It's useful for making weights that are small but very heavy, such as those worn by scuba divers. The weights cancel out the buoyancy (the tendency to float) of their wetsuits and breathing tanks so that they can dive deep underwater.

83
Bi

Bismuth
(BIZ-MUTH)

POST-TRANSITION METAL

FOR AN ELEMENT NESTLED NEXT TO SOME OF THE NASTIEST ELEMENTS IN THE PERIODIC TABLE, BISMUTH IS SURPRISINGLY FRIENDLY TO BOTH HUMANS AND THE ENVIRONMENT!

KEY PROPERTIES

- solid
- pinkish-white metal
- forms beautiful crystals
- brittle
- poor **conductor** of heat

WHERE IT'S FOUND

- **minerals**: bismuthinite, bismite
- as crystals of pure bismuth
- rocks that contain copper or lead or tin

HUMAN BODY

TRACE

ALL ABOUT BISMUTH

Bismuth is a very heavy metal, with 83 **protons** and at least the same number of **neutrons** crammed into the **nucleus** of each atom. Most other heavy metals are either very **toxic** or very **radioactive**, or both. But bismuth is surprisingly safe. Humans have been using it for thousands of years, not only as a metal, but also as a medicine. Drinking a solution of bismuth subsalicylate can calm an upset stomach. It's thought that it coats the walls of the stomach so that it's not irritated by the strong **acid** we produce to digest food. It is also used in make-up. If you spot anyone wearing shimmering eyeshadow or pearlescent nail polish, it probably contains ground-up crystals of bismuth oxychloride.

Bismuth behaves differently around **magnets** than most other metals. Instead of being attracted, bismuth and a magnet always push each other away. This strange property can be used to make small pieces of bismuth hover above a magnet—a phenomenon known as **magnetic** levitation. Exotic materials containing bismuth have been used to make magnetic levitation or "Maglev" trains. In the past, bismuth metal was often confused with lead because the two have very similar **densities**, so similar-sized lumps of lead and bismuth would weigh about the same. As lead is very toxic for living things, bismuth has replaced lead in many of the jobs lead used to do. One of these is in **solder**, a soft **alloy** with a very low **melting point** that can be easily melted and used to join pieces of metal together, such as copper water pipes.

SECRET CHEMISTRY

Bismuth was once thought to be the heaviest element with stable atoms that did not break apart over time. Today we know it is radioactive, but with one of the longest **half-lives**, of 20 billion, billion years!

INSIDE THE ATOM

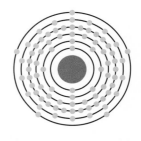

● 83   ⊕ 83   ○ 126

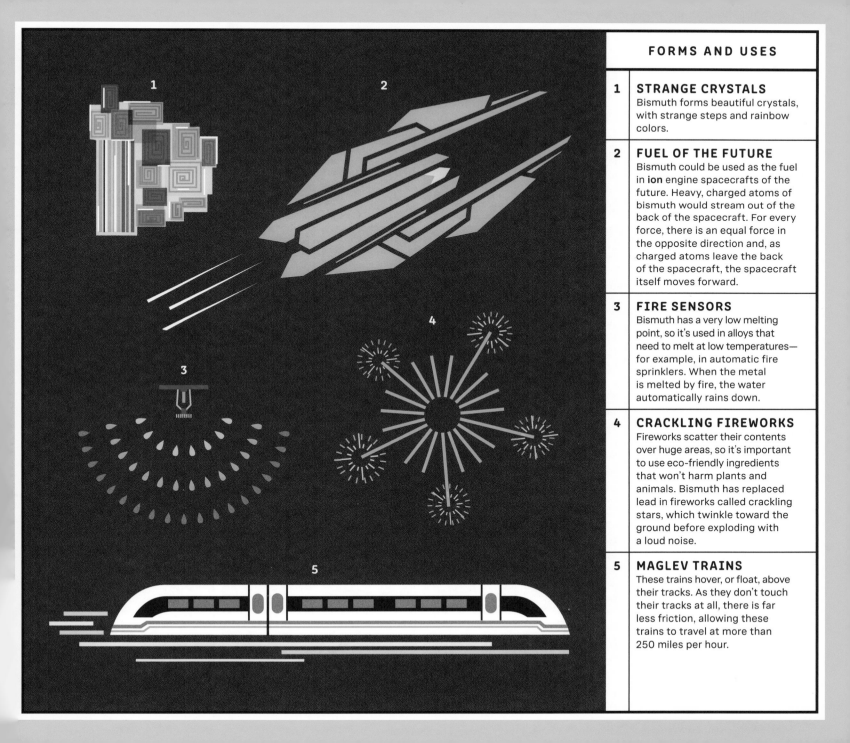

FORMS AND USES

1 STRANGE CRYSTALS
Bismuth forms beautiful crystals, with strange steps and rainbow colors.

2 FUEL OF THE FUTURE
Bismuth could be used as the fuel in **ion** engine spacecrafts of the future. Heavy, charged atoms of bismuth would stream out of the back of the spacecraft. For every force, there is an equal force in the opposite direction and, as charged atoms leave the back of the spacecraft, the spacecraft itself moves forward.

3 FIRE SENSORS
Bismuth has a very low melting point, so it's used in alloys that need to melt at low temperatures—for example, in automatic fire sprinklers. When the metal is melted by fire, the water automatically rains down.

4 CRACKLING FIREWORKS
Fireworks scatter their contents over huge areas, so it's important to use eco-friendly ingredients that won't harm plants and animals. Bismuth has replaced lead in fireworks called crackling stars, which twinkle toward the ground before exploding with a loud noise.

5 MAGLEV TRAINS
These trains hover, or float, above their tracks. As they don't touch their tracks at all, there is far less friction, allowing these trains to travel at more than 250 miles per hour.

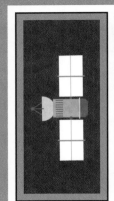

5

B

Boron

14

Si

Silicon

32

Ge

Germanium

33

As

Arsenic

51

Sb

Antimony

52

Te

Tellurium

84

Po

Polonium

Metalloids

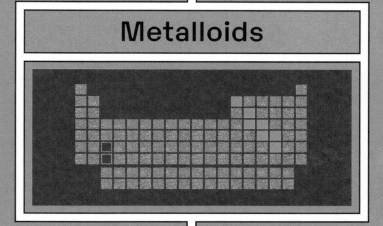

THE METALLOIDS INCLUDE SOME OF THE SMELLIEST, MOST POISONOUS ELEMENTS IN THE PERIODIC TABLE! THEY ARE THE ONLY ELEMENTS WITH PROPERTIES OF BOTH METALS AND NON-METALS. THE BEST-KNOWN IS SILICON, ONE OF THE MOST USEFUL ELEMENTS ON THE PLANET.

Boron, silicon, germanium, arsenic, antimony, tellurium, and polonium behave a bit like metals and a bit like non-metals. Unlike most other elements, metalloids can exist in different forms, known as **allotropes**. For example, pure boron can take the form of black and shiny crystals, or a dull brown powder. Allotropes of the same element not only look different, they behave differently too. For example,

black, shiny boron **conducts electricity** like a metal at high temperatures. But brown, powdery boron is an **insulator**—it barely lets electricity flow through it at all.

Most metalloids have at least one allotrope that is a **semiconductor**. This is the name for a substance that conducts electricity in certain conditions, but not in others. In the last 100 years, semiconductors have changed the world. They are the materials at the heart of radios, computer chips, solar panels, and every hi-tech, electronic device. Silicon is the most widely used semiconducting element and one of the most useful elements of all.

Because the metalloids are "in-between" elements, no one agrees for certain which elements belong in this category. Some scientists include bismuth and astatine too.

Boron

(BORE-ON)

5
B

METALLOID

⚡

BORON IS A RARE ELEMENT, FORMED BY COSMIC COLLISIONS IN SPACE. ON EARTH IT'S USED TO MAKE CLOTHES, FACES, AND TEETH SPARKLE.

KEY PROPERTIES

- solid
- four **allotropes**
- liquid boron is a **semiconductor**
- high **melting point**

WHERE IT'S FOUND

- **minerals**: kernite, tincalconite, borax soils
- seawater
- some plants

HUMAN BODY

TRACE

ALL ABOUT BORON

Boron is one of just a handful of elements that are not formed inside stars or even when stars explode, but when cosmic rays collide with atoms of heavier elements in space, splitting them apart. Like other metalloids, pure boron can exist in several forms, known as allotropes, which may look and behave totally differently from one another. Long before we discovered these pure forms of the element, humans used boron in the form of borax, a white mineral made of boron joined with sodium and oxygen. Borax is used to make all kinds of everyday chemicals and objects, including glass, ceramics, fertilizers, laundry detergents, and antiseptics. It can also be used to make a gloopy liquid known as slime, which is fun to play with because it behaves like both a solid and a liquid!

Other boron **compounds** are used to make fiberglass (the fluffy insulation used in roofs), bleach, and flame retardants. Sparkly, super-hard crystals of boron nitride are used as abrasives (substances that can scratch or wear away other materials). Boron carbide is so hard that it can be used to make bulletproof armor. Boron itself is **alloyed** with metals to make them better at **conducting electricity**, to give them a higher melting point, or as part of ultra-strong **magnets**. Many **nuclear power** stations use boron in the control rods used to adjust the speed of nuclear **reactions** so that they release energy safely. Boron is also added to silicon to make it better at conducting electricity (see page 120).

SECRET CHEMISTRY

Boron atoms form very strong **bonds** to each other, which make boron crystals very hard compared to metals. Breaking these bonds takes a lot of energy, so boron is unreactive unless it's heated.

INSIDE THE ATOM

⊖ 5   ⊕ 5   ◯ 6

FORMS AND USES

1 ESSENTIAL FOR PLANTS
All plants need boron to grow. It's added to fertilizers, but it's important to get the balance just right. Too much can be **toxic** for some plants.

2 PYREX® GLASS
Boric oxide is added to glass and ceramic glazes to stop cookware from cracking at high temperatures—like when hot water is suddenly poured into a glass jug.

3 HEALTHY BONES
Inside our bodies, a small amount of boron is thought to carry out some BIG jobs, such as helping bones to grow and stay strong, helping wounds to heal, and helping us to soak up magnesium from our food (see page 38). Fruits are good sources of the boron we need in our diets.

4 CLOTHES WASHING
Borax (sodium borate) is used in laundry detergents. It reacts with water to form hydrogen peroxide to clean clothes and make them whiter.

5 COSMETICS
Boron nitride is the world's second-hardest material, after diamond. It's also very sparkly, so tiny amounts are added to some face powders, eye make-up, and lipsticks.

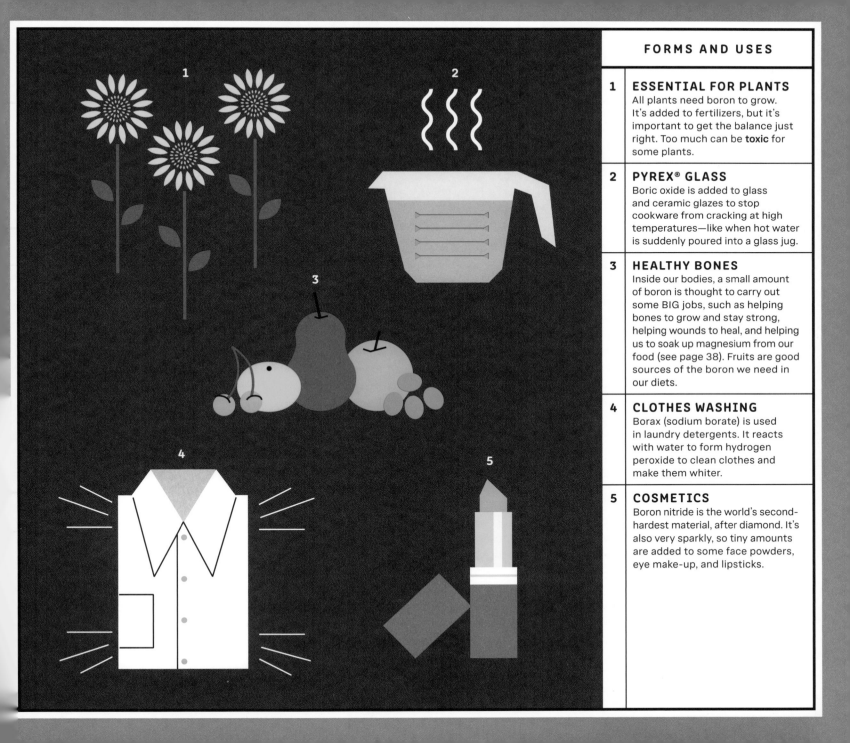

14
Si

Silicon
(SILL-EH-CON)

METALLOID

HUMAN HISTORY IS OFTEN DESCRIBED IN TERMS OF THE KEY MATERIALS BEHIND CHANGING TECHNOLOGY, SUCH AS THE STONE AGE, BRONZE AGE, AND IRON AGE. ARE WE NOW LIVING IN THE SILICON AGE?

KEY PROPERTIES

- solid
- two **allotropes**

WHERE IT'S FOUND

- almost all rocks!
- **minerals**: quartz, talc
- gemstones: opal, amethyst
- sand and soils
- water
- some plants and animals

HUMAN BODY

 0.001%

ALL ABOUT SILICON

Silicon is Earth's second most abundant element. Most of the Earth's crust is made of rocks that contain silicon, and most of the world's sand—on beaches and in soil—is tiny pieces of silicon dioxide, known as silica. Humans have come up with hundreds of different ways to use this easy-to-find element. Silicon is an important part of the **alloys**, concrete, cement, and bricks used in constructing buildings, bridges, dams, and roads. Silicon is also used to make glass, and substances called silicones, made from long chains of silicon and oxygen atoms with other chemicals stuck on. Like plastics, silicones can be runny or solid, soft like rubber or hard. Silicones are found in hundreds of objects and products in our homes. One of their earliest uses was in boots to protect the feet of the first astronauts to walk on the Moon. The footprints from these silicone boots are still on the Moon today!

In the last 75 years, silicon has changed the world as the material used to make computer chips. Silicon is a **semiconductor**—a material that lets **electricity** flow through it in certain conditions. Semiconductors can be used to make tiny devices called transistors, which are an important part of every electronic circuit. A transistor can either be "on," letting electricity flow through it, or "off." A computer chip is a tiny piece of silicon that holds circuits containing millions and millions of transistors. The path that electricity takes through these circuits depends on the combination of transistors that are "on" and "off." A different input of information leads to a different path for the electricity, which in turn leads to a different "answer" or output. This is how computers process information incredibly quickly.

SECRET CHEMISTRY

Electricity is a flow of **electrons**. Electrons can't flow through silicon, unless a tiny amount of another element—such as boron—is added to the silicon. This helps free up electrons, which can then flow as electricity.

INSIDE THE ATOM

— 14   + 14   O 14

FORMS AND USES

1 AMAZING SAND
Sand is fun to play with, but it's also the raw material for hundreds of different things, from sandpaper and molds for shaping molten metal to ceramic toilets and artificial grass.

2 CLEAR GLASS
Silica sand is the main raw material used to make clear glass for windows, cups, eyeglasses, lightbulbs, screens, and other objects.

3 SILKY HAIR
Silicone oils have a smooth, silky feel, so they are used in products that we put on our skin and hair, such as shampoo and conditioner.

4 STINGING SHARDS
The tiny hairs on a stinging nettle are made from glass-like silica. The tips break easily when an animal brushes against them, scratching the animal's skin and releasing stinging chemicals.

5 KEEPING TIME
Quartz is a hard mineral made of silicon and oxygen. Digital clocks and watches contain tiny crystals of quartz that vibrate in a very regular way when electricity is passed through them. These vibrations can be used to measure time!

6 KITCHEN HERO
Solid silicones don't **conduct** heat well, so they are used to make kitchen equipment such as baking sheets and molds.

7 SILICON CHIPS
Silicon chips lie at the heart of all our computer technology. Silicon is also used to make the glass screens and the optical fibers that carry digital information around the world.

32
Ge

Germanium
(JER-MAIN-EE-UM)

METALLOID

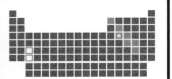

⚡

GERMANIUM SHARES THE STRANGE PROPERTIES THAT HAVE PUT SILICON AT THE CENTER OF OUR ELECTRONIC WORLD. IT'S NOT AS WELL KNOWN OR AS WIDELY USED AS SILICON BECAUSE IT'S MUCH RARER AND MORE EXPENSIVE.

KEY PROPERTIES

- solid
- two **allotropes**

WHERE IT'S FOUND

- rare **minerals** such as germanite
- **ores** of other metals
- some coals
- some soils
- some plants

HUMAN BODY

TRACE

ALL ABOUT GERMANIUM

When germanium was first discovered, people thought that it was just a useless metal that didn't **conduct electricity** very well. This changed during World War II, when inventors used germanium to create better devices to detect radio waves in the air and convert them into sound. As they tried to improve radios, engineers discovered that germanium is a **semiconductor**. This means that in certain conditions, germanium lets lots of electricity flow through it, while in other conditions it doesn't let any electricity flow at all. This strange property was used to invent the very first transistors: devices that act like tiny switches, controlling the path that electricity takes through an electronic circuit. Transistors were used to build the very first computer circuits.

Almost every electronic device that we use today, from televisions to smartphones, has a computer chip inside, which includes millions of tiny transistors. However, very few of these use germanium, because it's rare and expensive. When engineers discovered that the cheaper silicon has the same properties, silicon soon took over as the element of choice for making transistors. However, as scientists look for ways to make computer chips smaller and faster, germanium is being used once again. Germanium semiconductors are also used in devices that can detect different types of **radiation**—such as the scanners at airports, which check luggage to make sure there is nothing dangerous inside.

SECRET CHEMISTRY

When radiation hits germanium it changes how well this element conducts electricity. We can measure a flow of electricity very precisely, so this tells us how much radiation is present.

INSIDE THE ATOM

– 32 + 32 ○ 42

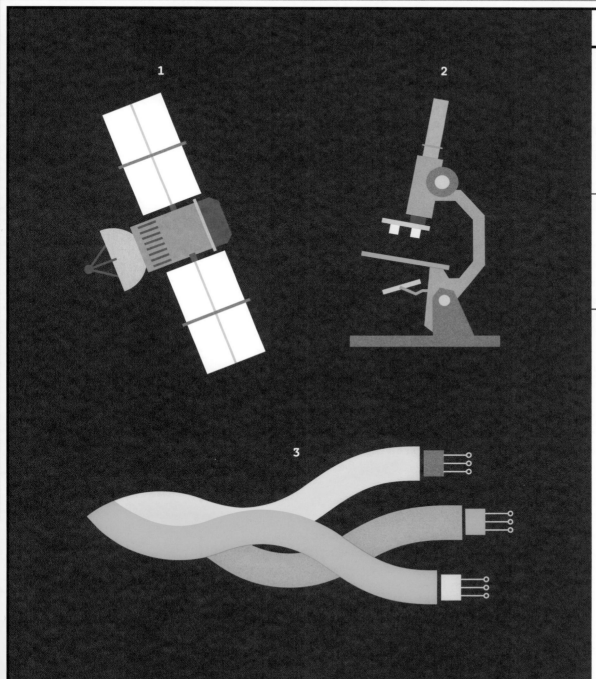

FORMS AND USES

1 POWERING SATELLITES
Semiconductors such as silicon and germanium are used in solar panels that convert sunlight energy into electrical energy. A little germanium makes a silicon solar panel work even better, converting more of the sunlight that hits it into electricity. This kind of solar panel is used to power satellites orbiting Earth.

2 SEEING SMALL THINGS
When light travels from air into glass, it changes direction. Adding germanium dioxide to glass makes it bend light even more strongly than usual. This type of glass is used in the lenses that focus light in a microscope.

3 INFORMATION AGE
Germanium is used in the glass of optical fibers—the thin glass tubes that carry pictures, messages, video calls, and other types of information all around the planet, and into homes, schools, and offices.

33
As

Arsenic
(ARE-SUH-NICK)

METALLOID

ARSENIC CAN BE A DEADLY POISON, BUT IT CAN ALSO SAVE LIVES BY HELPING TO TREAT CERTAIN TYPES OF CANCER.

KEY PROPERTIES

- solid
- three **allotropes**: one form **conducts electricity**
- no taste or smell

WHERE IT'S FOUND

- **minerals**: arsenopyrite
- volcanoes
- some groundwater
- soils
- some plants
- released burning fossil fuels

HUMAN BODY

TRACE

ALL ABOUT ARSENIC

Arsenic was once used to make green paints and dyes, which were used to color everything from wallpapers to fireworks. However, people gradually realized that arsenic is very **toxic**, and that it wasn't a good idea to paint bedrooms with it or to put it inside explosive rockets that scattered it across the sky. In the 19th century, arsenic was used in weed-killers and flypapers (sheets of sticky paper designed to trap and kill insects). The arsenic from these was sometimes collected and used as a poison! Just 200 milligrams of arsenic can be deadly for an adult. Inside a person's body, arsenic **bonds** easily with sulfur. The protein keratin, which hair is made from, is especially high in sulfur. Looking for traces of arsenic in a person's hair is one way that police can tell a person has been poisoned by arsenic, even many years after their death.

Today we are far less likely to come across arsenic in our homes, at least in a way that could poison us. It's still added to glass (to make it clear, rather than green) and is an important part of **semiconductors** used in all kinds of computers and electronic devices. When tiny amounts of arsenic are added to silicon, it frees **electrons**, which can then flow as electricity. Although arsenic can be very poisonous, many animals actually need a tiny amount of it to stay healthy! It's one of the building blocks for important proteins that build our nervous systems. Doctors also use arsenic to treat certain illnesses—for example, arsenic trioxide is used to treat a blood cancer called leukemia, by making the patient's body produce more blood **cells**.

SECRET CHEMISTRY

Most elements change from solid to liquid to gas as they are heated. Arsenic is different. It **sublimes** from a solid straight into a gas at 1141°F, without melting first!

INSIDE THE ATOM

- 33 + 33 O 42

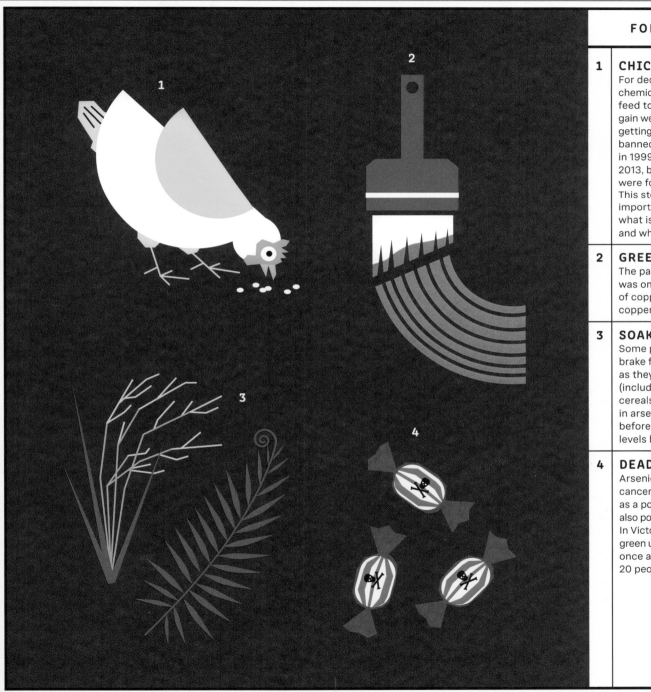

FORMS AND USES

1 CHICKEN FEED
For decades, arsenic-based chemicals were added to poultry feed to help chickens and turkeys gain weight and stop them from getting infections. This was banned in the European Union in 1999 and in North America in 2013, because traces of arsenic were found in the cooked meat. This story is a reminder that it's important to pay attention to what is in the foods that we eat, and where they come from.

2 GREEN PIGMENTS
The paint color Scheele's Green was once made with a **compound** of copper and arsenic called copper arsenite.

3 SOAKING RICE
Some plants—such as rice and brake ferns—soak up arsenic as they grow. This makes rice (including puffed rice breakfast cereals) one of the foods highest in arsenic. Soaking rice overnight before cooking it can cut arsenic levels by 80%.

4 DEADLY MISTAKE
Arsenic is toxic and also causes cancer. It has famously been used as a poison by criminals, but has also poisoned people by mistake. In Victorian Britain, sweets dyed green using an arsenic compound once accidentally killed about 20 people.

51
Sb

Antimony
(ANT-UH-MO-NEE)

METALLOID

ANTIMONY IS A HARD-WORKING METALLOID WITH A LONG HISTORY, FROM WEAPONRY AND PRINTING TO BATTERIES.

KEY PROPERTIES

- solid
- bright and silvery
- brittle and flaky
- several **allotropes**

WHERE IT'S FOUND

- **minerals**: stibnite, kermesite, tetrahedrite
- rocks containing copper or lead or silver
- traces in soils

HUMAN BODY

TRACE

ALL ABOUT ANTIMONY

Although antimony looks a lot like lead, it doesn't behave like a metal. For example, it doesn't **conduct electricity** very well. But for thousands of years, antimony was thought of as a mysterious metal. It's believed that the Ancient Greeks used it to make one of their most terrifying weapons, a liquid that burned with a flame that was impossible to put out with water. Antimony was ideal for casting metal letters used on old-fashioned printing presses. This is because, unlike other metals, molten antimony gets bigger when it cools down. The molten **alloy** was poured into molds of each letter, and as it set, it expanded and filled every last corner so none of the detail was missed.

Today's printing presses work in a different way, but antimony is still useful in alloys, especially lead alloys. Most lead alloys are used to produce parts for lead-**acid** batteries, and about half of the antimony produced each year comes from recycling old batteries. Antimony is also alloyed with tin in pewter and Babbitt metals, which are used to coat the moving parts of some machines. As the parts move, the alloy reduces friction and helps the machine to work smoothly. Very pure antimony is also used to make parts such as infrared detectors for electronic devices, such as night-vision cameras.

SECRET CHEMISTRY

Antimony atoms really like to react with sulfur atoms. Although it's safe to eat the tiny amount of antimony found in plants, a bigger dose can be poisonous because it clings to sulfur atoms in proteins, stopping them from working properly.

INSIDE THE ATOM

⊖ 51 ⊕ 51 ◯ 70

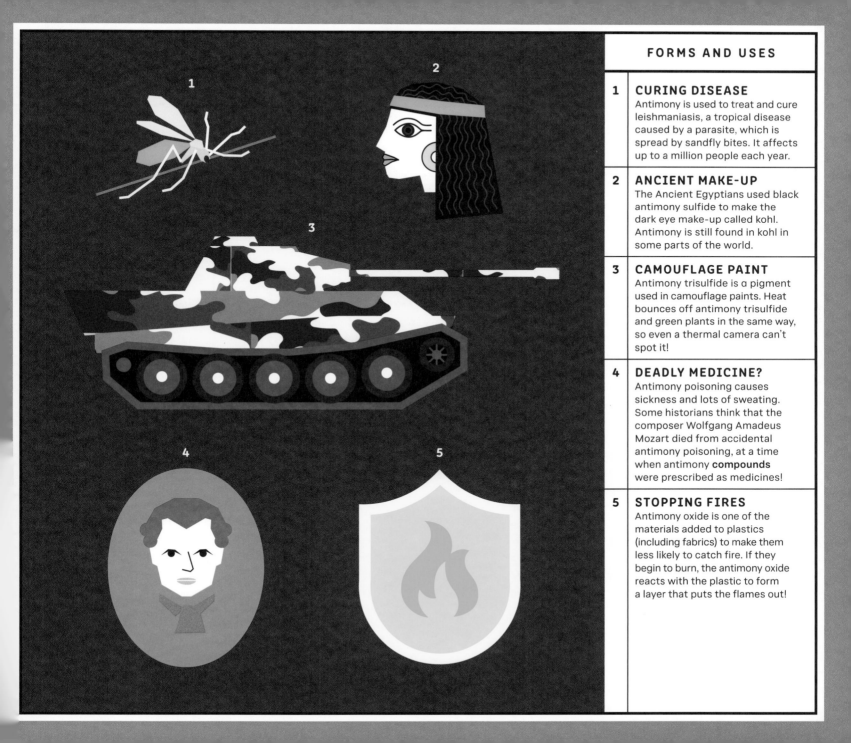

FORMS AND USES

1 CURING DISEASE
Antimony is used to treat and cure leishmaniasis, a tropical disease caused by a parasite, which is spread by sandfly bites. It affects up to a million people each year.

2 ANCIENT MAKE-UP
The Ancient Egyptians used black antimony sulfide to make the dark eye make-up called kohl. Antimony is still found in kohl in some parts of the world.

3 CAMOUFLAGE PAINT
Antimony trisulfide is a pigment used in camouflage paints. Heat bounces off antimony trisulfide and green plants in the same way, so even a thermal camera can't spot it!

4 DEADLY MEDICINE?
Antimony poisoning causes sickness and lots of sweating. Some historians think that the composer Wolfgang Amadeus Mozart died from accidental antimony poisoning, at a time when antimony **compounds** were prescribed as medicines!

5 STOPPING FIRES
Antimony oxide is one of the materials added to plastics (including fabrics) to make them less likely to catch fire. If they begin to burn, the antimony oxide reacts with the plastic to form a layer that puts the flames out!

Tellurium

52 Te

(TE-LUH-REE-UM)

METALLOID

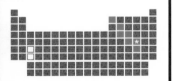

TELLURIUM IS INFAMOUS FOR MAKING PEOPLE SMELL DISGUSTING! BUT IT MAY ALSO BE THE KEY TO A FUTURE WITHOUT FOSSIL FUELS.

KEY PROPERTIES

- solid
- two **allotropes**

WHERE IT'S FOUND

- **minerals**: calaverite, sylvanite, tellurite
- rocks containing copper
- coal
- soil
- **microbes**

HUMAN BODY

TRACE

ALL ABOUT TELLURIUM

Pure tellurium doesn't do anything useful in our bodies, and it's not very **toxic**. If we eat a lot of it, our bodies treat it like sulfur or selenium—the elements just above tellurium in the periodic table—and most of it comes out in our urine. However, a tiny amount of it will also leave our bodies in our breath and sweat as a substance called dimethyl telluride. In this form, tellurium smells absolutely disgusting—like rotting garlic, rotten eggs, and skunks all in one! In one experiment, people who ate 15 milligrams of tellurium in one go (the weight of half a grain of rice) suffered garlic breath for eight months!

It's no surprise that people avoid using tellurium where possible! Sometimes it's used in **alloys** (mixtures of two or more metals), to make copper and stainless steel easier to bend, shape, and cut. Adding tellurium to lead makes the lead harder and more resistant to **acids**, so tellurium is often found in batteries that contain lead. Cadmium telluride is one of the best **semiconductors** for making "thin film" solar panels—devices that convert sunlight straight into **electricity** using a layer of semiconducting material just a tenth as thick as a human hair! These "CdTe" solar panels are much cheaper and easier to make than traditional silicon solar panels, and they also work better when it's dusty, shady, or very hot. As solar power becomes more and more important for replacing fossil fuels and tackling climate change, unpopular tellurium might have a very bright future.

SECRET CHEMISTRY

Surprisingly for such an unpopular element, when tellurium is found in nature it's often combined with platinum, gold, or silver! For example, calaverite is gold telluride. Calaverite is one of the few tellurium **compounds** that doesn't smell of rotting garlic!

INSIDE THE ATOM

● 52 ✚ 52 ○ 78

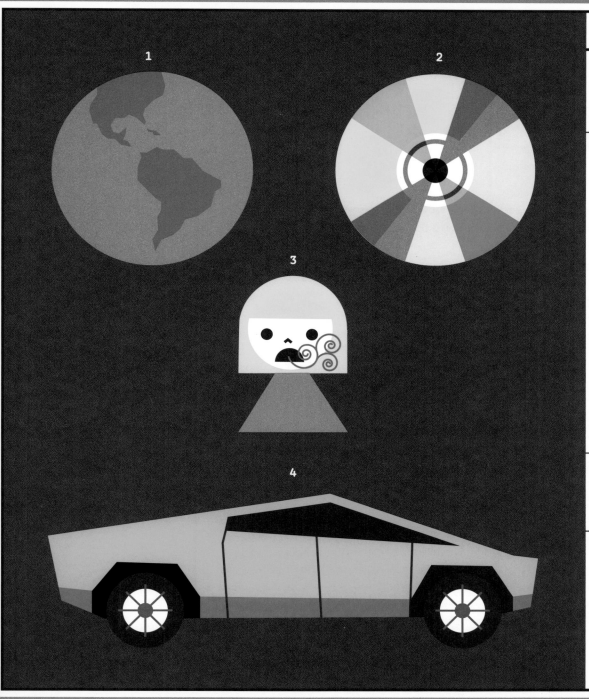

FORMS AND USES

1 EARTHLY MEANING
Like uranium, neptunium, and plutonium, tellurium is named after a planet. *Tellus* is the Latin word for Earth!

2 RECORDING DATA
The surface of a rewritable disc is coated with a thin layer of tellurium. To record data, a high-powered laser beam is used to heat up tiny areas of the surface. Everywhere the laser strikes, the tellurium in that spot is changed from one of its allotropes to the other—from dull to shiny. A device reads the CD or DVD by shining a different type of laser light at the disc. This time the laser light doesn't have enough energy to heat the tellurium. But every time the laser light hits one of the shiny patches, some light bounces back and gets detected. The pattern of dull and shiny areas is recorded as "0s" (no light bounced back) and "1s" (light bounced back)—a code that can be understood by computers, and translated into sounds and pictures.

3 GARLIC BREATH
Swallowing or breathing in even a tiny speck of tellurium can make a person's breath and sweat stink for days.

4 FUTURE BATTERIES
Tellurium plays a small role in batteries that contain lead. In the future, it's likely to play a starring role in ultra-high capacity, rechargeable batteries that will allow us to store renewable energy better. We'll need these batteries to make electric vehicles more practical.

84
Po

Polonium
(PUH-LO-NEE-UM)

METALLOID

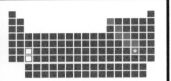

POLONIUM IS ONE OF THE RAREST ELEMENTS, WHICH IS LUCKY BECAUSE IT'S ALSO ONE OF THE DEADLIEST.

KEY PROPERTIES

- solid
- two **allotropes**

WHERE IT'S FOUND

- rocks containing uranium
- traces in soil
- plants and animals
- tobacco smoke
- seafood

HUMAN BODY

NONE

ALL ABOUT POLONIUM

Just over 120 years ago, a scientist named Marie Curie began investigating a strange rock called pitchblende. It was the source of a **radioactive** metal called uranium, but strangely the pitchblende was far more radioactive than pure uranium! Marie realized there must be at least one other very radioactive element hidden in the pitchblende. Along with her husband, Pierre, she set out to find it, grinding the pitchblende into powder, dissolving it in **acid**, and separating out the different elements it was made from. They ended up with a tiny amount of black powder 330 times more radioactive than uranium—so radioactive that it glowed in the dark! She named it after Poland, the country where she was born.

Atoms of polonium naturally break apart or **decay** over time. As they do this, they release a type of **radiation** that has lots of energy but doesn't travel very far. This type of radiation bounces off skin and can even be stopped by a piece of paper, so it can't harm anyone if it's outside their body. But if even a speck of polonium gets into a person's body—through their nose, mouth, or a cut—it's one of the deadliest substances in the world. The billions of atoms in the speck quickly travel around the body and make their way into all kinds of different **cells**. Then, as they break apart, the radiation they release damages the cells from the inside. In 2006, polonium made headlines around the world when it was used to poison a former spy.

SECRET CHEMISTRY

Marie Curie's daughter Irene Curie also became a scientist and worked with polonium. Irene died of cancer caused by tiny amounts of polonium getting into her body.

INSIDE THE ATOM

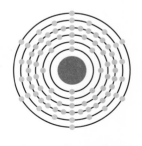

− 84　＋ 84　○ 125

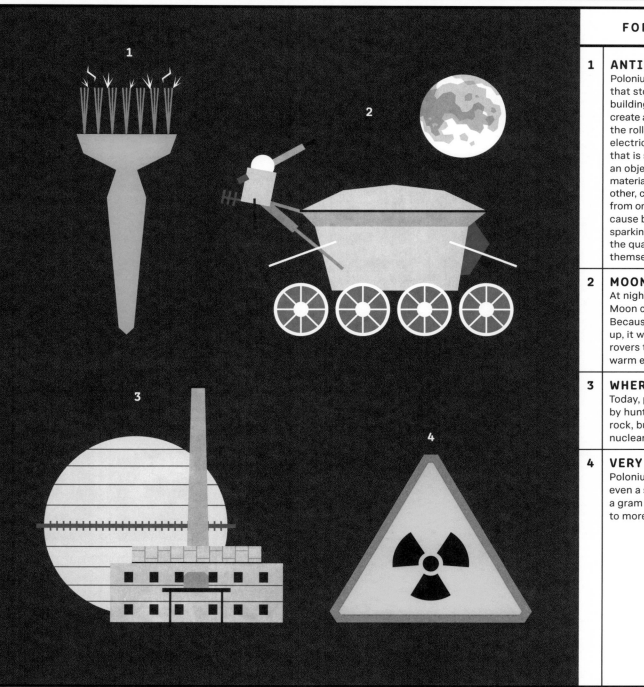

FORMS AND USES

1 ANTISTATIC DEVICES
Polonium is used to make devices that stop static electricity building up on machines that create a lot of friction, such as the rollers in paper mills. Static electricity is an electrical charge that is stuck at the surface of an object. It builds up when two materials are rubbed against each other, causing electrons to move from one object the other. It can cause big problems in a factory, by sparking, causing fires, or affecting the quality of the products themselves.

2 MOON HEATER
At night, temperatures on the Moon can drop below –274°F. Because polonium heats itself up, it was carried onboard Moon rovers to keep their instruments warm enough to work.

3 WHERE IT'S MADE
Today, polonium is not extracted by hunting through tons of rock, but produced inside nuclear reactors.

4 VERY RADIOACTIVE
Polonium is so radioactive that even a small lump weighing half a gram quickly heats itself up to more than 930°F!

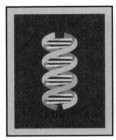

6

C

Carbon

7

N

Nitrogen

8

O

Oxygen

15

P

Phosphorus

16

S

Sulfur

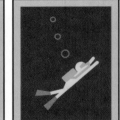

34

Se

Selenium

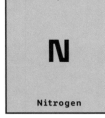

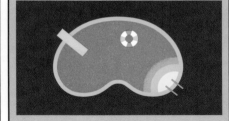

Non-Metals

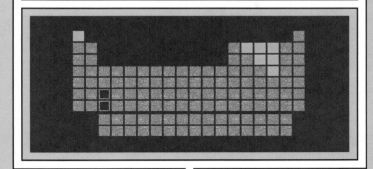

ALONG WITH HYDROGEN, THE NON-METALS CARBON, NITROGEN, OXYGEN, PHOSPHORUS, SULFUR, AND SELENIUM ARE ALL KEY BUILDING BLOCKS OF LIVING THINGS.

Most of the elements in the periodic table are metals—they are shiny or **lustrous**, soft and easy to shape, and **conduct** heat and **electricity**. They also react with elements and more complex chemicals in a certain way, being willing to share some of their **electrons** with other elements, or give them up altogether. The metalloids share some of these properties too. The remaining elements of the periodic table are non-metals. They include the halogens (see page 146), the noble gases (see page 158), and the special collection of six elements explored in this chapter: carbon, nitrogen, oxygen, phosphorus, sulfur, and selenium. Non-metals are less willing to give up their electrons. This means they react with other elements and chemicals in a different way to metals, and that they don't conduct electricity well (although one form of carbon breaks this rule).

Carbon, nitrogen, oxygen, phosphorus, sulfur, and selenium have something else in common. They are constantly on the move, from the environment to living things and back again. These great natural cycles, such as the carbon cycle, constantly recycle the elements that are the building blocks of life on Earth. Humans rely on these cycles too, but in the past few hundred years our activities have upset the balance of many of these elements in the environment. This has disrupted the natural cycles, leading to problems such as pollution, **acid** rain, the hole in the ozone layer, global warming, and climate change. Science has helped us to understand these natural cycles well, so we know what we must do to solve these problems. Now it is up to us to take action to restore the delicate balance of life on Earth.

6
C

Carbon
(CAR-BUN)

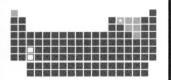

NON-METAL

CARBON IS THE MAIN BUILDING BLOCK OF ALL LIVING THINGS. IT'S ALSO AN ESSENTIAL PART OF ALMOST EVERY OBJECT, FUEL, AND FOOD ON THE PLANET.

KEY PROPERTIES

- solid
- several **allotropes:** diamond and graphite
- graphite **conducts electricity**

WHERE IT'S FOUND

- many rocks/**minerals**
- pure, as coal and soot
- pure, as graphite
- pure, as diamond
- fossil fuels
- all living things
- air (as carbon dioxide)

HUMAN BODY

 18.5%

ALL ABOUT CARBON

People have known about coal, soot, charcoal, graphite, and diamond for hundreds or even thousands of years, but it was only in the 1700s that chemists realized they were all different forms of the same element. It was even longer before we realized that carbon is the key element of life itself. This means that carbon is the basis of almost everything: of your clothes and shoes; of the walls and floors of your home and the fuels burned to light and heat it; of objects made from wood and plastic; of the pages in this book and the ink of these words. Carbon is also the main building block of your body, so you need to eat hundreds of grams every day to live and grow. For most people this is easy because carbon is also the main element in most foods, from sugars and fats to proteins and fiber.

Humans dig more carbon out of the ground than any other element, and we've found thousands of ways to use it to improve our lives. We build grand structures with limestone and marble (the **compound** calcium carbonate). We burn coal, oil, and natural gas to release the energy trapped in their long chains of carbon atoms. We also turn carbon-based fossil fuels into plastics and fibers, including carbon fibers that are stronger than steel. We rely on carbon in the form of coke to make steel itself, and we handle molten metals in containers lined with another form of carbon—graphite. Carbon is also a part of thousands of other materials and chemicals that make everyday life possible. Scientists are still discovering exciting new ways to use carbon, including engineering "nanostructures" (tiny structures built with **particles**) using carbon atoms themselves!

SECRET CHEMISTRY

Carbon atoms can **bond** with other elements (and with each other) to form nearly ten million different compounds—more than any other element! These compounds include very large and complex **molecules** with long chains of carbon atoms.

INSIDE THE ATOM

— 6   + 6   ○ 6

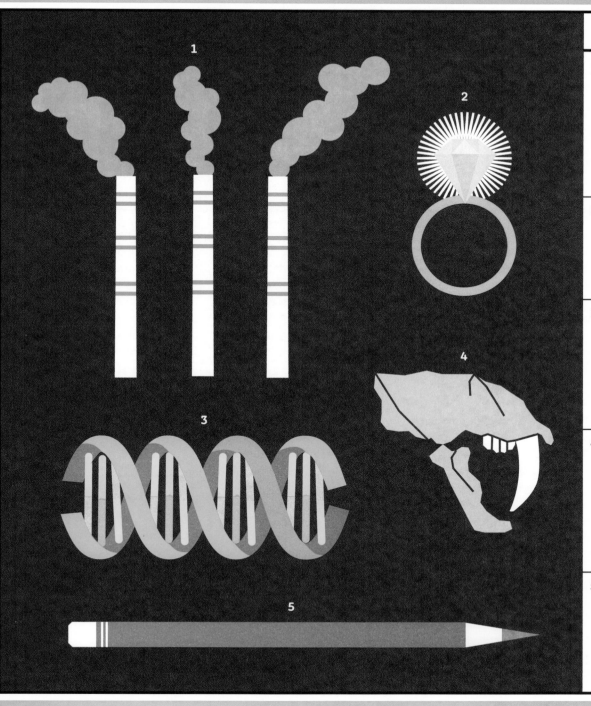

FORMS AND USES

1 FOSSIL FUELS
When we burn fossil fuels, we break long chains of carbon and hydrogen atoms, releasing their chemical energy as heat and light. Burning fossil fuels releases more carbon dioxide (CO_2) and methane (CH_4) into the atmosphere than is normal. These are two of the main "greenhouse gases" causing global warming.

2 HARD DIAMOND
Diamond is made of carbon atoms. Instead of being soft and slippery—like its allotrope, graphite—it's the hardest substance in nature! The difference comes from the way the atoms are arranged inside.

3 LIFE ON EARTH
Molecules that include lots of carbon atoms are the basis of all living things. These molecules include **chlorophyll** (used by plants to absorb the energy in sunlight, in order to make food) and **DNA** (which encodes the "instructions" for building living things).

4 CARBON DATING
Carbon-14 is a natural **radioactive** form of carbon. Its unstable atoms break apart over time, at a very steady rate. By measuring the amount of carbon-14 left in an ancient object, we can tell how old it is. Carbon dating tells us that saber-toothed cats were alive at the time the first humans moved to Europe!

5 SOFT GRAPHITE
The graphite in pencils is a form of carbon. In graphite, the carbon atoms are organized into different layers. The bonds between layers are weak, which is why graphite easily rubs off—layer by layer—onto the paper when you write.

Nitrogen

(NIGH-TRO-GIN)

7

N

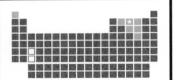

NITROGEN IS BEST KNOWN FOR BEING THE MAIN GAS IN AIR. BUT IT'S ALSO USED TO HELP FEED THE PLANET, AND TO MAKE SOME OF THE MOST EXPLOSIVE CHEMICALS IN HISTORY.

KEY PROPERTIES

- gas
- colorless
- no taste
- no smell
- one **allotrope**

WHERE IT'S FOUND

- some **minerals**
- air
- **salts** called nitrates

HUMAN BODY

 3.2%

ALL ABOUT NITROGEN

Nitrogen is an essential part of the proteins, **DNA**, and hundreds of other building blocks of living things—including us! Although 78% of the air around us is nitrogen, plants and animals can't soak up nitrogen gas and use it. Only certain bacteria and algae have the power to "fix" nitrogen from the air and soil. These **microbes** trap nitrogen in **compounds** that other living things *can* use, such as ammonia (NH_3) and nitrates. Plants can soak up ammonia and nitrates from soil. Animals then get hold of nitrogen by eating plants, or other animals.

Crops grow better when extra ammonia and nitrates are added to the soil. Farmers and gardeners have done this for thousands of years, by adding manure (animal poop) and mulch (**decaying** plants) to the soil, which act as natural fertilizers. But as demand for food increased, people wanted to find a way to make artificial fertilizers. Although we can extract nitrogen gas from the air, it's much harder to copy what nitrogen-fixing microbes do and turn it into ammonia, which is a compound of nitrogen and hydrogen! Getting nitrogen to **bond** with hydrogen is very hard, because pure nitrogen gas is very unreactive. Its atoms are joined together in pairs, as N_2 **molecules**. These pairs of atoms are very stable—it's very hard to separate them so they can form bonds with hydrogen atoms. When chemists finally worked out how to do this, it changed farming. It allows us to make artificial nitrogen fertilizers that help us grow enough crops to feed the world. It also helps us to make thousands of other useful chemicals. Nitrogen is also a key ingredient in many different explosives, from gunpowder and dynamite to the sodium azide that explodes to inflate car airbags.

SECRET CHEMISTRY

Pure nitrogen is used as a gas to surround things that would decay or explode if they came into contact with oxygen in air. If it is squeezed enough, nitrogen becomes a liquid. At normal pressure, pure liquid nitrogen is incredibly cold and is used to preserve other things by cooling them to less than –321°F.

INSIDE THE ATOM

 7   7 ○ 7

FORMS AND USES

1 USEFUL GAS
Nitrous oxide, also known as laughing gas, is used as an anesthetic in hospitals, because when people breathe it in it helps them to ignore pain. It's also used to make cream fluffy and bubbly as it comes out of a can.

2 MAKING THINGS
Nitrogen is used to make thousands of different chemicals and materials, from dyes and medicines to plastics and fabrics, such as nylon. Nylon is strong and lightweight, making it perfect for stretchy sportswear, but also things like seatbelts and tents!

3 EXPLOSIVES
Some nitrogen compounds explode when a small burst of energy from a detonator allows the nitrogen atoms to break free and bond with each other to form nitrogen gas (N_2). This **reaction** releases energy as heat, causing the newly formed nitrogen gas to expand quickly.

4 DANGER FOR DIVERS
If divers breathe air deep underwater, the high pressure causes some nitrogen to dissolve in their blood. If they swim back up too quickly, the nitrogen in their blood forms bubbles of gas, which can be deadly.

5 ELEMENT OF LIFE
All living things need nitrogen. By making nitrogen react with hydrogen to produce ammonia, the "Haber-Bosch" process is the first step in producing the nitrogen fertilizers that make it possible to grow enough crops to feed billions of humans.

O

8

Oxygen

(OX-EH-GIN)

NON-METAL

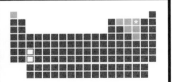

OXYGEN IS NEEDED BY MOST LIVING THINGS ON EARTH. ITS ABILITY TO REACT WITH ALL KINDS OF OTHER CHEMICALS—FROM FUELS TO FOOD— IS THE KEY TO UNLOCKING STORED ENERGY.

KEY PROPERTIES

- gas
- colorless
- no taste
- no smell
- two **allotropes**

WHERE IT'S FOUND

- most rocks/**minerals**
- air
- water
- sand and soil
- living things

HUMAN BODY

65%

ALL ABOUT OXYGEN

There are more atoms of oxygen on Earth than any other element. Along with silicon it's the most abundant element in rocks and minerals. Combined with hydrogen, it makes up water that drifts across the sky as clouds, pours down as rain, flows in rivers, and sloshes around the world's oceans. All living things need this water, and many also rely on the oxygen in the air. We get oxygen from the air as we breathe, and our bodies use it for respiration. This is the name for the chemical **reaction** that releases the energy trapped inside food. In respiration, oxygen reacts with glucose ($C_6H_{12}O_6$), breaking the sugar apart to form water and carbon dioxide, and releasing the energy that was stored in their chemical **bonds**. Plants and animals need this energy to live and grow.

Other substances react with oxygen more dramatically, by burning. We rely on the energy released by combustion to heat our homes, produce **electricity**, and power cars, trucks, trains, and planes. Most machines powered by burning fuel only work because of the oxygen in the air around the machine. Most of this oxygen is in the form of O_2 **molecules**—each one a pair of oxygen atoms clinging together. We can get hold of pure oxygen by cooling air until it becomes liquid, then heating it slowly to boil off the nitrogen, leaving pale blue liquid oxygen behind. Pure oxygen is used for making steel and many other materials and chemicals, for supporting patients whose heart or lungs aren't working properly, and for sterilizing water. Oxygen can also exist as O_3 molecules, known as ozone. You can smell traces of ozone in the air after a thunderstorm—a crisp, sweet smell, as if the air has been burned.

SECRET CHEMISTRY

Oxygen is the most reactive non-metal and will combine with every element except a few noble gases. This can happen very slowly in a reaction such as rusting, or very quickly in combustion (burning) and explosions.

INSIDE THE ATOM

$-$ 8 $+$ 8   ○ 8

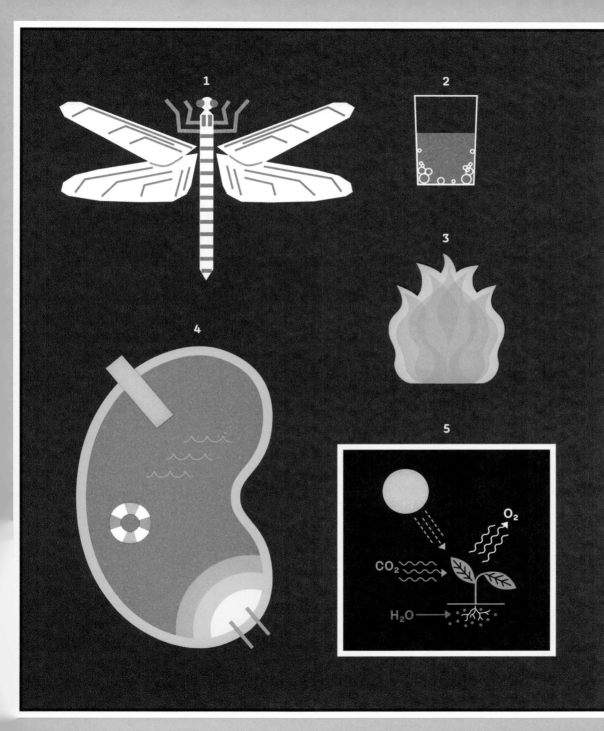

FORMS AND USES

1 OXYGEN IN AIR
Each time an animal takes a breath, oxygen is collected from their lungs and carried around their body. About 300 million years ago, the air was richer in oxygen than it is today. This extra oxygen allowed giant insects to exist, including dragonflies the size of today's birds!

2 OXYGEN IN WATER
Oxygen is one of the building blocks of water molecules, H_2O. However, aquatic creatures rely on oxygen gas dissolved in water. You can prove this dissolved oxygen is there by leaving a glass of tap water standing for a few days. The bubbles that form on the sides are bubbles of dissolved oxygen (and nitrogen) that have come out of solution.

3 BURNING FUEL
Burning is a very fast reaction between a fuel and oxygen in the air. It releases energy as light and heat. There is no air in space, which means rockets and other spacecraft must carry their own oxygen in order to burn fuel.

4 OZONE SHIELD
Oxygen can also exist as O_3 molecules, known as ozone. High in the atmosphere, ozone absorbs **UV radiation** in sunlight, shielding living things from its dangerous energy. Down on the ground, ozone is used to purify swimming pool and drinking water.

5 OXYGEN CYCLE
Most plants and animals take in oxygen constantly, using it to release energy from their food. Plants also give out oxygen as they make their own food by **photosynthesis**.

Phosphorus

15

P

(FOSS-FUR-US)

NON-METAL

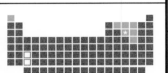

WHEN PHOSPHORUS IS COMBINED WITH OXYGEN AS PHOSPHATE, IT'S COMPLETELY SAFE AND A BUILDING BLOCK OF LIFE. BUT PURE PHOSPHORUS CAN BE DEADLY.

KEY PROPERTIES

- solid
- smells like garlic
- several **allotropes**
- one allotrope **conducts electricity**

WHERE IT'S FOUND

- many rocks/**minerals**
- bird and bat poop
- deep sea waters
- meteorites

HUMAN BODY

1%

ALL ABOUT PHOSPHORUS

Phosphorus was discovered by accident, by an alchemist named Hennig Brand, who was actually hunting for a way to turn cheap metals into gold. He believed that all he needed to do was to discover the right **catalyst**, known as the philosopher's stone. Brand had somehow decided that human urine was a good place to hunt for this mythical material! He collected 50 buckets of it and heated it gently to get rid of all the water. This left behind a gloopy substance that he then heated with sand in order to make it red hot. Finally, Hennig collected the glowing gas that evaporated and cooled it down until it became liquid, and then a soft, white solid.

Hennig hadn't found the philosopher's stone (there is no such thing), but he had discovered an element that glows in the dark. He named it phosphorus, after the Greek word for "light-bringing." Electricity hadn't been invented in the 1600s, so Hennig began selling his new, glowing element to make lamps. Today, we get phosphorus from rocks rather than urine, and it's used to make all sorts of useful things. Most is used to make chemicals, from food additives and cleaning products, to fertilizers that provide the phosphates that crops need in order to grow. Pure phosphorus is also used to make LEDs—tiny devices that glow when electricity is passed through them. However, pure phosphorus has a dangerous side too. In warm, damp air, white phosphorus spontaneously bursts into flames, which reach incredibly hot temperatures.

SECRET CHEMISTRY

In nature, phosphorus is only found in the form of phosphates, where each phosphorus atom is joined to four oxygen atoms. Phosphates are important building blocks of living things, especially brains, bones, and **DNA**, the **molecule** that codes life itself.

INSIDE THE ATOM

− 15   + 15   ○ 16

FORMS AND USES

1 MADE OF METEORITES
Most phosphorus on Earth is locked away inside rocks. Much of the phosphorus in living things came from meteorites that crashed to Earth billions of years ago!

2 PRECIOUS POOP
Guano (bird and bat droppings) is such a good source of the phosphates that plants need, it was once nicknamed "white gold"! The world's 800 million seabirds and their chicks are thought to poop out about 100,000 tons of phosphorus every year.

3 BUILDING BONES
Bones are mostly calcium phosphate, so our body can use them as a store of phosphates. In the 1800s, people dug up dinosaur bones and ground them up to use as fertilizer!

4 IN AND OUT AGAIN
Our bodies are constantly using phosphates, and they are found in many of the foods that we eat every day, such as fish, meat, eggs, and cheese. If we collected the phosphates peed out by a human in one day, it would weigh as much as two jellybeans! Urine is such a good source of phosphates that it can be used as fertilizer!

5 ESSENTIAL ELEMENT
Phosphate fertilizers are really important in helping to grow enough food to feed the world's enormous population. However, when they are washed off fields and into rivers, streams, lakes, and oceans, fertilizers can upset the balance of nature very quickly.

Sulfur
(SULL-FUR)

16
S

NON-METAL

SULFUR IS AN ESSENTIAL BUILDING BLOCK OF LIFE, THOUGH IT'S MOST FAMOUS FOR THE SMELLS RELEASED WHEN THINGS THAT USED TO BE ALIVE ARE DIGESTED OR DECAYED.

KEY PROPERTIES

- solid
- several **allotropes**

WHERE IT'S FOUND

- many rocks/**minerals**
- as pure sulfur
- meteorites
- fossil fuels
- plants and animals

HUMAN BODY

 0.25%

ALL ABOUT SULFUR

Bright yellow crystals of pure sulfur can be found inside rocks, especially near volcanoes, so it was one of the first elements to be named by humans. All living things need sulfur. Plants get it from the soil, and animals get it by eating plants or other animals. It's a building block of many proteins—the complex **molecules** that carry out jobs in our bodies. One of the proteins that contains the most sulfur is keratin, which is the material of hair, horns, and fingernails. Although pure sulfur is not **toxic** and has no smell, some of its **compounds** are a different story! Gases such as sulfur dioxide and hydrogen sulfide are produced when living things die and **decay**, and their sulfur-containing molecules are broken down. These gases are also behind the smell of bad breath, rotting eggs, farts, and raw sewage. This probably explains why we have evolved to find their smell so disgusting, because touching sewage or decaying things risks making us ill.

Sulfur reacts easily with lots of other elements, including metals. That's why a lot of the minerals we dig up to get hold of metals such as lead, zinc, iron, and copper also contain sulfur. Sulfur is a big part of the natural cycle of life on Earth, passing from soil to living things to air to water, over and over again. When humans mess with this natural cycle, it causes problems. Burning fossil fuels releases sulfur dioxide into the air, where it forms **acid** rain that harms the environment—especially forests and lakes. Today we collect sulfur dioxide as it leaves power stations and use it as a source of sulfur. Most is used to make sulfuric acid, an important chemical used to make thousands of products we rely on in everyday life, including fertilizers, metal objects, explosives, fuels, plastics, paints, detergents, dyes, and batteries.

SECRET CHEMISTRY

Sulfur will readily form **bonds** with every metal except gold and platinum. Inside our bodies sulfur atoms help to transport essential metals around our bodies, and to get rid of harmful heavy metals such as cadmium.

INSIDE THE ATOM

− 16   + 16   ○ 16

FORMS AND USES

1 GUNPOWDER
Sulfur is a key ingredient of gunpowder, an explosive that changed the world when it was used in weapons of war. Today it is mainly used in fireworks.

2 YELLOW MOON
Jupiter's moon Io is covered with volcanoes that eject huge plumes of pure sulfur gas that rise around 185 miles high. The sulfur then settles on the moon's cold surface, giving it a yellow color.

3 VULCANIZING RUBBER
Sulfur reacts with natural rubber, changing it from a sticky goo that oozes out of trees to the tough but flexible material that tires and shoes are made from.

4 FOOD ADDITIVES
Sulfur dioxide and sulfites are added to some foods as preservatives. They kill bacteria and can stop fruits and vegetables from turning brown.

5 TOXIC STENCH
Toxic sulfur dioxide and hydrogen sulfide gases waft out from molten magma and volcanoes on Earth too. They can be extremely toxic in large doses, which can make volcanoes deadly even when they are not erupting.

6 STINKY SULFUR
Sulfur compounds are responsible for some of the stinkiest odors, from the smell of onions and garlic to the smell of skunk spray.

34
Se

Selenium
(SUH-LEE-NEE-UM)

NON-METAL

SELENIUM IS RESPONSIBLE FOR THE WORLD'S WORST SMELL, BUT IN SMALL AMOUNTS THIS ELEMENT IS ESSENTIAL FOR HUMAN LIFE.

KEY PROPERTIES

- solid
- three **allotropes**
- some allotropes are **semiconductors**

WHERE IT'S FOUND

- some **minerals**
- rocks containing copper
- some soils

HUMAN BODY

TRACE

ALL ABOUT SELENIUM

Selenium is thought to be essential for humans, helping our bodies to build important proteins. Most of us get the selenium we need from our food, but some people take selenium supplements too, for example if they are trying to have a baby. Although we need selenium to stay alive, too much can be **toxic**. Certain selenium **compounds**, such as hydrogen selenide gas, are deadly. The first sign that someone has been poisoned by selenium is a disgusting smell. This is caused by methyl selenium, which evaporates easily in a person's sweat, as their body desperately tries to get rid of the selenium.

Selenium is unique because some forms behave like a non-metal and others like a metalloid. One form of selenium has the strange property of **conducting electricity** more than a thousand times better in the light than in the dark! This makes it a useful semiconductor for building electronic devices that can sense tiny changes in the level of light. In the past it has been used in alarms, doors that open and close automatically, safety systems, and photocopiers. However, selenium is rare—far rarer than silver—and many of these jobs are now done by different materials. Old photocopiers are still a major source of recycled selenium, most of which is added to glass to make it totally colorless, or to make special kinds of glass for coating buildings. Selenium is also used to help extract and process metals such as manganese. It is used to color paints, ceramics, and plastics red and orange. It also helps make fertilizers and animal feeds to make sure that crops and livestock get exactly the right amount to help them grow.

SECRET CHEMISTRY

Selenium atoms like to react with heavy metal atoms, such as mercury and lead. This means selenium can be used a bit like an antidote, to help remove these toxic heavy metals from a patient's body.

INSIDE THE ATOM

● 34 ✚ 34 ○ 46

FORMS AND USES

1 FATAL TO FUNGUS
Selenium is toxic to the fungus that likes to feed on the dead skin that collects on human scalps, so it's used in some anti-dandruff shampoos.

2 MOON LINK
Selenium has lots of similarities to tellurium, the metalloid below it in the periodic table. Selenium was even named after the Greek goddess of the Moon, because tellurium had been named after Earth.

3 ESSENTIAL ELEMENT
Humans need selenium to build their bodies, and to grow new babies. It's thought that every **cell** in our body contains more than a million atoms of selenium! We get the selenium we need from foods such as nuts, garlic, onions, and broccoli. Eating too many Brazil nuts at once can cause selenium poisoning.

4 WORLD'S WORST SMELL
If you think hydrogen sulfide smells bad (see page 143), hydrogen selenide is said to smell a hundred times worse! It's also very toxic to sniff. Breathing air that contains just six atoms of selenium for every million atoms of other kinds is enough to kill some small animals.

5 TOXIC DOSE
Some plants, such as milk vetches, soak up so much selenium from the soil that they may one day be grown just to use as a source of selenium! However, they can be toxic if animals such as cattle graze on them, so they are seen as problematic plants.

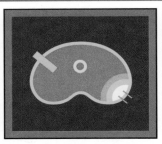

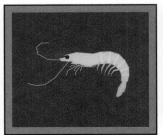
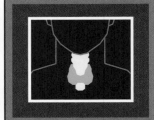

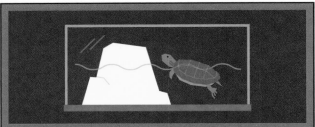
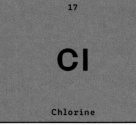
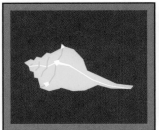
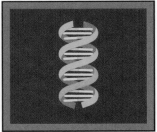

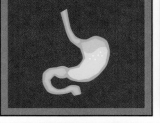

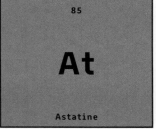

Halogens

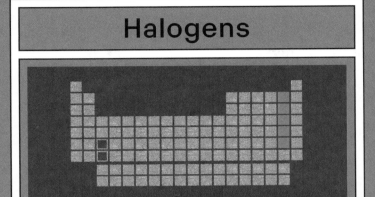

THE ELEMENTS IN THIS GROUP EXIST IN TWO FORMS. THE HIGHLY REACTIVE HALOGENS ARE NASTY AND **TOXIC**. THE MORE STABLE HALIDES ARE ESSENTIAL FOR LIFE.

The halogens form group 17 of the periodic table. These elements are all non-metals that don't **conduct** heat or **electricity** well, and have low **melting** and **boiling points**. The halogens are the most reactive of the non-metals. Each halogen atom is just one **electron** short of filling its outer orbit. Atoms are most stable when their outer orbit is full, so halogens will try to grab this missing electron from almost anything they come across! This makes the halogens very reactive, and happy to combine with almost every other element.

Because they are so reactive, we don't come across pure halogens in nature. We wouldn't want to either—pure fluorine, chlorine, bromine, and iodine are very toxic, and astatine is **radioactive**. All halogens will combine with other elements to form halides. In this form, their atoms each gain an extra electron, filling their outer orbit and making them much more stable and far less reactive. For example, chlorine(Cl) reacts with sodium(Na) metal to produce sodium chloride, the **salt** that we add to food. During the **reaction**, each chlorine atom takes the lonely outer electron of a sodium atom, and both atoms become more stable as a result. The atoms are now electrically charged **ions**, with opposite charges, so they are attracted to each other to form NaCl **molecules** (see page 211).

Many other important salts are also halides, and the word *halogen* means "salt-producing." Fluorides, chlorides, bromides, and iodides have thousands of different everyday uses, from medicines and toothpaste to chemicals and plastics with incredible properties.

Tennessine (Ts) is also a member of the halogen group, but it doesn't occur in nature. In this book, you'll find it listed with the other superheavy elements (see page 204).

9
F

Fluorine
(FLOOR-EEN)

FLUORINE HAS BEEN CALLED "THE MOST SAVAGE OF ALL" ELEMENTS. IT CAN BE INCREDIBLY DANGEROUS, BUT WE ALSO PUT IT INTO OUR MOUTHS AT LEAST TWICE A DAY!

KEY PROPERTIES

- gas
- pungent smell

WHERE IT'S FOUND

- **minerals**: fluorspar
- animal bones
- teeth and tusks
- coal and clay
- dust from volcanoes
- soils (especially near heavy industry)
- seawater

HUMAN BODY

0.004%

ALL ABOUT FLUORINE

Fluorine is the most reactive element of all. It will combine with almost anything! The **bonds** it forms with carbon are the strongest bonds ever seen in living things, and very hard to break. This makes fluorine very **toxic** for living things, which are mainly made of carbon. The fluorine atoms grab onto carbon atoms, refusing to let go and messing up thousands of different processes. Breathing in just a tiny amount of fluorine gas for a few minutes is deadly. Even a small splash of hydrofluoric **acid** on skin can kill. However, in small doses, fluorine is thought to be essential for humans and other animals. Toothpaste contains a safer form of fluorine known as fluoride. Inside our bodies, fluoride heads for our bones and teeth, where it reacts with calcium phosphate and turns it into a harder mineral. This makes bones and teeth stronger.

Chemists have found hundreds of thousands of other ways to use fluorine and fluoride. An amazing quarter of all medicines contain those mega-strong carbon-fluorine bonds, and are used to treat serious infections, cancer, and many other conditions. Other "fluorochemicals" are used for extracting aluminum from rocks and making steel. Fluorine is also used to make the world's strongest acids, used in industry and for etching glass and silicon computer chips. All these jobs rely on fluorine's amazing reactivity. However, there are also chemicals called fluorocarbons that are useful because they *don't* react with other things. Their carbon-fluorine bonds are so strong that they are happy to ignore everything else. Hydrofluorocarbons are used in air-conditioning units, refrigerators, and spray cans, and to make foams and fire extinguishers.

SECRET CHEMISTRY

Fluorine gas is made up of **molecules** of two fluorine atoms (F_2), and reacts with every element except argon, neon, and helium—often so quickly it causes an explosion. Fluoride is a form of fluorine where each atom has an extra **electron**. It isn't as reactive as fluorine, and is the form found in nature.

INSIDE THE ATOM

 9   ⊕ 9   ○ 10

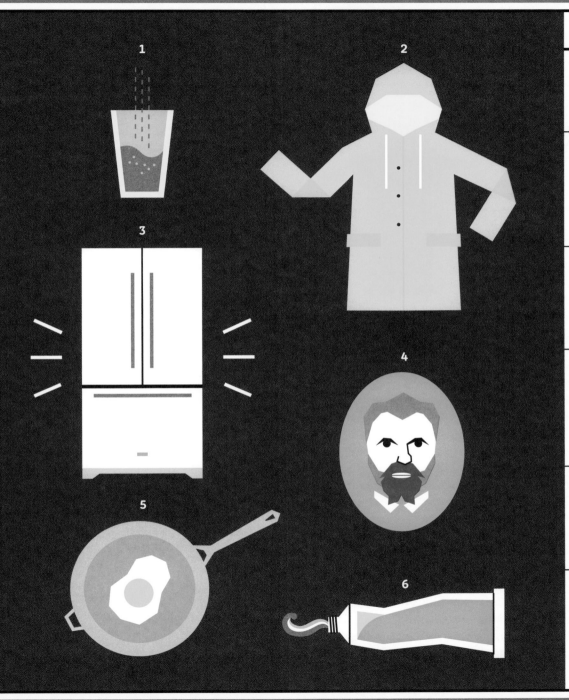

FORMS AND USES

1 DRINKING WATER
In some places, tiny amounts of fluoride (about 1 part per million) are added to drinking water to help prevent tooth **decay**.

2 WEATHERPROOF
Teflon plastic is used to make GORE-TEX® fabric for weatherproof clothing. GORE-TEX® has holes so tiny they can let sweat out but stop drops of rain from getting in! It's also used for making artificial veins and arteries.

3 GREENHOUSE GASES
Although they don't poison wildlife directly, the hydrofluorocarbons found in refrigerators are very strong greenhouse gases. When they escape into the atmosphere, they contribute to global warming.

4 NOBEL PRIZE
Because fluorine is so reactive, it was incredibly difficult and dangerous to extract the pure element. Henri Moissan won a Nobel Prize for succeeding, opening the way for humans to learn more about fluorine.

5 NON-STICK SAUCEPANS
Plastics that contain fluorine are very strong because they include unbreakable carbon-fluorine bonds. An example is Teflon, used to make non-stick pans. It doesn't react with anything, so foods don't stick to it.

6 TOOTHPASTE
Fluoride is added to many toothpastes to help teeth develop and stay strong. However, swallowing fluoride can damage growing teeth. Always follow the instructions to spit toothpaste out after brushing.

17
Cl

Chlorine
(CLOOR-EEN)

HALOGEN

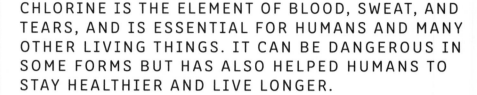

CHLORINE IS THE ELEMENT OF BLOOD, SWEAT, AND TEARS, AND IS ESSENTIAL FOR HUMANS AND MANY OTHER LIVING THINGS. IT CAN BE DANGEROUS IN SOME FORMS BUT HAS ALSO HELPED HUMANS TO STAY HEALTHIER AND LIVE LONGER.

KEY PROPERTIES

- gas
- greenish yellow
- more than twice as heavy as air
- antiseptic taste

WHERE IT'S FOUND

- **minerals**: carnallite, sylvite
- tap water
- animals
- rock **salt**
- seawater/soils

HUMAN BODY

 0.2%

ALL ABOUT CHLORINE

Chlorine is one of the two elements in salt, so there are vast quantities on Earth, including trillions of tons dissolved in seas and oceans. However, it's very reactive so it takes a lot of energy to extract pure chlorine gas. This is needed to make hundreds of different things, including chemicals, PVC plastics, bleaches, flame retardants, and pesticides. Chlorine is also used to kill any harmful **microbes** in tap water and swimming pools. Thousands of other chlorine chemicals are used in the process of making medicines, silicones, paper, textiles, and paints. In fact, chlorine plays a part in making an amazing 85% of all medicines and other substances used to keep us healthy! One of the most common chlorine chemicals is household bleach, sodium hypochlorite (NaOCl). It works by breaking up the chemicals in a stain such as ketchup, or in a colorful dye. The stain or dye is still there, but it is now white! Bleach can break apart and destroy bacteria and viruses in the same way, which is why it's used to clean toilets.

Over the past few decades, research has shown that some chlorine—based chemicals may harm the environment. Chlorofluorocarbons (CFCs) used to be found in air-conditioning units, fridges, and spray cans, and seemed to be harmless until scientists realized they were silently destroying the ozone layer—a part of the atmosphere that protects Earth from harmful rays from the Sun. CFCs have been banned around the world, but they are still being used in some places. This is worrying because even a single chlorine atom that escapes into the atmosphere can destroy up to 100,000 ozone **molecules**.

SECRET CHEMISTRY

In pure chlorine gas, the chlorine atoms are **bonded** together in pairs, as Cl_2. In this form, chlorine is very reactive and dangerous. Chloride is a more stable, safer form of chlorine, where each chlorine atom has an extra **electron**.

INSIDE THE ATOM

● 17   ⊕ 17   ○ 18

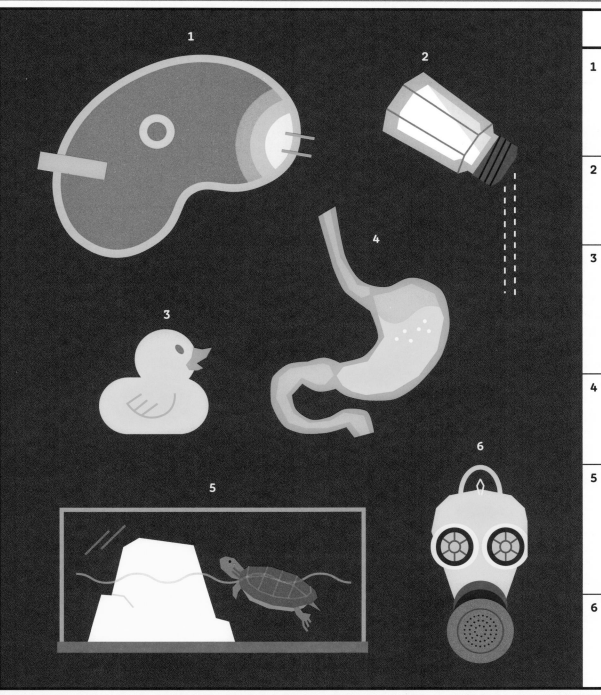

FORMS AND USES

1 SWIMMING POOLS
Chlorine is used to kill microbes in swimming pools. It also reacts with urine to form a substance called trichloramine—it's this chemical that you can smell in swimming pools.

2 PART OF SALT
Table salt (sodium chloride) is essential for humans. Eating too much salt is thought to be dangerous, but it's the sodium that seems to cause problems.

3 PLASTIC INGREDIENT
Polyvinyl chloride (PVC) is one of the world's most popular plastics. It's used around our homes and schools, in window frames and doors, pipes, electrical cables, garden furniture, vinyl floors, shoes, bags, raincoats, and bath toys! It's also easy to recycle.

4 STOMACH ACID
Our bodies use chlorine to make hydrochloric **acid** in our stomachs. This acid destroys most microbes that make it into our stomach. It also helps us to digest food.

5 STERILIZING WATER
A tiny amount of chlorine is added to tap water to kill germs. In some parts of the world, this has wiped out deadly diseases such as cholera. Even a low level of chlorine can harm aquatic animals, so tap water has to be treated before it's added to aquariums and ponds.

6 DEADLY WEAPON
In World War I, chlorine gas was used as a weapon, killing and injuring thousands of soldiers. This led to the invention of the gas mask to protect troops.

Br

35

Bromine

(BRO-MEAN)

HALOGEN

THIS IS THE ONLY NON-METALLIC ELEMENT THAT IS LIQUID IN NORMAL CONDITIONS, AND IT'S ALSO ONE OF THE WORST SMELLING.

KEY PROPERTIES

- liquid
- orange red
- bitter, medicinal taste
- strong, sharp smell

WHERE IT'S FOUND

- brine deposits
- seaweed/algae
- **mineral** water
- seawater
- briny lakes (Dead Sea)
- volcanic soils

HUMAN BODY

TRACE

ALL ABOUT BROMINE

Bromine doesn't just smell unpleasant; its vapor would burn your nose and throat, and sting your eyes. It was even named after the Greek word *bromos*, meaning "bad smell"! Bromine is very **toxic**—just 100 milligrams (the weight of 20 grains of sand) could kill a person. Bromide **salts** are much safer, and an adult could eat up to 3,000 milligrams without being poisoned. Bromine is found in our bodies because it's also found in the things we eat, but, unlike chlorine, it doesn't seems to be essential for life.

Outside our bodies, bromine has been useful. It's used to make dyes and medicines, to disinfect water, and in **DNA** sequencing—this is when scientists "read" the DNA of a living thing, to understand the "instructions" that living **cells** follow as they grow and develop. Bromine-based rechargeable batteries such as zinc-bromine (Zn-Br) and hydrogen bromide (HBr) batteries are used to store and release energy in some electric vehicles. Bromine finds its way into the tires of these cars too, because it's added to rubber to make it stronger and more weatherproof. A newer use of bromide is in power stations, where it helps to capture the toxic metal mercury that is released by burning coal. Chemists keep coming up with new uses for bromine, though, like some fluorine and chlorine **compounds**, they have to be carefully monitored to make sure they aren't harmful to people or the environment.

SECRET CHEMISTRY

Bromine is very reactive. If you dropped a piece of aluminum foil into a beaker of bromine, it would burst into flames.

INSIDE THE ATOM

● 35 ⊕ 35 ○ 44

FORMS AND USES

1 DNA DETECTIVES
Scientists use a chemical called ethidium bromide to study DNA, the **molecule** that acts as the "instructions" for every living thing. Understanding DNA better will lead to new kinds of medicine in the future.

2 PURPLE DYE
Some shellfish absorb bromine from seawater. The Romans were fans of a dye called Tyrian purple, which contains bromine. This wasn't made in a lab, but by boiling large cauldrons of sea snails!

3 MEDICAL HERO
Bromine is an ingredient in many medicines and is used to speed up the process of making lots of others, from sunscreen to pain medication.

4 EXTINGUISHING FIRES
Bromine's high reactivity can be used to prevent fires. Most fires are **reactions** between a fuel and oxygen in the air. Bromine will always react with the fuel first, pushing less-reactive oxygen to the back of the line. It was once widely used in halon fire extinguishers, for putting out fires where water would make things worse or do damage. However, the gases released by these extinguishers damage the ozone layer, so today they are only allowed where there is no good alternative, such as onboard aircraft. Bromine is also added to the casings of electrical gadgets such as televisions, computers, and plug sockets, to the stuffing of sofas and mattresses, and even to the insulation inside our walls.

53

I

Iodine
(EYE-O-DINE)

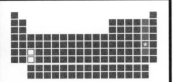

HALOGEN

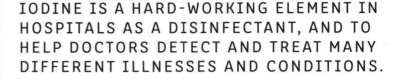

IODINE IS A HARD-WORKING ELEMENT IN HOSPITALS AS A DISINFECTANT, AND TO HELP DOCTORS DETECT AND TREAT MANY DIFFERENT ILLNESSES AND CONDITIONS.

KEY PROPERTIES

- solid
- black, shiny crystals
- purple vapor when heated
- sharp smell

WHERE IT'S FOUND

- **minerals**: lautarite, iodargyrite
- natural brines
- seawater/rainwater
- soils
- seaweed

HUMAN BODY

TRACE

ALL ABOUT IODINE

The name iodine means violet-colored, but its pinkish-purple vapor only appears when pure iodine is heated. In everyday life, we are more likely to come across the orange-brown color of iodine dissolved in water. This is an important antiseptic in hospitals, where it's used to clean wounds or kill any germs living on the skin before a surgeon makes a cut. On dairy farms, it's used to sterilize a cow's udders after it has been milked.

Like other animals, we need iodine in our bodies, though not to kill germs. Most of it collects in the thyroid gland, where it's used to make **hormones** that control how our body uses energy. We lose iodine in our urine, so we need to eat around 70 micrograms every day. This is so important that in many countries, table **salt** has to have iodine added to it by law. Around 2 billion people still don't get enough iodine, and this can cause a condition where a person's body and brain do not grow and develop properly.

Iodine is used in medicines to treat iodine deficiency and thyroid problems. It's also used to help detect certain types of cancer, such as cervical cancer, and to find out how well a person's thyroid gland is working. In this case, the patient eats a **radioactive** form of iodine that collects in the thyroid gland and shows up on certain types of scan. A different type of radioactive iodine is used to treat certain cancers.

SECRET CHEMISTRY

Iodine is the least reactive halogen apart from astatine. This makes it less dangerous than fluorine, chlorine, and bromine but it's still **toxic** in large doses—3 grams of iodine could be fatal. 3 grams is the weight of two paperclips! The iodide form is much safer.

INSIDE THE ATOM

— 53   + 53   ○ 74

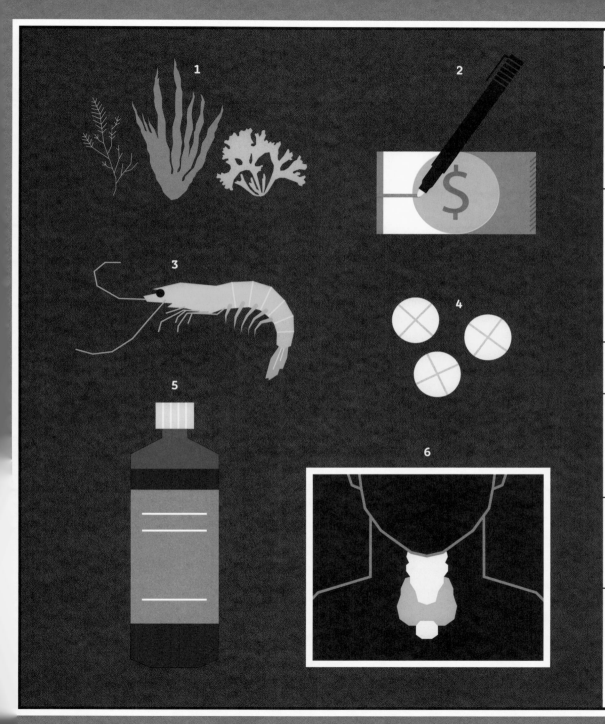

FORMS AND USES

1 SEAWEED SUNSCREEN
Seaweed soaks up and stores iodine from the oceans. The iodine is thought to protect the seaweed from being damaged by **UV** light from the Sun. Much of the world's iodine was once extracted from seaweed ashes!

2 STAINS AND DYES
Iodine turns deep blue when it reacts with starch—a type of **molecule** found in plants. This is useful for making pens to test if banknotes are real or fake. Banknotes in the USA, Canada, and the European Union are made from fabric or plastic, so they don't turn blue. Forged banknotes printed on paper are stained.

3 ESSENTIAL ELEMENT
People who eat lots of seafood will get plenty of iodine in their diet.

4 PROTECTIVE POWERS
Potassium iodide tablets are used to protect people from **radiation** poisoning after a nuclear accident. The safe iodide in the tablets stops the person's body from absorbing radioactive iodine-131.

5 MEDICAL MARVEL
Iodine disinfectant is the orange-brown disinfectant used in hospitals. It is often made by dissolving potassium iodide in alcohol and water.

6 THYROID GLAND
Eating too much or too little iodine can cause thyroid problems. Your thyroid is a butterfly-shaped gland in your neck. It takes iodine and uses it to make two hormones needed for every **cell** in your body to work properly.

85
At

Astatine
(AS-TUH-TEEN)

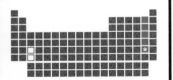

IT'S HARD TO GET HOLD OF ASTATINE, BUT CHEMISTS ARE KEEN TO FIND OUT MORE ABOUT THIS ELEMENT. IT COULD BE THE KEY TO NEW WAYS TO TREAT CANCER.

KEY PROPERTIES

- solid
- can only be predicted, but probably black

WHERE IT'S FOUND

- a tiny amount in rocks that contain uranium and thorium
- nuclear reactors

HUMAN BODY

NONE

ALL ABOUT ASTATINE

Scientists began hunting for "element 85" to fill a gap in the periodic table. Over several decades, many teams claimed to have found the missing element, and each one suggested a different name, including alabamine, dakin, helvetium, and viennium. Yvette Cauchois and Horia Hulubei were two of these scientists. Yvette had invented a new type of **spectroscopy**—a way to separate out and examine the different kinds of **radiation** coming from an element. In 1939, they used this to study the kinds of radiation coming from radon. They spotted signs of an element that wasn't radon, and were convinced it was the missing element 85, hiding in their sample of radon. Horia did years of work to try to confirm this, even though World War II made this incredibly hard.

In 1944, they announced the new element and named it "dor," from a Romanian word meaning longing. Horia explained that they named it "dor," or longing, because "It was identified during a period of terrible suffering for humanity. The name would ... recall a longing for the time when peace will bring an end to the most hateful war history has ever known." However, astatine is so rare in nature that other scientists decided it probably wouldn't have been possible for Yvette and Horai to detect astatine in radon. The credit went to someone else. Yvette's work improving spectroscopy was still incredibly important in helping scientists detect elements and find out more about them. She became the second woman president of the French Society of Physical Chemistry after Marie Curie.

SECRET CHEMISTRY

No one has ever seen a lump of pure astatine, so chemists use what they know about the other halogens to predict how astatine behaves. Experiments with tiny amounts of astatine dissolved in other substances confirmed that astatine is the least reactive halogen.

INSIDE THE ATOM

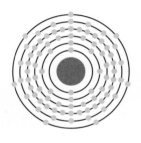

● 85 ✚ 85 ○ 125

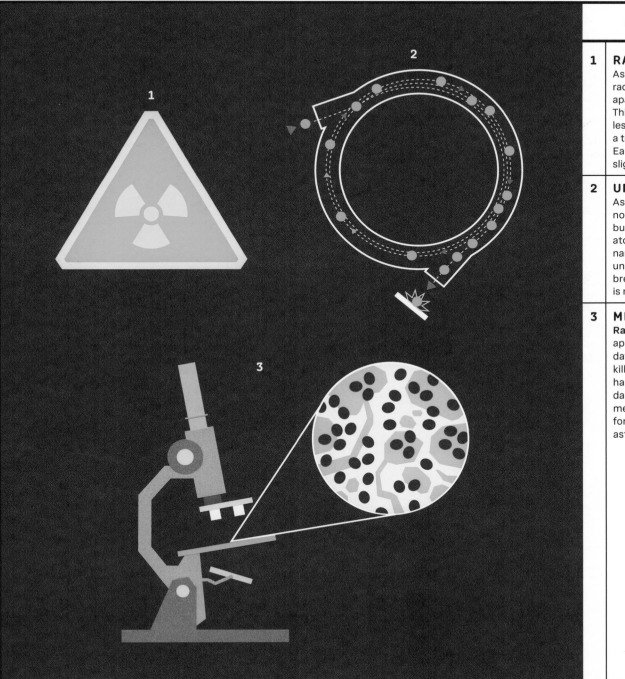

FORMS AND USES

1 | RARE ELEMENT
Astatine is so unstable and radioactive that its atoms break apart soon after they are formed. This means there are likely to be less than 30 grams (less than a tenth of a pound) in all of the Earth's rocks at any time—only slightly heavier than an AA battery!

2 | UNSTABLE ELEMENT
Astatine was officially discovered not by extracting it from nature, but by bombarding bismuth atoms with radiation. It was named after the Greek word for unstable, because its atoms break apart so quickly. Today it is made in a **particle accelerator**.

3 | MEDICAL RESEARCH
Radioactive atoms that break apart (**decay**) in a few hours or days can be very useful. They can kill cancer **cells** quickly, but don't hang around in a patient's body, damaging healthy cells. This is why medical researchers are hunting for new ways to use radioactive astatine for treating cancers.

2

He

Helium

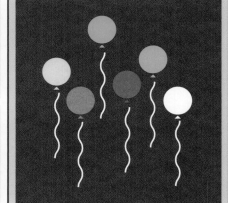

10

Ne

Neon

18

Ar

Argon

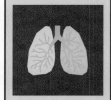

36

Kr

Krypton

54

Xe

Xenon

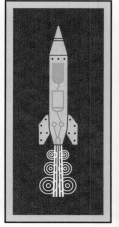

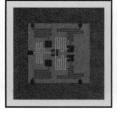

86

Rn

Radon

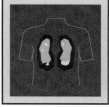
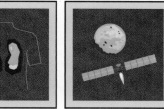

Noble Gases

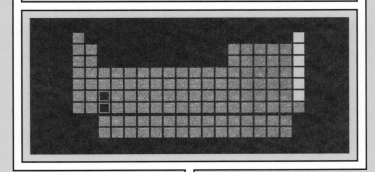

ATOMS OF THE NOBLE GASES ARE DRIFTING AROUND YOU RIGHT NOW, MOVING IN AND OUT OF YOUR LUNGS AS YOU BREATHE! HOWEVER, THEY ARE INCREDIBLY HARD TO DETECT.

When Dmitri Mendeleev put together the first periodic table, none of the noble gases had yet been discovered. Dmitri didn't even predict that this group existed. This turned out to be quite embarrassing because there's actually quite a lot of argon in the air around us—it's the third most abundant gas on Earth! John William Strutt and William Ramsay finally managed to get hold of argon in 1894. They did this by cooling air until it became liquid, then warming it up very, very slowly. Argon has a very low **boiling point**, so it evaporated first and could be trapped. When he discovered neon, krypton, and xenon in 1898, William realized they all belonged together as a brand-new group of elements—group 18 of the periodic table. Radon was discovered in 1900, completing the group.

Helium shares many properties of noble gases, so it's included in group 18. However, some scientists argue that helium belongs elsewhere in the table.

The noble gases were so hard to detect because they are very stable and quite happy to hang around on their own rather than react with other elements. They were even named after lazy "nobles" who keep to themselves. But the noble gases actually work hard for us in all kinds of different jobs, from making lightbulbs and lasers to putting patients to sleep during operations. Noble gases may be invisible to the eye, but when **electricity** is passed through them, they glow brightly—each one with a different color—so they are also used to make bright lights. Ever since the noble gases were discovered, chemists have tried to get them to react with other elements, something that doesn't happen naturally on Earth. In 1962 a chemist finally got xenon and fluorine to join together and form a new substance. Since then, several hundred noble gas **compounds** have been created in labs and some are being used in exciting ways.

2
He

Helium
(HE-LEE-UM)

HELIUM WAS FIRST SPOTTED INSIDE THE SCORCHING SUN, BUT HERE ON EARTH, LIQUID HELIUM CAN BE THE COLDEST SUBSTANCE ON THE PLANET. IT'S ALSO ONE OF THE MOST USEFUL.

KEY PROPERTIES

- gas
- lighter than air
- colorless
- no taste
- no smell

WHERE IT'S FOUND

- the Sun
- other stars
- natural gas
- air
- rocks containing thorium or uranium

HUMAN BODY

TRACE

ALL ABOUT HELIUM

Helium makes up almost a quarter of the matter in the universe, but on Earth it's rare. This explains why it was discovered by astronomers rather than chemists. It was named after Helios, the Greek god of the Sun. Inside the Sun, atoms of hydrogen are fused together to make atoms of helium. The helium found on Earth is made in a different way—when larger **radioactive** atoms inside rocks deep underground **decay** or split up into smaller parts. Helium is the second-lightest element after hydrogen and is lighter than air. Although radioactive decay is releasing a little helium into the air all the time, it tends to float up through the atmosphere and escape into space. However, we do find pockets of helium trapped underground, as part of natural gas. These pockets are one of the main sources of the helium used in party balloons, hospitals, weather balloons, and lab equipment such as lasers and powerful microscopes. Because helium is lighter than air, airships and balloons filled with helium will float upward, in the same way that air-filled bath toys bob to the surface of the water.

We can also extract helium from liquid air, but it takes about 990 tons of air to get enough helium to fill just seven large balloons! Scientists have warned that we are running out of helium, but it may be possible to exploit a different source in the future. There is a lot more helium on the Moon than there is on Earth. Some scientists have suggested that, one day, humans could mine the Moon for helium. It would be used as a fuel in **fusion** reactors, either here on Earth or to power long-distance space voyages. This element of the stars could one day help us to reach the stars!

SECRET CHEMISTRY

A helium atom is very unreactive because its outer **shell** of **electrons** is full. It doesn't need to share electrons with anything else. It's perfectly happy and stable on its own. Because it is unreactive, it is safer than hydrogen, which can react with other substances so quickly that it explodes.

INSIDE THE ATOM

− 2   + 2   ○ 2

FORMS AND USES

1 ROCKET SCIENCE
Helium is used to push propellants out of tanks and into a rocket's engines, because it won't react with the propellants.

2 BALLOONS
Helium is the most popular gas for filling lighter-than-air balloons.

3 BARCODE SCANNERS
A mixture of helium and neon gases is used to make the red lasers that scan barcodes in supermarkets.

4 UNDER PRESSURE
Researchers have forced helium to react with sodium, by squeezing atoms of helium and sodium together between two diamonds, the hardest material on Earth.

5 AIRSHIPS
The biggest helium balloons inflate to the size of a football stadium and carry scientific instruments to the edge of space.

6 DEEP SEA DIVING
Deep sea divers breathe a mixture of oxygen and helium. Unlike nitrogen in air, helium doesn't dissolve in a diver's blood, and because it's so unreactive it doesn't harm the diver.

7 COOLING THINGS DOWN
No matter how much you cool helium, it won't freeze solid unless it's also squeezed. This makes liquid helium the coldest substance on Earth. It's used to cool the huge **magnets** used in MRI scanners and **particle accelerators**. Low temperatures are key to making these magnets work.

10
Ne

Neon
(NEE-ON)

NOBLE GAS

NEON WAS NAMED WITH THE HELP OF A 13-YEAR-OLD. IT'S PROBABLY THE MOST UNREACTIVE ELEMENT OF ALL BUT HAS BECOME FAMOUS FOR ITS ROLE IN GLOWING "NEON" LIGHTS.

KEY PROPERTIES

- gas
- lighter than air
- colorless
- no taste
- no smell

WHERE IT'S FOUND

- the Sun and other stars
- air
- volcanic gases
- rocks such as granite

HUMAN BODY

NONE

ALL ABOUT NEON

Neon is the least reactive of all the elements. Nothing seems to be able to persuade it to share its **electrons** with other elements. However, when neon atoms get a boost of energy, they do something extraordinary. When **electricity** is passed through neon gas, its atoms begin to rush around and bump into each other. Their electrons gain a little more energy than usual. Eventually the electrons settle back to normal, and release the extra energy as bright orange-red light. This dazzled the scientists who first discovered neon, as well as a child named Willie who happened to be visiting his father in the lab that day. Willie suggested that the Latin word for "new" would be a brilliant name for this element because no one had ever seen anything like it. The scientists liked this idea but chose the Greek word for "new": *neos*.

Neon's bright glow is used to make neon lights, but it's also very useful for making lasers. In a laser, the light is focused into a single beam, which can be used to zap things with exactly the right amount of energy. As well as being used in barcode scanners (see page 161), the precise beam of light from a helium-neon laser has all kinds of uses, from measuring how much rain is falling to lining materials up on cutting machines, from helping wounds heal faster to zapping seeds to make them grow better. Although neon is the fifth most common element in the universe, it's rare on Earth. All the neon we use has to be extracted from air. It takes about 88,000 pounds of air to get just 1 pound of neon—that's roughly enough air to fill 13 Olympic swimming pools.

SECRET CHEMISTRY

Despite years of trying, scientists haven't been able to coax neon into reacting with other substances to form proper **compounds**. For this reason it has been called the most noble of the noble gases!

INSIDE THE ATOM

- 10   + 10   O 10

FORMS AND USES

1 UNCHANGING ELEMENT
Neon from deep inside Earth is being used to understand our planet's history. Because neon doesn't react with anything, all neon on Earth has stayed exactly the same ever since our planet formed!

2 NEON SIGNS
In the early 1900s, a French entrepreneur realized that glowing tubes filled with neon could be bent to form words and pictures.

3 NOT NEON!
Only bright red-orange "neon" lights actually contain neon—other colors are made using different noble gases.

4 PLASMA GLOBES
In a plasma globe, electricity flows through a mixture of neon and other noble gases, passing on some extra energy to the atoms of gas, which then release this energy as light as they settle back down again. If you put your fingers on the glass, the arcs of **electric current** are attracted to them, because the current wants to take the easiest path to Earth—through you!

5 NANO-ENGINEERING
Nano-engineers build miniscule structures out of **particles**. For example, carbon atoms can be used to build "buckyballs"—incredibly tiny but strong spheres made from 60 carbon atoms linked together. Nano-engineers can't build with normal tools—they would be far too big! Instead, they use special tools such as a beam of neon **ions**.

18
Ar

Argon
(ARE-GONE)

NOBLE GAS

IN GREEK MYTH, ARGOS WAS A DOG WHO DIDN'T DO MUCH. BUT ARGON THE "LAZY GAS" NOW WORKS HARD FOR HUMANS, DOING A HUGE RANGE OF USEFUL JOBS.

KEY PROPERTIES

- gas
- heavier than air
- colorless
- no taste
- no smell

WHERE IT'S FOUND

- air
- some bacteria
- in some **minerals** that contain potassium

HUMAN BODY

NONE

ALL ABOUT ARGON

Argon forms inside stars, but most of Earth's argon was formed as atoms of **radioactive** potassium changed or **decayed** over time. There's lots of potassium on our planet—in rocks and minerals underground, in seawater and in living things—so there's lots of argon in the air compared to other noble gases. By comparing the amounts of potassium and argon in rocks, we can work out how long the potassium has been decaying for, which tells us how old the rocks are. Strangely there is not as much argon as we'd expect after four and a half billion years of potassium decay on Earth! The missing argon is still a mystery that scientists are trying to solve!

Argon is useful because it's relatively cheap and easy to extract from air, and it refuses to react with metals, no matter how hot it gets. For example, it is a good choice for replacing air when doing jobs such as **welding** metals at high temperatures. This stops oxygen in the air from reacting with the hot metals. For the same reason, argon is used to fill lightbulbs, protecting the metal filament that heats up as **electricity** flows through it. In air, the filament would react with oxygen and burn, but in argon, it just glows. Argon also sits between the panes of glass in double-glazed windows and doors. It's chosen for this job because heat doesn't travel through argon very easily. Museums and archives also make use of argon's lazy nature, by surrounding old documents with the gas. This protects the documents by stopping them from coming into contact with oxygen, which would otherwise react with both paper and ink, causing ancient documents to deteriorate.

SECRET CHEMISTRY

Scientists have managed to make argon react with some elements, but only by creating unusual conditions, such as very high heat and pressure!

INSIDE THE ATOM

− 18 + 18 ○ 22

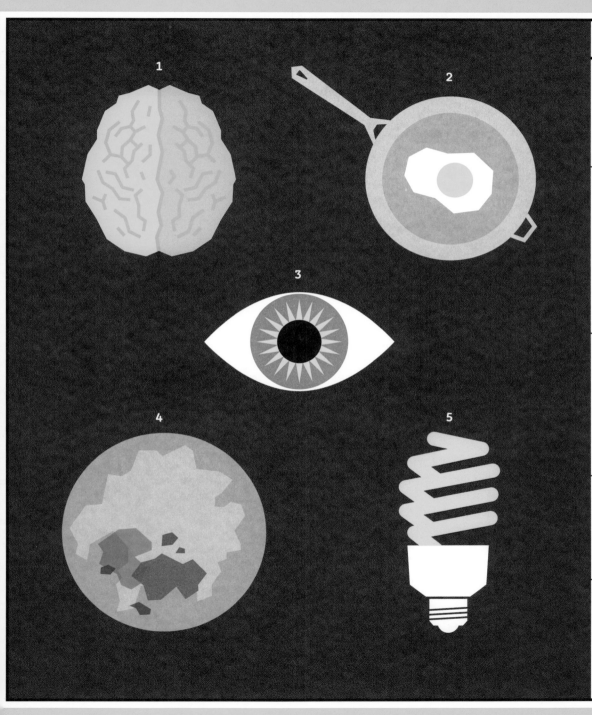

FORMS AND USES

1 FUTURE FIRST AID
In the future, argon may be used to help prevent brain damage. Researchers have found that if a rat is given argon to breathe after a brain injury, it stops brain **cells** from dying from a lack of oxygen.

2 STAINLESS STEEL
Stainless-steel objects, such as saucepans, are made with the help of argon. The steel is melted in a furnace, and a mixture of argon and oxygen gas is blown through it. The oxygen helps remove some of the carbon from the steel by reacting with it, but the argon stops the oxygen from grabbing onto elements such as chromium, which need to stay put.

3 BLUE LASERS
Argon lasers produce a beam of blue light that delivers a very precise amount of energy to the target. Often the target is a human eye, as these lasers are used for laser eye surgery to correct problems with vision. A laser makes much more precise cuts than a scalpel.

4 THE PLANET MERCURY
The planet Mercury doesn't have much of an atmosphere but what is there includes argon! As on Earth, it's produced by the radioactive decay of elements inside rocks.

5 LIGHTBULBS
Argon is used in low-energy lightbulb designs. Electricity is passed through a mixture of mercury and argon gas, producing invisible **UV** light, which makes the material coating the inside of the bulb glow brightly.

36
Kr

Krypton
(KRIP-TAWN)

NOBLE GAS

SINCE THIS "HIDDEN" GAS WAS DISCOVERED, IT HAS HELPED REVEAL SCORES OF OTHER SECRETS, FROM ANSWERS LOCKED AWAY IN ANCIENT AIR, TO THE SUPERFAST MOVEMENTS OF INSECTS, AND EVEN HIDDEN NUCLEAR WEAPON TESTS.

KEY PROPERTIES

- gas
- colorless
- no taste
- no smell

WHERE IT'S FOUND

- traces in air
- groundwater
- some **radioactive minerals**

HUMAN BODY

NONE

ALL ABOUT KRYPTON

Krypton is very rare, which makes it expensive. It could be useful for lots of things, but using other noble gases is usually cheaper. However, there are special missions that only krypton can carry out. These include ultra-high-energy lasers used by surgeons and superbright lights that light up airport runways. Krypton lights up incredibly quickly when **electricity** passes through it. This makes it perfect for high-speed photography, which uses a superfast flashing light to take thousands of different pictures in a second. It can let us see things that happen too quickly for our eyes or a normal camera to capture.

Some natural forms of krypton are radioactive, which means that they change and disappear over time. Measuring the amount of these radioactive **isotopes** in ancient ice tells us how old it is. This is really useful for finding out the age of ice cores drilled from deep below the Antarctic. Bubbles of ancient air trapped in the ice tell us what the climate was like all those years ago, so if we know exactly how old the ice is, we can understand climate change better. A different radioactive form of krypton, called krypton-85, is produced in **nuclear power** plants when uranium atoms are split apart to release energy. If people try to collect dangerous plutonium from the used fuel, the krypton-85 escapes into the air. In the past, traces in unexpected places have been a warning sign that plutonium is being collected to make nuclear weapons.

SECRET CHEMISTRY

Chemists have been able to get krypton to react with fluorine, to form substances that would never occur in nature. One of these is only stable when it's very cold. If it warms up to –58°F it explodes.

INSIDE THE ATOM

- 36   + 36   O 48

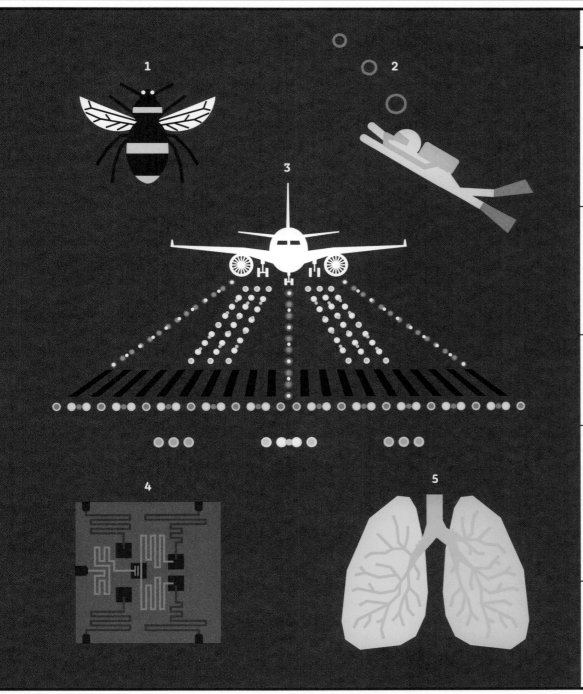

FORMS AND USES

1 INSECT FLIGHT
Krypton begins to glow incredibly quickly when electricity passes through it. This makes it perfect for high-speed photography, which uses a superfast flashing light to take thousands of different pictures in a second. It lets us see things that happen too quickly for our eyes to see, such as the movement of a bee's wings.

2 BETTER WETSUITS
Wetsuits work by trapping tiny pockets of air. If the air is replaced with krypton (by leaving the suit in a tank of krypton for a day), then the wetsuit becomes much better at trapping heat. In the future, this may help Arctic explorers or rescue divers to work for longer underwater.

3 SAFE LANDING
Krypton can be made to glow with an ultra-bright light that is perfect for lighting up airport runways. Even on a foggy day, they can be seen by planes several hundred feet away.

4 POWERFUL LASERS
Krypton-fluorine lasers release a beam of **UV** light, which is used to etch the circuits on tiny computer chips. One day, these high-energy lasers may be used to trigger **nuclear fusion reactions**. These are the reactions that happen in the Sun, releasing lots of energy, but they also take lots of energy to start them off.

5 DIAGNOSING DISEASE
If a patient breathes in specially treated krypton gas, it makes the hidden spaces inside their lungs show up on an MRI scan, which can be used to diagnose lung diseases.

54
Xe

Xenon
(ZEE-NON)

XENON IS A GAS OF EXTREMES: IT'S USED IN SUPERFAST SPACECRAFT AND THE ULTRA-BRIGHT PROJECTORS IN IMAX CINEMAS.

NOBLE GAS

KEY PROPERTIES

- gas
- heavier than air
- colorless
- no taste
- no smell

WHERE IT'S FOUND

- traces in air
- some meteorites
- some natural gas
- some spring water
- seawater

HUMAN BODY

NONE

ALL ABOUT XENON

Like the other noble gases, xenon glows brightly—this time with a blue light—when its atoms are given a boost of extra energy. Xenon lamps are used to make ultra-bright car headlights and IMAX projectors. They are also found in vast kitchens and food factories, because xenon's bright blue glow includes some invisible **UV** light, which can kill **microbes** without changing the taste of the food! Xenon is also the best fuel for spacecraft **ion** engines, and the best anesthetic in hospitals. When someone needs an operation, doctors use anesthetics to "pause" everything that's happening in their body, putting them to sleep and stopping an operation from being painful. Xenon makes a perfect anesthetic. However, it's so rare and difficult to extract from air that xenon is currently many times more expensive than other noble gases.

Traces of xenon found in meteorites are evidence that when the solar system was forming, it contained much more xenon than we find on Earth. Xenon is heavier than air, so, unlike helium, it hasn't escaped into space. So where is the missing xenon? One theory is that it might be trapped deep inside Earth's crust or core, where the heat and pressure has squished it into **compounds** that would never form on Earth's surface. Experiments have shown that xenon can be forced to combine with iron when the pressure is about one and a half million times the pressure of the air pressing down on you right now. If we ever get hold of this missing xenon, it will be very useful! Chemists have made xenon react with fluorine and other non-metals and metals, to form more than 100 different compounds.

SECRET CHEMISTRY

Making new xenon compounds is exciting, because each one may have totally new and useful properties. For example, xenon difluoride is used to make computer chips, and a medicine for treating cancer.

INSIDE THE ATOM

— 54　➕ 54　◯ 78

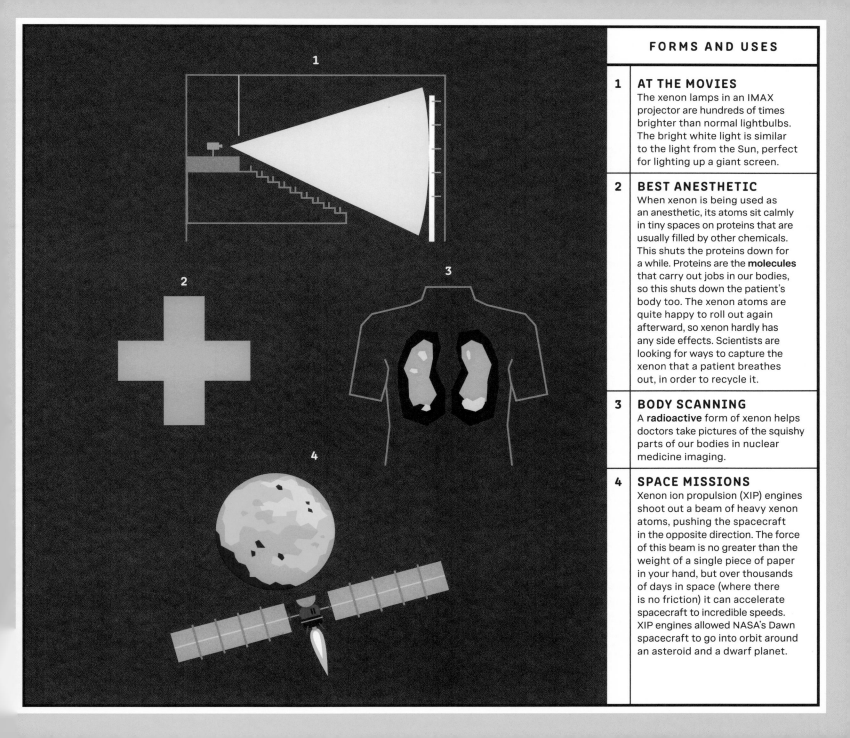

FORMS AND USES

1 AT THE MOVIES
The xenon lamps in an IMAX projector are hundreds of times brighter than normal lightbulbs. The bright white light is similar to the light from the Sun, perfect for lighting up a giant screen.

2 BEST ANESTHETIC
When xenon is being used as an anesthetic, its atoms sit calmly in tiny spaces on proteins that are usually filled by other chemicals. This shuts the proteins down for a while. Proteins are the **molecules** that carry out jobs in our bodies, so this shuts down the patient's body too. The xenon atoms are quite happy to roll out again afterward, so xenon hardly has any side effects. Scientists are looking for ways to capture the xenon that a patient breathes out, in order to recycle it.

3 BODY SCANNING
A **radioactive** form of xenon helps doctors take pictures of the squishy parts of our bodies in nuclear medicine imaging.

4 SPACE MISSIONS
Xenon ion propulsion (XIP) engines shoot out a beam of heavy xenon atoms, pushing the spacecraft in the opposite direction. The force of this beam is no greater than the weight of a single piece of paper in your hand, but over thousands of days in space (where there is no friction) it can accelerate spacecraft to incredible speeds. XIP engines allowed NASA's Dawn spacecraft to go into orbit around an asteroid and a dwarf planet.

86
Rn

Radon
(RAY-DON)

NOBLE GAS

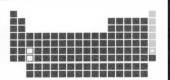

RADON VANISHES IN DAYS, HOURS, OR SECONDS AFTER IT FORMS. IT IS RARE IN FRESH AIR, BUT IF IT BUILDS UP IN A HOME IT CAN BE HARMFUL TO HUMANS.

KEY PROPERTIES

- gas
- colorless
- the heaviest gas
- no taste
- no smell

WHERE IT'S FOUND

- **radioactive** rocks and **minerals**: granite, shale, phosphate
- air (tiny amounts)
- some groundwater

HUMAN BODY

NONE

ALL ABOUT RADON

The noble gas radon is formed when other radioactive elements, such as uranium and radium, break apart over time. There is a small amount of uranium in rocks and soils, so radon is always being released into the air. Radon is also radioactive, and it **decays** (breaks apart) very quickly. The longest-lasting type of radon has a **half-life** of less than four days, which means that every four days, half of the radon has broken up to form different kinds of atoms. Some types of radon have a half-life of just four seconds! This means radon is incredibly rare—all the radon in the world's air at any one time adds up to less than the weight of an apple. However, some granite rocks contain uranium, so underground mines and buildings built on (or out of) granite can contain much higher levels of radon than normal. Breathing in this radon is harmful, because the elements that it forms as it decays include a radioactive form of lead, which can sit in a person's lungs for years and cause cancer. Good ventilation can blow the radon away and stop dangerous levels from building up.

Radon gas was detected by several scientists before it was properly discovered. Marie and Pierre Curie (see page 46) noticed it in a sample of radium and wondered if it was a new element. But it was a German chemist named Friedrich Dorn who collected enough of it to study and got the credit. A fourth scientist, William Ramsay, worked out that it belonged with the noble gases in the periodic table.

SECRET CHEMISTRY

Radon changes into other elements so fast that it's hard to experiment with. It's a noble gas, which tells us it's probably quite unreactive. The first **compound** scientists managed to make was radon fluoride.

INSIDE THE ATOM

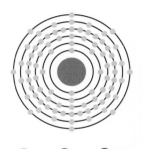

– 86 + 86 ◯ 136

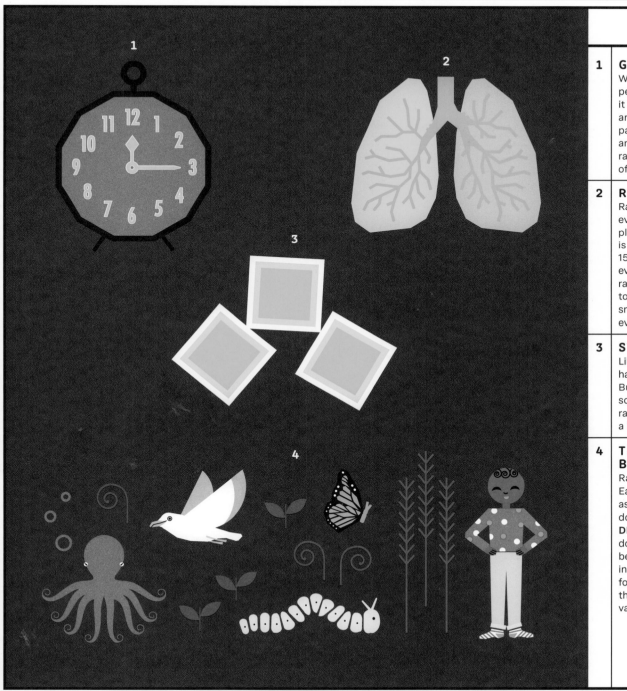

FORMS AND USES

1 GLOWING PAINT

When radium was first discovered, people were excited about the way it made certain substances glow, and added it to glow-in-the-dark paints used on clocks, watches, and even toys. Now we know that radium and the radon gas it gives off are dangerous.

2 RELATIVE RISK

Radon is present in the air nearly everywhere, but levels vary from place to place. In the US, radon is thought to cause more than 15,000 deaths from lung cancer every year. However, the risks from radon are very small compared to the risk from smoking tobacco—smoking causes 480,000 deaths every year in the US.

3 STRANGE SOLID

Like the other noble gases, radon has no color at room temperature. But if it's cooled until it freezes solid (–96°F), radon's natural radioactivity causes it to glow with a brilliant orange-yellow light.

4 THE SECRET OF BIODIVERSITY?

Radon is the source of lots of Earth's natural **radiation** (known as background radiation). At high doses radiation can harm the **DNA** in living things. But at low doses, background radiation may be the cause of the tiny changes in DNA that are the "raw material" for natural selection and evolution—the processes behind the great variety of life on Earth.

57	58	59	60	61
La	**Ce**	**Pr**	**Nd**	**Pm**
Lanthanum	Cerium	Praseodymium	Neodymium	Promethium

62	63	64	65	66
Sm	**Eu**	**Gd**	**Tb**	**Dy**
Samarium	Europium	Gadolinium	Terbium	Dysprosium

67	68	69	70	71
Ho	**Er**	**Tm**	**Yb**	**Lu**
Holmium	Erbium	Thulium	Ytterbium	Lutetium

Lanthanides

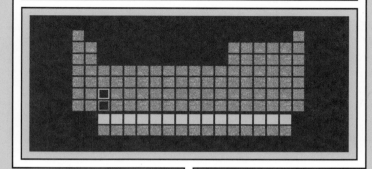

DESPITE BEING EXPENSIVE TO PRODUCE, THE LANTHANIDES ARE IN DEMAND. THEY'RE USED IN OUR CELL PHONES, LAPTOPS, FLAT SCREENS, AND FLUORESCENT LIGHTS. OUR HIGH-SPEED TELEPHONE AND INTERNET NETWORKS RELY ON THEM. WE ALSO USE THEM TO GENERATE **ELECTRICITY** AND TO MAKE ELECTRIC MOTORS.

These 15 fairly soft, silvery metals have lots in common with each other. At first, they were known as the "rare-earth" elements, but they turned out not to be rare after all—just very hard to get hold of. Even the rarest lanthanides are many times more common than silver or platinum, and traces are found in all kinds of rocks, including granite and shale. However, only **minerals** such as monazite, bastnäsite, and cerite contain enough of these metals to extract. Some of these minerals contain almost every lanthanide, but these metals are so similar it can be difficult to separate them.

Their similarity is explained by their quirky atoms. Like most other elements in the periodic table, each lanthanide has atoms with one more **electron** than the element to its left. These extra electrons usually sit farther away from the center of an atom, completely changing the way the element behaves. In lanthanide atoms, the extra electrons get tucked away deep inside the atom instead. As a result, atoms of all the lanthanides react with other substances in an identical way. This is a nightmare if you're trying to separate elements. Lots of different processes have to be used to tease them apart, which is expensive. Producing the lanthanides can also be very harmful to the environment.

The name "lanthanide" means "like lanthanum." Although lanthanum isn't therefore really a lanthanide, it's often included in this collection.

57

La

Lanthanum
(LAN-THA-NUM)

LANTHANIDE

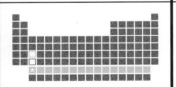

INSIDE THE ATOM

- − 57
- + 57
- ○ 82

ALL ABOUT LANTHANUM

Lanthanum is all around us—in iron and steel **alloys** and in the glass lenses of cameras and telescopes, where its large atoms help to slow and bend light. Hybrid cars with nickel-metal hydride batteries contain several kilograms of lanthanum. Lanthanum is very reactive, which makes it a useful chemical "sponge." If phosphorous fertilizer gets into fresh water, it causes algae to grow too quickly, harming other wildlife. Lanthanum will react with the phosphorus, removing it from the water. In medicines it can mop up extra phosphorus from blood, which could harm a person's kidneys. An alloy of lanthanum and nickel is brilliant at soaking up hydrogen gas and could be used to store fuel in hydrogen-powered vehicles of the future.

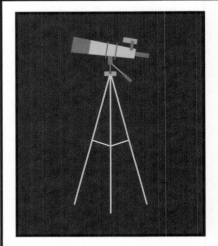

59

Pr

Praseodymium
(PRAY-ZEE-O-DIM-EE-UM)

LANTHANIDE

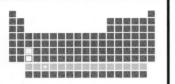

INSIDE THE ATOM

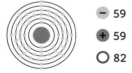

- − 59
- + 59
- ○ 82

ALL ABOUT PRASEODYMIUM

A lump of this silvery-gray metal reacts slowly with oxygen in the air to form a green coating of praseodymium oxide. This is where its name, meaning "green twin," comes from. Praseodymium **salts** are used to color fake gemstones, ceramics, and glass green or yellow. It's also used in safety goggles and visors, to protect eyes from the glare of very hot objects. Praseodymium is combined with other metals to make alloys, such as the superstrong magnesium alloys used in aircraft engines. One praseodymium nickel alloy becomes incredibly cold when it's near strong **magnets**. Scientists use this quirk to cool experiments down to close to absolute zero (-459.67°F).

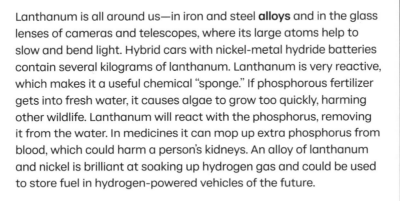

Cerium

(SEAR-EE-UM)

58
Ce

LANTHANIDE

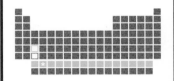

1 CLEANER CARS

Cerium oxide does an important job in catalytic converters, the devices that make car exhaust fumes less polluting. The cerium oxide gives up oxygen atoms so the burning fuel forms carbon dioxide (CO_2) instead of **toxic** carbon monoxide (CO), which can be deadly to breathe in.

Cerium was named after the dwarf planet Ceres, which, like cerium, was discovered in the early 1800s. There's more cerium on Earth than the other lanthanides, and it's easier to extract from rocks. Like lanthanum, cerium is very reactive. Just scratching the metal with a knife can create tiny sparks of burning metal (burning is just a speedy **reaction** between the metal and oxygen in the air). Cerium is the main lanthanide in mischmetal, which is used in fire-lighting devices, and to create showers of sparks in film special effects. Cerium oxide is added to diesel fuel, and is also found in self-cleaning ovens, where it provides extra oxygen for burning any splashes of food and grease to a crisp. Once burned, these simply flake off without scrubbing.

INSIDE THE ATOM

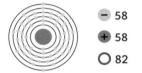

- 58
+ 58
O 82

1

Neodymium

(NEE-OH-DI-MEE-UM)

60
Nd

LANTHANIDE

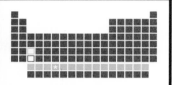

INSIDE THE ATOM

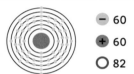

- − 60
- + 60
- ○ 82

ALL ABOUT NEODYMIUM

Neodymium was discovered in 1885, but for a hundred years it didn't seem to be very useful. Then, in 1983, it was used to make an **alloy** of neodymium, iron and boron (NIB for short). It turned out NIB alloys make the strongest permanent **magnets** known (permanent magnets are always magnetic, unlike electromagnets, which are only magnetic when switched on). NIB magnets are thousands of times more powerful than iron magnets. This made it possible to make smaller **electricity** generators, motors, speakers and other devices. NIB magnets are at the heart of wind turbines, cell phones, cordless tools, robots, computer hard disks and many electric vehicle motors. Neodymium is also used to make very powerful lasers that can cut through metal.

1 **CLEANER ENERGY**
As well as being found in electric cars and wind turbines, neodymium may help with the quest to find cleaner sources of energy in a different way. One day, neodymium lasers may be used to heat substances to 180 million degrees Fahrenheit in order to start **nuclear fusion**—this is the same process that releases energy in the Sun.

1

Promethium
(PRO-MEETH-EE-UM)

ALL ABOUT PROMETHIUM

Natural promethium has never been found in the Earth's crust. Its atoms only form when heavier uranium atoms break apart. Even then, promethium is so **radioactive** that its atoms quickly break apart themselves. Rocks that contain uranium may have traces of promethium, but only about a picogram for every ton of rock. That's the weight of a **microbe** and would be impossible to track down. We can collect promethium from nuclear reactors, which break uranium atoms apart to release energy. The element has been used to make nuclear-powered batteries, which last for a few years. In the future they could be useful on robotic spacecraft, where there won't be anyone around to change the batteries.

LANTHANIDE

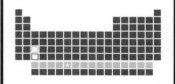

INSIDE THE ATOM

- − 61
- + 61
- ○ 84

Samarium
(SUH-MARE-EE-UM)

ALL ABOUT SAMARIUM

Magnets made from samarium and cobalt are incredibly powerful. They are found inside things that rely on tiny magnets, such as headphones and some electric musical instruments. Neodymium magnets are more widely used, but samarium-cobalt magnets stay magnetic at much higher temperatures—up to 1292°F. Samarium is also used in treating cancer, in **nuclear power** stations, and to make powerful lasers. A **compound** of samarium and sulfur that has strange and exciting properties could be used in the future to make devices that can store huge amounts of data.

LANTHANIDE

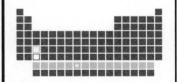

INSIDE THE ATOM

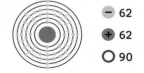

- − 62
- + 62
- ○ 90

63
Eu

Europium
(YOUR-ROW-PEA-UM)

LANTHANIDE

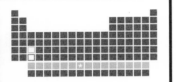

INSIDE THE ATOM

- – 63
- + 63
- ○ 90

ALL ABOUT EUROPIUM

Europium is one of the most reactive lanthanides. Although there's twice as much europium as tin in the Earth's crust, its reactivity makes it far harder to separate from the rocks and **minerals** it's found in. These include fluorite (calcium fluoride), which glows green when it's heated—even by the heat of a person's hand! Other europium **compounds** glow under **UV** light. The europium atoms absorb the energy of the UV light and release it as lower-energy light that we can see. This property makes europium useful as a tracer to help us understand how living **cells** work. Europium is attached to chemicals that get taken into cells. Under a microscope, UV light makes the europium glow brightly so a scientist can track the journey of chemicals inside the cells.

1 CATCHING CRIMINALS

Europium was discovered in France in 1901 and named after the continent of Europe. The element is used to make some banknotes, including euros! It makes the banknotes glow under a UV light—proving the money is real, as rare europium would be expensive for a forger to get hold of.

Gadolinium
(GAD-O-LIN-EE-UM)

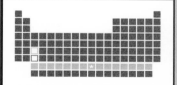

64
Gd

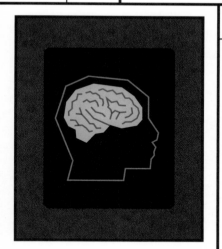

ALL ABOUT GADOLINIUM

LANTHANIDE

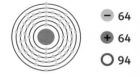

This element is named after the scientist whose curiosity led to the discovery of many of the other lanthanides. Johan Gadolin spent two years investigating a strange, black mineral found in a quarry near Ytterby, Sweden, in 1780. He managed to extract the element yttrium from it. Later, this led to the discovery of erbium, terbium, and ytterbium. Gadolinium is special because it's one of the only **ferromagnetic** elements—meaning that it's naturally attracted to **magnets** and acts as a permanent magnet itself. This property can be used by doctors to find out what is happening inside a patient's body. Gadolinium collects in tissues such as the brain and makes them **magnetic**, so they show up in the strong **magnetic field** created by an MRI scanner.

INSIDE THE ATOM

- − 64
- + 64
- ◯ 94

Terbium
(TER-BEE-UM)

65
Tb

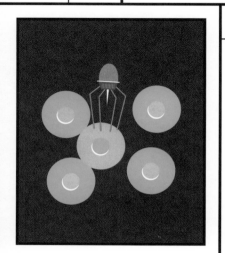

ALL ABOUT TERBIUM

LANTHANIDE

Under UV light, terbium atoms become excited, glowing green as they settle down again. This means atoms of terbium can be used to "tag" different chemicals and track their journey through an animal or its cells, helping scientists to understand how living cells work, and why they sometimes go wrong. Terbium is also used in "dynamic" or moving **X-rays**, which could help with healthcare in a new way. Terbium can be controlled by magnets. One day, it could be attached to tiny swimming **microbes** that could be steered to the correct part of a patient's body to deliver medicines. Because terbium glows under UV light, these micro-robots would also be easy to track, and could be collected afterward using magnets.

INSIDE THE ATOM

- − 65
- + 65
- ◯ 94

Dysprosium
(DIS-PRO-ZHEE-UM)

66

Dy

LANTHANIDE

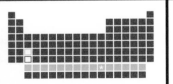

INSIDE THE ATOM

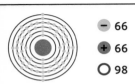

- − 66
- + 66
- ○ 98

ALL ABOUT DYSPROSIUM

Dysprosium is added to powerful neodymium **magnets** to make sure they stay **magnetic** even at high temperatures. This makes it important in electrical generators and motors. Dysprosium is one of the hardest lanthanides to extract from rocks—it's named after a Greek word meaning "difficult to get." This makes it very expensive, so scientists are looking for ways to make these magnets using cheaper lanthanum and cerium. Dysprosium has another important job—it's used to make safety badges worn by people who work closely with **radioactive** materials. The dysprosium atoms get excited by **radiation**, glowing green as they return to normal. This glow can be measured to check if the "dose" of radiation is safe.

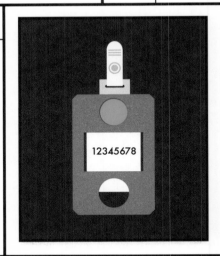

Holmium
(HOLE-ME-UM)

67

Ho

LANTHANIDE

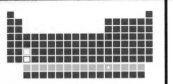

INSIDE THE ATOM

- − 67
- + 67
- ○ 98

ALL ABOUT HOLMIUM

Holmium was discovered by a Swedish chemist, who named it after the Swedish capital Stockholm. Like other lanthanides, holmium can be used to make powerful lasers. The energy of a holmium laser beam is just right for being absorbed by water **molecules**. As the water molecules absorb this energy, they begin to vibrate very quickly and heat up. Our bodies contain lots of water, which means the lasers can be used by surgeons to make very precise cuts and carry out 'keyhole' operations. The laser makes blood vessels (the capillaries, veins, and arteries that blood flows through) so hot that they seal themselves.

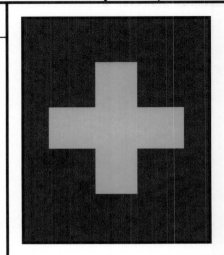

Erbium
(ER-BEE-UM)

ALL ABOUT ERBIUM

LANTHANIDE

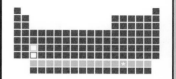

INSIDE THE ATOM

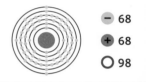

- 68
+ 68
○ 98

1 INFORMATION AGE

Thanks to erbium, fiber-optic cables can carry information at incredible speeds over land and under oceans. They have changed the way we communicate and make high-speed internet possible by carrying far more data than metal cables can. The first copper cable to cross the Pacific Ocean could carry just 91 phone calls at once.

Erbium was one of four lanthanide elements discovered in a mysterious black **mineral** found near Ytterby in Sweden. Like other lanthanides, erbium is used to add color to glass, and to make lasers. However its main job is keeping the world connected. Erbium is added to optical fibers—the thin glass tubes that carry messages around the world. Coded messages are beamed through these tubes as pulses (flashes) of laser light. Each pulse enters a fiber at one end, and travels to the other end by "bouncing" repeatedly off the sides of the tube. As light travels along the tube, it gets scattered and the signal gradually gets weaker. Erbium atoms absorb the light of a weakened signal and reemit it at the original energy, boosting the signal so it can continue its long journey.

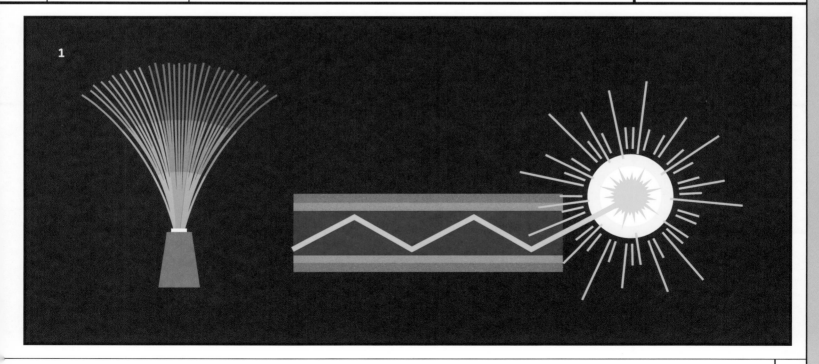

69
Tm

Thulium
(THOOL-EE-UM)

LANTHANIDE

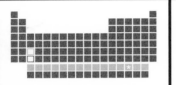

INSIDE THE ATOM

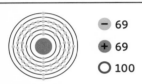

- − 69
- + 69
- ○ 100

ALL ABOUT THULIUM

A Swedish chemist spotted signs that a new element was hidden inside a sample of erbium, and named it thulium after an ancient word for Scandinavia. Even once scientists knew where to find thulium, it proved very difficult to extract a totally pure piece of the metal. An American chemist finally cracked it by dissolving thulium bromate, drying it out, collecting the crystals left behind, and testing them 15,000 times! This hard work helped him to win a Nobel Prize for chemistry. Today around 55 tons are extracted every year. Thulium can be turned into a **radioactive** substance that gives out **X-rays** for up to a year. It's easy to store safely, so it's used in X-ray machines that need to be moved from place to place, such as the ones used by dentists.

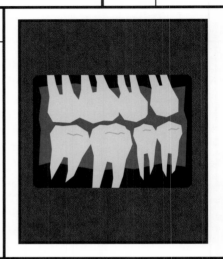

70
Yb

Ytterbium
(IT-TER-BEE-UM)

LANTHANIDE

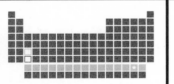

INSIDE THE ATOM

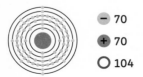

- − 70
- + 70
- ○ 104

ALL ABOUT YTTERBIUM

Ytterbium is another element found hidden inside erbium, which itself was found in yttrium—an element discovered in a black rock found near Ytterby in Sweden. Many of the jobs that ytterbium could do—such as strengthening steel and making lights and lasers—are left to cheaper lanthanides. However, ytterbium might have an important role in quantum computers of the future. Today's computers store information by altering materials such as **semiconductors** and **magnetic** metals. Quantum computers will be much tinier, because they will store information by altering individual atoms! Ytterbium atoms seem to be good candidates, because they can be controlled by **magnetic fields**.

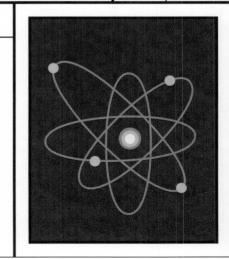

Lutetium
(LOO-TEE-SHEE-UM)

ALL ABOUT LUTETIUM

LANTHANIDE

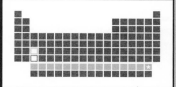

1 MAKING PLASTICS
The high cost of this element means it's only used where no other element would do—mainly in the process of turning **crude oil** (a hydrocarbon) into the substances used to make plastics. The lutetium is used to break up long chains of hydrogen and carbon atoms up into smaller, more useful **molecules**.

Lutetium is often included in the lanthanide group because it reacts with other elements in a similar way. It was the last element to be discovered hidden in samples of yttrium, like many of the other lanthanides. However, lutetium is harder and denser than the other lanthanides, and some chemists feel it really belongs with the transition metals. Either way, pure lutetium is one of the rarest and most expensive metals in the world. Like yttrium, lutetium can be used to help certain parts of the body show up on CT and PET scans. Lutetium can be made radioactive by firing **neutrons** at it. This form of lutetium is used as a source of **radiation** to kill cancer **cells** that are difficult to treat in other ways.

INSIDE THE ATOM

- 71
+ 71
○ 104

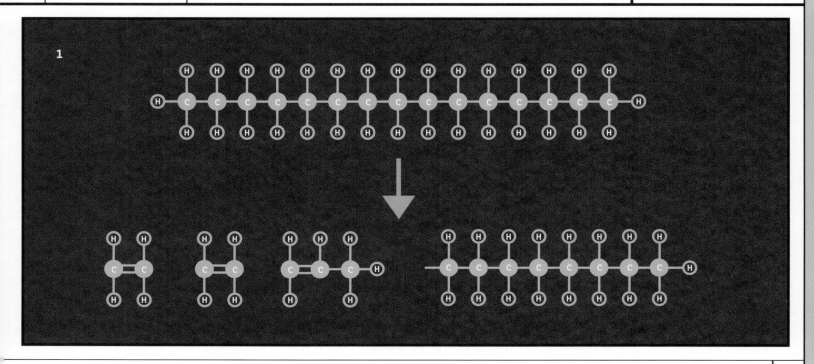

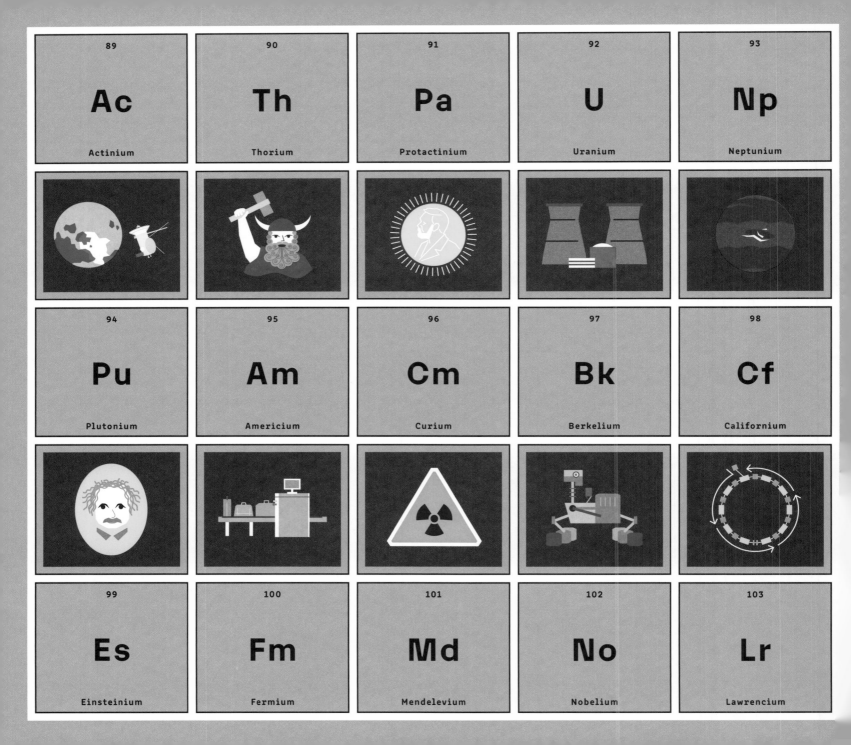

89	90	91	92	93
Ac	**Th**	**Pa**	**U**	**Np**
Actinium	Thorium	Protactinium	Uranium	Neptunium

94	95	96	97	98
Pu	**Am**	**Cm**	**Bk**	**Cf**
Plutonium	Americium	Curium	Berkelium	Californium

99	100	101	102	103
Es	**Fm**	**Md**	**No**	**Lr**
Einsteinium	Fermium	Mendelevium	Nobelium	Lawrencium

Actinides

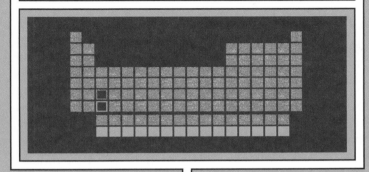

THE ACTINIDES ARE ALL VERY HEAVY, SILVER-COLORED, **RADIOACTIVE** METALS. SOME, SUCH AS THORIUM AND URANIUM, ARE COMMON AND CAN BE EXTRACTED FROM ROCKS OR EVEN SEAWATER. OTHERS CAN ONLY BE MADE IN A LAB OR A NUCLEAR REACTOR.

Like the lanthanides, the actinides are grouped together in the periodic table because they share similar properties. However, the actinides are far more diverse than the lanthanides. They range from californium, soft enough to cut with a knife, to uranium, which is so hard it can punch a hole through a tank. The actinides all behave differently when they meet other elements too. For example, thorium refuses to dissolve in water, but about 4.4 billion tons of uranium are dissolved in the world's oceans.

They are so different that scientists are still debating which elements are truly actinides. However, one property they all have in common is radioactivity. Their heavy atoms are unstable. They naturally break apart or **decay**, turning themselves into different, more stable elements. As they break apart, the atoms release energy in the form of **radiation**. This radiation can be useful, but it can also be deadly to living things. Some actinides are so radioactive that every atom that was once on Earth is long gone, breaking apart over billions of years to form lighter, smaller atoms. These actinides were only discovered when scientists learned how to make them in a lab or in a nuclear reactor.

As new "human-made" elements were discovered, the periodic table had to be redesigned to fit them all in! Some were named after planets. Others were paired with the lanthanide sitting just above them in the periodic table, for example americium below europium. The heaviest actinides were named after famous scientists.

We've only just started finding out about these extremely heavy elements, and there are sure to be more secrets to discover.

Actinium
(ACK-TIN-EE-UM)

89
Ac

ACTINIDE

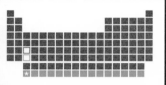

INSIDE THE ATOM

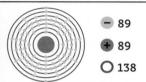

- − 89
- + 89
- ○ 138

ALL ABOUT ACTINIUM

Actinium is a very rare, very **radioactive** metal. All the actinium in a ton of uranium **ore** would weigh about the same as five grains of rice! Despite this, the element was discovered by two different scientists at separate times. One of them discovered it in the waste rock left over after the Curies had extracted radium (see page 46). Because it was so radioactive, actinium was almost ignored for 100 years, but scientists and doctors are now carrying out research into how it might be used to treat cancer. If some actinium-225 is placed inside cancer **cells**, the high-energy **radiation** it releases quickly kills the cancer cells. The actinium atoms break apart in a few days, so they don't harm healthy cells. All that is left behind is atoms of bismuth (see page 114), an element that is not radioactive or **toxic**.

1 GLOWING ELEMENT
Actinium is about 150 times as radioactive as radium, and was named after the Greek word for ray. It's one of the only radioactive elements that actually glows in the dark, when the radiation it gives out excites atoms in air.

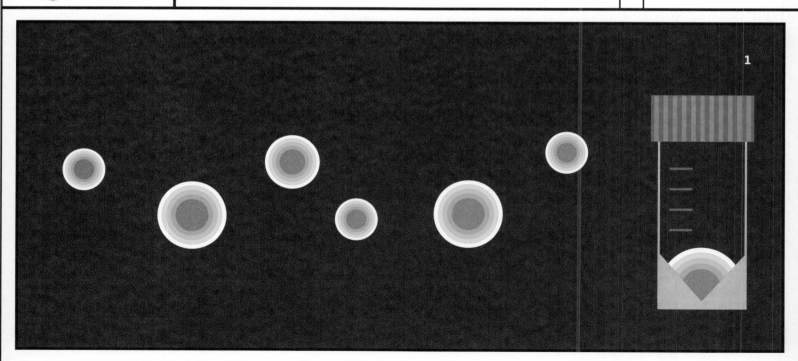

Thorium
(THOR-EE-UM)

ALL ABOUT THORIUM

Thorium is three times more common than uranium, and found in most rocks and soils. It has some very useful properties and was used widely before the dangers of radioactivity were properly understood. Thorium is still used for making tools needed in metal **welding**, which can be heated to more than 5970°F without melting. It's also added to glass to make camera and telescope lenses better at focusing light. Thorium can be converted to uranium, the fuel used to generate heat and then **electricity** in **nuclear power** stations. The world's supply of uranium will one day run out, but the same thorium could potentially be used over and over again to generate nuclear power. That's fitting for an element named after Thor, the Norse god of thunder.

ACTINIDE

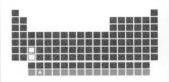

INSIDE THE ATOM

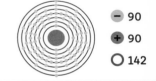

- − 90
- + 90
- ○ 142

Protactinium
(PRO-TACK-TIN-EE-UM)

91
Pa

ALL ABOUT PROTACTINIUM

Protactinium is so rare it remained undiscovered for almost 50 years after Mendeleev predicted an element between thorium and uranium. It was Lise Meitner who finally extracted protactinium from the rock pitchblende. Along with Otto Hahn she named the new element "parent of actinium" because it forms actinium when it **decays**. Protactinium is still very hard to produce. If you collected enough ore to fill a tractor trailer, all the protactinium in it would weigh about the same as an apple. Even then, it would disappear in hours or days. This means it's only useful for research.

ACTINIDE

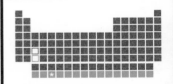

INSIDE THE ATOM

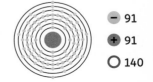

- − 91
- + 91
- ○ 140

U

Uranium
(YOUR-RAY-NEE-UM)

ACTINIDE

URANIUM IS FAMOUS FOR ITS **RADIOACTIVITY** AND ITS ROLE IN PROVIDING **NUCLEAR POWER**, BUT IT HAS ALSO BEEN USED TO MAKE DEVASTATING WEAPONS.

KEY PROPERTIES

- solid
- silvery metal
- extremely hard
- some **compounds** are pungent

WHERE IT'S FOUND

- **minerals:** uraninite, brannerite, coffinite
- rocks: granite, phosphate
- monazite sands
- seawater
- coal and plant ashes

HUMAN BODY

TRACE

ALL ABOUT URANIUM

Uranium was found first in a rock known as pitchblende more than 200 years ago, and was named after the planet Uranus, which had also just been discovered. For a long time, there seemed to be nothing special about this metal, apart from its ability to make glass more colorful. Then in 1896, Henri Becquerel left some uranium **salts** on top of photographic film and noticed that a foggy mark appeared, as if the film had been hit by bright light. Henri's "invisible rays" attracted the attention of Marie and Pierre Curie (see page 46), who discovered two other elements that gave out these invisible rays and came up with the word "radioactivity" to describe this strange property.

So what is radioactivity? Uranium is a very dense, heavy element—a die-sized piece would weigh about four and a half times as much as a normal die. Uranium's heavy atoms are unstable. They naturally break apart or **decay**, forming more stable atoms of different elements. As they break apart, the atoms release tiny **particles** and energy in the form of **radiation**. This energy can harm living things, but uranium is only harmful in large doses, which most people don't come across in everyday life.

SECRET CHEMISTRY

Uranium metal joins with oxygen to form colorful compounds. In the 1800s they were used to make stained glass and bright ceramics, including dinner plates. Uranium is not used like this anymore because we now know it's both **toxic** and **radioactive**.

INSIDE THE ATOM

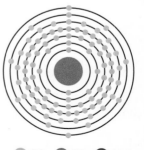

– 92   + 92   ○ 146

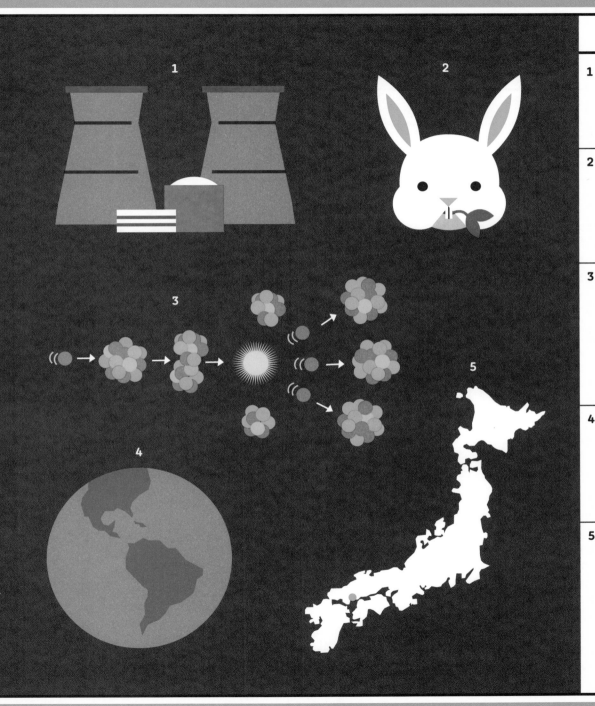

FORMS AND USES

1 NUCLEAR POWER

7,700 tons of uranium could release enough energy to power the whole world for a year. At the moment nuclear power produces about 11% of the world's **electricity**.

2 TRACES IN HUMANS

Plants soak up uranium from the soil and it passes up the food chain, so humans have around 100,000 trillion uranium atoms in their bodies. This is still a very tiny amount, about a third the weight of a poppy seed!

3 SPLITTING ATOMS

When a slow-moving **neutron** crashes into a heavy uranium atom, the atom splits apart into two pieces of roughly the same size. This **nuclear fission** releases energy but also more neutrons, which go on to split more uranium atoms. Once started, this "chain **reaction**" can release huge amounts of energy.

4 HEATING EARTH

There are billions of tons of uranium and thorium in Earth's crust. As they slowly decay, they release a huge amount of heat energy. In fact, it's one of the main sources of the heat that keeps our planet warm enough to live on.

5 NUCLEAR WEAPONS

Uranium was the fuel inside the first atomic bomb used in war. The bomb was dropped in 1945 by the USA on Hiroshima, Japan, during World War II. In a bomb the fission of uranium is not controlled, and so much energy was released that an estimated 70,000 people were killed at once. Another 70,000 died by the end of that year, from the effects of radiation.

93
Np

Neptunium
(NEP-TUNE-NEE-UM)

ACTINIDE

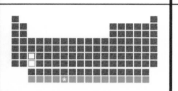

INSIDE THE ATOM

- − 93
- + 93
- ○ 144

ALL ABOUT NEPTUNIUM

Neptunium was discovered in 1940, less than 100 years ago. It was found in uranium that had been bombarded with **particles** called **neutrons**. Like uranium it was named after a planet—Neptune. At first scientists thought neptunium could only be produced in a lab. However, neptunium is also found in rocks that contain uranium. There is far too little of it in nature to find and extract, so all the neptunium used by scientists has to be made by humans. A few atoms of neptunium also form inside smoke detectors, as americium atoms break apart (see below).

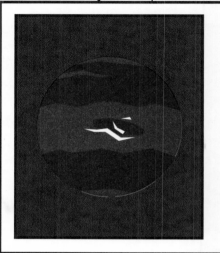

95
Am

Americium
(AM-ER-EE-SHE-UM)

ACTINIDE

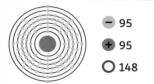

INSIDE THE ATOM

- − 95
- + 95
- ○ 148

ALL ABOUT AMERICIUM

Americium is not found anywhere in nature, not in the highest mountain nor the deepest ocean. It can only be made by humans, by firing neutrons at plutonium atoms to turn them into even heavier atoms. This was first done during World War II but it was kept a secret…until the brilliant chemist Glenn Seaborg went on a children's radio show called Quiz Kids. After a child asked about new elements, Glenn announced that the very first human-made element had been discovered. Americium has proved to be useful. Many smoke detectors contain a tiny piece of this metal. The **radiation** makes air inside the alarm **conduct electricity** across a small gap. The electricity stops flowing if smoke mixes with the air, triggering the alarm.

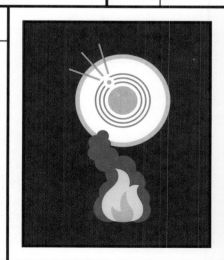

Plutonium

(PLOO-TONE-EE-UM)

ALL ABOUT PLUTONIUM

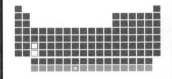

INSIDE THE ATOM

- 94
+ 94
○ 150

1 | PLUTO

Plutonium was named after the dwarf planet Pluto, and has visited this planet itself! It is the power source on the New Horizons mission, which took the first-ever close-up pictures of Pluto, and has now traveled even farther from the Sun. In this part of the solar system, the Sun's light is too weak for solar panels to work.

Plutonium is the heaviest element found naturally on Earth. Like neptunium, traces of it are found in rocks that contain uranium. However, most of the plutonium on Earth has been made by humans, by bombarding uranium with neutrons—either in a lab, a **nuclear power** station, or a nuclear weapon. This breaks uranium atoms apart to form neptunium atoms, which break apart themselves to form plutonium. Like uranium, a nuclear chain **reaction** can be started in a lump of plutonium metal to release huge amounts of energy. Plutonium was the fuel in the second atomic bomb dropped on Japan, on the city of Nagasaki on August 9, 1945, during World War II. The energy released from just 13.7 pounds of plutonium destroyed the city and killed at least 70,000 people.

1

96
Cm

Curium
(CURE-EE-UM)

ACTINIDE

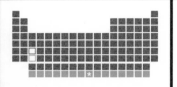

INSIDE THE ATOM

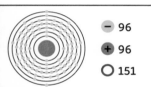

- − 96
- + 96
- ○ 151

ALL ABOUT CURIUM

Curium is another artificial element made by bombarding plutonium with **particles** to create heavier atoms. It was named after Marie and Pierre Curie, the scientists who discovered **radioactivity** (see page 46). Curium is so radioactive that it glows in the dark with a purple light. Although very rare and expensive, curium is useful because the **radiation** it releases generates lots of heat. If you held a lump in your hands it would feel very warm. It could one day be used as a source of power for space probes and satellites. Curium has already been to the Moon and to Mars, as part of instruments called **X-ray** spectrometers, which use radiation to find out what rocks are made of.

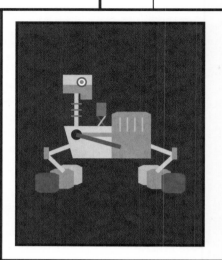

97
Bk

Berkelium
(BERK-LEE-UM)

ACTINIDE

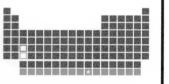

INSIDE THE ATOM

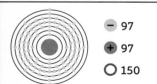

- − 97
- + 97
- ○ 150

ALL ABOUT BERKELIUM

Berkelium was named after the place where many of the elements heavier than uranium were first made—the University of California at Berkeley. Glenn Seaborg and his team made berkelium by bombarding americium with particles called **neutrons**. The first sample of berkelium wasn't big enough to see with their own eyes but was detected using instruments. Although more than 70 years have passed, it has been impossible to make and collect enough berkelium to make things with it, but even small samples are useful for finding out more about heavy elements—and for making even heavier elements!

ACTINIDES

Californium
(CAL-UH-FOR-NEE-UM)

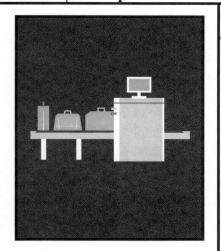

ALL ABOUT CALIFORNIUM

Californium can only be made in nuclear reactors, but it's easier and cheaper to get hold of than most other elements heavier than uranium, so it's useful. As atoms of californium break apart they release lots and lots of neutrons. A piece of californium weighing as much as a grain of table **salt** releases around 165 million neutrons every second! These neutrons can be put to use in many different ways—to start **reactions** in **nuclear power** stations, to make instruments that measure things, in airport metal detectors, and in cancer treatment. Scientists have been able to find out more about californium than other harder-to-get actinides, and the results have been exciting.

ACTINIDE

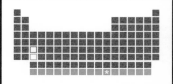

INSIDE THE ATOM

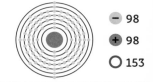

- – 98
- + 98
- ○ 153

Einsteinium
(EINE-STY-NEE-UM)

ALL ABOUT EINSTEINIUM

This element was discovered in the cloud of particles produced by a nuclear bomb test in 1952. It was named after the scientist Albert Einstein, who realized that matter (physical "stuff" made of particles) and energy are really different forms of the same thing, so one can be changed into the other. This was used to predict that huge amounts of energy could be released by breaking up lots of heavy atoms at once. Einsteinium isn't found in nature, so we don't know much about it except that it is incredibly radioactive. A single gram of einsteinium releases as much energy as a household iron turned up to maximum heat.

ACTINIDE

INSIDE THE ATOM

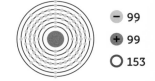

- – 99
- + 99
- ○ 153

<table>
<tr><td>

100

Fm
</td><td>

Fermium
(FUR-ME-UM)
</td><td>

</td></tr>
</table>

<table>
<tr><td>

ACTINIDE

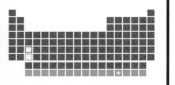

INSIDE THE ATOM

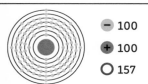

— 100
+ 100
O 157
</td><td>

ALL ABOUT FERMIUM

Along with einsteinium, fermium was first discovered in the waste thrown across the Pacific Ocean when a powerful nuclear bomb was tested in 1952. It was named after Enrico Fermi, the scientist who built the world's first **nuclear fission** reactor (the type of reactor that is used to generate **nuclear power**). The reactor—known as Chicago Pile 1—was built underneath a football stadium, by piling up layers of pure graphite (carbon) blocks (see page 134), alternated with blocks that contained uranium metal and uranium oxide (see page 188). A little fermium is made in nuclear reactors every year. It's the heaviest element that humans can make enough of to actually see, but no one has found any uses for it yet.
</td><td>

</td></tr>
</table>

<table>
<tr><td>

101

Md
</td><td>

Mendelevium
(MEN-DUH-LEE-VEE-UM)
</td><td>

</td></tr>
</table>

<table>
<tr><td>

ACTINIDE

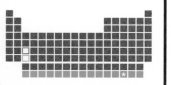

INSIDE THE ATOM

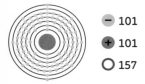

— 101
+ 101
O 157
</td><td>

ALL ABOUT MENDELEVIUM

This metal was named in honor of Dmitri Mendeleev, the creator of the first periodic table (see page 208). Only a few atoms of mendelevium are made every year, by firing alpha **particles** (two **protons** and two **neutrons**) at einsteinium atoms. Once they've been made, most of the atoms break apart in minutes, hours, or days. This means they're only useful to help scientists find out more about heavy elements.
</td><td>

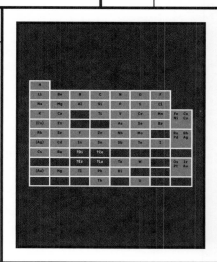
</td></tr>
</table>

Nobelium

(NO-BELL-EE-UM)

102

No

ALL ABOUT NOBELIUM

Three different groups of scientists argued for almost 40 years about who made nobelium first. In the end the International Union of Pure and Applied Chemistry (IUPAC) ended the argument by awarding the credit for discovery to one group, but keeping the name chosen by another. Nobelium is named for Alfred Nobel, the Swedish chemist who invented dynamite but is even more famous for leaving his fortune to fund the Nobel Prizes. These awards are given each year to scientists and others who have done the most to benefit humankind. Every year there are Nobel Prizes for physics, chemistry, medicine, economics, peace, and literature.

ACTINIDE

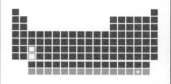

INSIDE THE ATOM

- 102
+ 102
○ 157

Lawrencium

(LAW-REN-SEE-UM)

103

Lr

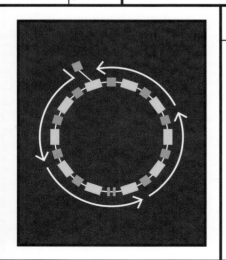

ALL ABOUT LAWRENCIUM

Lawrencium is another human-made element named after a person. Ernest Lawrence won a Nobel Prize for inventing the cyclotron, the first device that could get particles moving so fast that when they smashed into atoms, they actually changed them into totally different atoms. **Particle accelerators** based on Lawrence's design, such as the synchrotron, transformed physics and the way we understand the universe. Lawrence and his colleagues also used a similar technology to invent some of the first color televisions, which used to work like miniature particle accelerators! Today's flatscreen color televisions work in a totally different way.

ACTINIDE

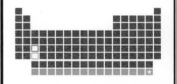

INSIDE THE ATOM

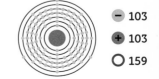

- 103
+ 103
○ 159

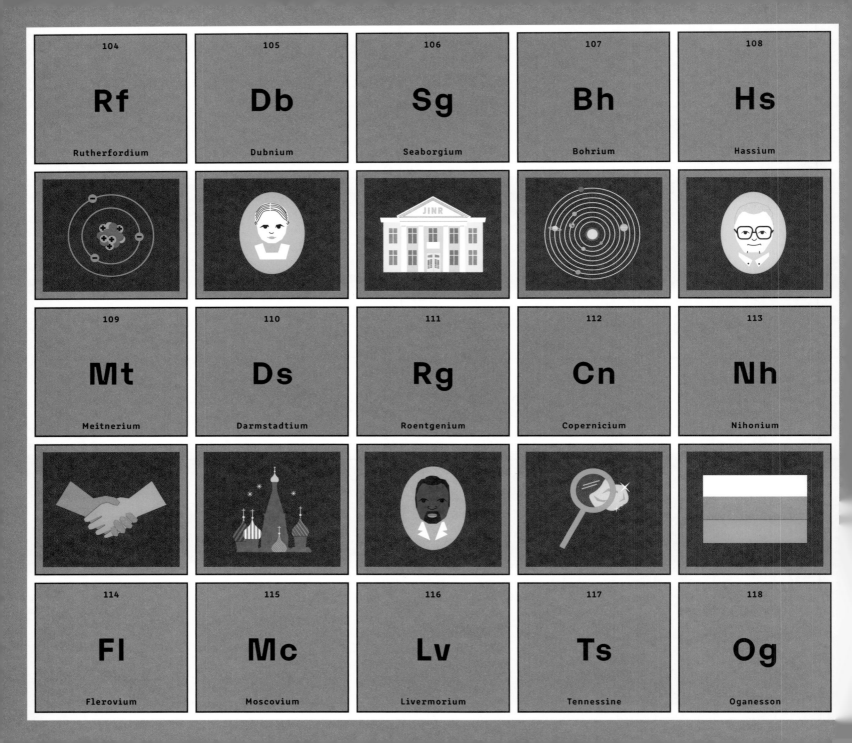

104	105	106	107	108
Rf	**Db**	**Sg**	**Bh**	**Hs**
Rutherfordium	Dubnium	Seaborgium	Bohrium	Hassium

109	110	111	112	113
Mt	**Ds**	**Rg**	**Cn**	**Nh**
Meitnerium	Darmstadtium	Roentgenium	Copernicium	Nihonium

114	115	116	117	118
Fl	**Mc**	**Lv**	**Ts**	**Og**
Flerovium	Moscovium	Livermorium	Tennessine	Oganesson

Superheavy Elements

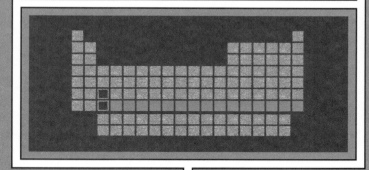

ELEMENTS WITH AN **ATOMIC NUMBER** GREATER THAN 103 ARE KNOWN AS SUPERHEAVY ELEMENTS.

The superheavy elements include elements from the transition metals, post-transition metals, metalloids, halogens, and noble gases. However, none of the superheavy elements is found naturally on Earth—they were all made by humans rather than discovered. Nor are the superheavy elements useful in everyday life. We can't make enough of them to see, and even if we did, they are incredibly **radioactive** and just don't stick around for long enough.

Superheavy elements are made in **particle accelerators**, by firing fast-moving **particles** at heavy atoms. Every so often the particles and atoms stick together to form even heavier atoms of new elements. However, these superheavy atoms are very unstable (radioactive). Most of them break apart in just a few seconds, minutes or hours. This doesn't give scientists very long to detect or study them. As a result, different teams of scientists have argued over who made each element first and who would get to choose its name. Sometimes it has taken decades to decide on an official name! In the meantime, the International Union of Pure and Applied Chemistry (IUPAC) gave the elements temporary names based on their atomic number. For example, *un-un-pent* is Latin for one-one-five, so for many years element 115 was known as ununpentium.

So far elements with up to 118 **protons** have been created in particle accelerators and officially named. Because scientists can only create a few superheavy atoms at a time, most of what we know about these elements is just a prediction based on the properties of elements in the same group. However, superheavy atoms can behave very strangely, so scientists try to carry out "fast chemistry" experiments to test their ideas about these elements and understand atoms better.

104
Rf

Rutherfordium
(RUH-THUR-FORD-EE-UM)

SUPERHEAVY ELEMENT

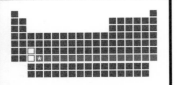

INSIDE THE ATOM

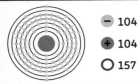

- − 104
- + 104
- ○ 157

ALL ABOUT RUTHERFORDIUM

The team of US scientists that created element 104 in the lab included nuclear chemist James Andrew Harris. He became the first African American credited with helping to discover a new element. After a long debate, Rutherfordium was eventually named after Ernest Rutherford, the scientist who taught us to think of atoms as tiny solar systems. We still use his idea that atoms are mostly empty space—with a tiny **nucleus** at the center, orbited by even tinier **electrons**. It helps us to understand why atoms behave as they do. More than a dozen different **isotopes** of Rutherfordium have been produced, by bombarding plutonium or californium with heavy **particles** so they combine to make new, heavier atoms.

105
Db

Dubnium
(DUBE-NEE-UM)

SUPERHEAVY ELEMENT

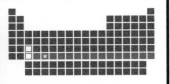

INSIDE THE ATOM

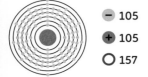

- − 105
- + 105
- ○ 157

ALL ABOUT DUBNIUM

Two teams of scientists discovered element 105 at about the same time in 1967. After a thirty-year argument, both teams shared the credit! The American team wanted to call it nielsbohrium, after a famous Danish nuclear physicist. The Russian team preferred hahnium, after a famous German chemist. In the end the International Union of Pure and Applied Chemistry (IUPAC) ended the argument by naming it after Dubna, Russia, the "town of science" that is home to the Joint Institute for Nuclear Research (JINR), where the Russian team was based.

Seaborgium

(SEE-BORG-EE-UM)

ALL ABOUT SEABORGIUM

Once again, scientists in Russia and the USA both claimed that they had discovered element 106 first. This time the team at the Lawrence Berkeley National Laboratory, in California, were best able to prove their discovery and got the credit. They named seaborgium after Glenn Seaborg, one of the most important scientists who worked at that lab. This made him the only living person up to that time to have an element named after them! Glenn had led teams that helped to discover plutonium and eight other heavier elements. He also discovered how to make **radioactive** iodine, which could then be used to treat thyroid cancer. Doctors even used it to save Glenn's mother's life!

SUPERHEAVY ELEMENT

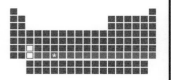

INSIDE THE ATOM

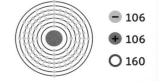

- 106
+ 106
O 160

Bohrium

(BORE-EE-UM)

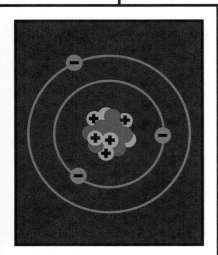

ALL ABOUT BOHRIUM

The team of scientists at the Joint Institute for Nuclear Research (JINR) finally got to name an element after Niels Bohr, when they discovered element 107. They did it by firing chromium atoms at a thin layer of bismuth atoms, to create a few atoms of bohrium that stuck around for less than a hundredth of a second! Since then other, longer-lasting bohrium atoms have been made, but they still break apart within minutes. This means it's only useful for research—we'll never be able to see what a solid lump of bohrium metal looks like.

SUPERHEAVY ELEMENT

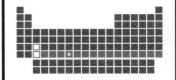

INSIDE THE ATOM

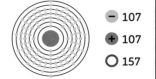

- 107
+ 107
O 157

108
Hs

Hassium
(HAH-SEE-UM)

SUPERHEAVY ELEMENT

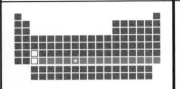

ALL ABOUT HASSIUM

For almost 25 years, scientists hunted for element 108 in nature, then tried to create it by smashing other elements together in a lab. So many teams claimed to have succeeded that it was hard to know who was first. As usual, it was up to the International Union of Pure and Applied Chemistry (IUPAC) to help decide, and the prize of naming it went to a team of scientists from Germany. The IUPAC were hoping to finally use the name hahnium, after the famous German scientist Otto Hahn, but the scientists chose hassium after Hesse, the area of Germany where their lab was based.

INSIDE THE ATOM

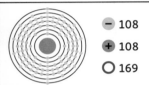

- − 108
- + 108
- ○ 169

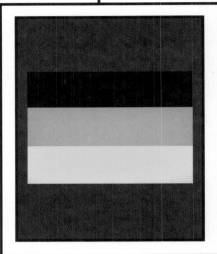

109
Mt

Meitnerium
(MIGHT-NEAR-EE-UM)

SUPERHEAVY ELEMENT

ALL ABOUT MEITNERIUM

The first meitnerium atoms were made in Germany, by firing the **nuclei** of iron atoms at bismuth. It took a week of this before the scientists detected a single, lonely atom of an element with 109 **protons**. Fifteen years later, this new element was named after Lise Meitner, an Austrian-Swedish physicist famous for helping the world to understand **radioactivity** better, and whose ideas led to the discovery of **nuclear fission**. During the Second World War, the US government invited Lise to join other leading scientists in a project to develop nuclear weapons. She refused, saying "I will have nothing to do with a bomb."

INSIDE THE ATOM

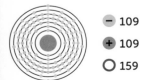

- − 109
- + 109
- ○ 159

Darmstadtium
(DARM-STAD-EE-UM)

ALL ABOUT DARMSTADTIUM

SUPERHEAVY ELEMENT

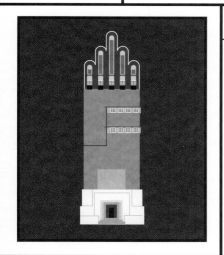

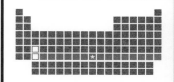

Element 110 is named after the city of Darmstadt in Germany, where it was first produced. Doing this was very difficult, even for a superheavy element. Eventually it was made by bombarding bismuth atoms with cobalt atoms, later by bombarding plutonium atoms with sulfur atoms, and again by bombarding lead atoms with nickel atoms. It doesn't matter which combination of atoms you smash together—if the final atom has 110 protons it's darmstadtium! We'll never be able to collect enough darmstadtium atoms in one place to see what the element looks like because they **decay** so quickly, but based on the elements above it in the periodic table—platinum, palladium, and nickel—chemists have predicted that it would be a silvery metal.

INSIDE THE ATOM

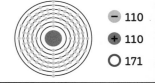

- – 110
- + 110
- ◯ 171

Roentgenium
(RENT-GEH-NEE-UM)

111

Rg

ALL ABOUT ROENTGENIUM

SUPERHEAVY ELEMENT

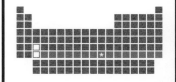

This element is named after Wilhelm Röntgen, a German scientist who discovered **X-rays.** It was first made in a German lab, by smashing together bismuth and nickel atoms. The handful of roentgenium atoms created lasted less than two milliseconds—not even long enough to blink! Then they began to break apart, first forming meitnerium, then bohrium, dubnium, and lawrencium. Most superheavy elements don't seem to occur naturally on Earth, but in 2010 a physicist based in Israel revealed that he had detected traces of it in gold—the element that sits just above roentgenium in the periodic table.

INSIDE THE ATOM

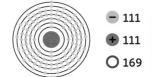

- – 111
- + 111
- ◯ 169

112
Cn
Copernicium
(CO-PER-NISS-EE-UM)

SUPERHEAVY ELEMENT

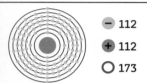

INSIDE THE ATOM

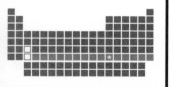

- − 112
- + 112
- ○ 173

ALL ABOUT COPERNICIUM

This element was first made in Germany, by firing charged zinc atoms at 18,600 miles per second toward a piece of lead! It is named after Nicolaus Copernicus, a Polish astronomer who studied the night sky around the year 1500. At that time, most people were convinced that the Sun, Moon, and stars orbited Earth. Copernicus came up with a new theory, that Earth travels around the Sun each year and also spins on its own axis once a day. After many years, he wrote his ideas down in what became the most important book in the history of astronomy!

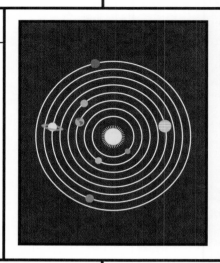

113
Nh
Nihonium
(NIH-HO-NEE-UM)

SUPERHEAVY ELEMENT

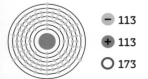

INSIDE THE ATOM

- − 113
- + 113
- ○ 173

ALL ABOUT NIHONIUM

Nihonium was first created by scientists based in Japan, by firing zinc atoms at bismuth atoms. It took eight months to produce the first atom of element 113, and the team repeated this twice more to confirm the discovery! Nihonium was named several years after this, in 2015. At first the team wanted to call it japonium, with the symbol Jp. This would have been the very first time the letter "J" was used in a chemical symbol! Eventually the team decided on a name based on the Japanese name for their country—*Nihon*. The team explained that they wanted to thank everyone in Japan for their support, in funding the research that led to the discovery.

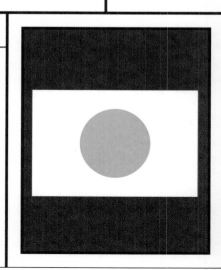

Flerovium
(FLUR-O-VEE-UM)

ALL ABOUT FLEROVIUM

A single atom of flerovium was created by scientists at the Joint Institute of Nuclear Research (JINR) in Russia, in 1998. They did it by firing a beam of charged calcium atoms (with 20 **protons**) at plutonium atoms (with 94 protons), until two of them combined to make an atom with 114 protons! The new element was named after the Russian scientist Georgy Flyorov, who founded JINR. Since then, at least five different **isotopes** of flerovium have been made but we don't know much about it. Even though flerovium atoms stick around for a bit longer than other superheavy elements, they still have **half-lives** of less than a second.

SUPERHEAVY ELEMENT

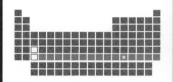

INSIDE THE ATOM

- 114
+ 114
O 175

Moscovium
(MOSS-COVE-EE-UM)

ALL ABOUT MOSCOVIUM

When scientists hear about the results of a new experiment, they look carefully at the methods that were used and try to repeat them. If they get the same result, they can be sure that the findings are accurate and real. Each time a team discovers a new element, other teams around the world repeat the experiment. If a second team gets the same result, the original discovery becomes official. This is why element 115 was only confirmed and named (after the Russian capital Moscow) ten years after it was first discovered by a team of scientists in Russia.

SUPERHEAVY ELEMENT

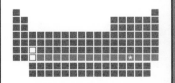

INSIDE THE ATOM

- 115
+ 115
O 174

116
Lv

Livermorium
(LIV-UR-MORE-EE-UM)

SUPERHEAVY ELEMENT

INSIDE THE ATOM

- − 116
- + 116
- ○ 177

ALL ABOUT LIVERMORIUM

Teams of scientists from Russia and the US worked together to try to create element 116. It was finally done in 2000, at the Joint Institute for Nuclear Research (JINR) in Russia, and the discovery was confirmed and announced at the Lawrence Livermore National Laboratory in California. The element was named after this lab. The building blocks of the new element were atoms of curium and calcium. At first just one atom was made, but almost a year later two more had been created.

117
Ts

Tennessine
(TEN-NESS-EEN)

SUPERHEAVY ELEMENT

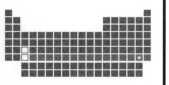

INSIDE THE ATOM

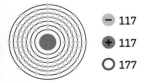

- − 117
- + 117
- ○ 177

ALL ABOUT TENNESSINE

Six atoms of element 117 were made in 2010 by smashing together atoms of calcium and berkelium, something that's very difficult to do because berkelium itself is hard to make and hold onto! To do it, dozens of scientists from around the world worked together to plan the 150-day experiment, which was carried out inside a **particle accelerator** in Russia. More than 70 different scientists then carried out experiments to confirm the discovery! The new element was named in 2016 after Tennessee, a US state that has several important laboratories devoted to researching elements heavier than uranium.

Oganesson

(O-GUH-NESS-ON)

ALL ABOUT OGANESSON

If we could ever collect enough oganesson to look at, it would probably be a non-metal, and a gas at room temperature. We know this because it lies in the noble gas group of the periodic table. Scientists aren't able to check this with experiments, because only three oganesson atoms have been made. The element is named after Yuri Oganessian, a Russian-Armenian physicist who has spent most of his life researching and discovering the superheavy elements. He was only the second living person to have an element named after them.

SUPERHEAVY ELEMENT

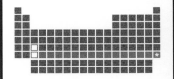

INSIDE THE ATOM

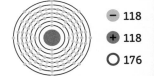

- − 118
- + 118
- ○ 176

Future Elements

?

?

ABOUT FUTURE ELEMENTS

The periodic table (probably) doesn't end here! Although 118 elements have been discovered and named so far, scientists around the world are busy hunting for more. The patterns in the periodic table help with planning these experiments and give us clues about what these future elements may be like. For example, element 119 will most likely be an **alkali** metal that behaves a bit like potassium. We probably won't be able to go on making heavier atoms forever—at some point, they will become too unstable to hold together even for a few milliseconds. We will one day reach the end of the periodic table, but for now there are still exciting new elements to discover and name. Perhaps one of them will even be discovered by you!

SUPERHEAVY ELEMENT

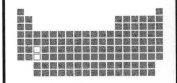

INSIDE THE ATOM

?

- − ?
- + ?
- ○ ?

More About
the Elements
and
Other Resources

A History of Exploring the Elements

FOR THOUSANDS OF YEARS, CURIOUS PEOPLE HAVE GAZED AT THE SUN AND STARS IN THE SKY, AND THE ROCKS, OCEANS, PLANTS, AND ANIMALS ON EARTH, AND ASKED THE SAME QUESTION—WHAT IS EVERYTHING MADE OF?

The Ancient Greeks did a lot of observing and thinking. They realized that the millions of different objects we see around us are made from a much smaller number of ingredients. They named these ingredients the "elements." They noticed that a burning log seems to split up into four parts—blazing flames, water, ashes, and smoke. So, the Ancient Greeks decided that there were four elements: fire, water, earth, and air. These "classical" elements weren't really the ingredients of everything on Earth, but the idea lasted for more than 1,600 years.

However, people began to notice that most things didn't fit neatly into the four categories. For example, iron and gold were both metals, which were said to be made of "earth." But if metals were made of the same thing, why was iron hard and silvery, while gold was soft and yellow? Why did iron rust easily, while gold kept its beautiful glow forever? People began to wonder if metals changed into one another over time. The idea of turning a cheap metal such as lead into a rare, expensive metal such as gold was exciting. It became known as alchemy.

Although alchemists worked for years to try to turn other metals into gold, they never succeeded. Today we know why. Lead and gold are not different versions of the same substance—they are completely different substances made up of different types of atoms. But the alchemists had not completely wasted their time. Their curiosity and careful investigations led to many new discoveries. They helped to show that experimentation was the best way to understand the natural world better.

THE BEGINNING OF CHEMISTRY

The first true chemistry, where chemists carried out careful experiments to test their ideas and to find answers, quickly led to new discoveries that challenged old ideas about elements. In 1783, a French chemist named Antoine Lavoisier discovered that water could be split apart into even simpler building blocks—the gases hydrogen and oxygen. By splitting water into simpler ingredients, he had shown that water was not an element. Lavoisier wrote a new definition for elements, which we still use today:

An element is any substance that cannot be broken apart into simpler substances.

Chemists realized that some of the substances they already knew about—such as oxygen, iron, lead, and gold—were elements. They could not be broken apart into simpler substances. The race was on to find more examples. From the late 1700s, the list of elements grew quickly as scientists found new ways to break up all sorts of substances and work out which elements they were made from. Scientists also began to learn more about the tiny **particles**— or atoms—of which the elements themselves were made.

ORGANIZING THE ELEMENTS

During the 1800s, dozens of new elements were being discovered, described, and named. Scientists began looking for ways to organize them into groups. They looked closely at the similarities and differences between the elements and tried to spot patterns. Many different scientists came up with schemes for organizing the elements, but the one we use today— the periodic table of the elements—was invented by a Russian scientist named Dmitri Mendeleev.

Mendeleev began by arranging all the elements that had been discovered in order of the weight of their atoms. He noticed that certain groups of elements with very different **average atomic masses** behaved in very similar ways—they had similar properties. Mendeleev drew a chart that showed this repeating pattern clearly. The elements were arranged in order of average atomic mass but placed in rows so that elements with similar properties appeared underneath each other in a vertical group. This system of rows (periods) and columns (groups) became the first "periodic table" of the elements.

What made Mendeleev's system brilliant was that he didn't just include the elements that had already been discovered.

He realized that there were elements that hadn't been discovered yet—like a jigsaw with pieces missing. He left gaps for these missing pieces, ready for the scientists of the future to fill. At first glance, today's version of the periodic table looks very different from Mendeleev's first chart. Over the last 150 years, all of the gaps left by Mendeleev have been filled. Scientists have also discovered many elements that he hadn't predicted. Gradually, the periodic table has been expanded and reshaped to fit these new discoveries. But it's still based on the repeating patterns that Mendeleev spotted.

ELEMENTS KNOWN TO MENDELEEV

Hydrogen	Calcium	Zirconium	Cerium
Lithium	Titanium	Niobium	Tantalum
Beryllium	Vanadium	Molybdenum	Tungsten
Boron	Chromium	Ruthenium	Osmium
Carbon	Manganese	Rhodium	Iridium
Nitrogen	Iron	Palladium	Platinum
Oxygen	Cobalt	Silver	Gold
Fluorine	Nickel	Cadmium	Mercury
Sodium	Copper	Indium	Thallium
Magnesium	Zinc	Tin	Lead
Aluminum	Arsenic	Antimony	Bismuth
Silicon	Selenium	Tellurium	Thorium
Phosphorus	Bromine	Iodine	Uranium
Sulfur	Rubidium	Cesium	
Chlorine	Strontium	Barium	
Potassium	Yttrium	Lanthanum	

Questions About Atoms, Elements, and Compounds

EACH ELEMENT IS MADE UP OF A CERTAIN TYPE OF ATOM. UNDERSTANDING THE STRUCTURE OF ATOMS HELPS US TO EXPLAIN WHY ELEMENTS LOOK AND BEHAVE AS THEY DO.

WHAT IS AN ISOTOPE?

Atoms are made up of even smaller particles, called **protons**, **neutrons**, and **electrons**. Each element has atoms with a certain number of protons (and electrons)—this is the element's **atomic number**. For example, carbon atoms have six protons, so carbon's atomic number is 6. The number of neutrons in an atom might match the number of protons and electrons, or it might be different. For example, a regular carbon atom has six protons and six neutrons, but some carbon atoms have six protons and eight neutrons.

These different forms of the same element are called **isotopes**. Extra neutrons don't change the way an atom behaves around other substances, but it does make the atom heavier, so different isotopes have slightly different **average atomic masses**.

An atom with six protons is always a carbon atom. But the number of neutrons in a carbon atom can vary. The number of protons and neutrons added together is known as the atomic mass number.

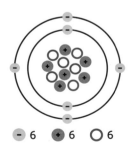

CARBON 12
This carbon atom has six protons and six neutrons. Six plus six is 12, so we call this form, or isotope, carbon-12.

- 6 + 6 ○ 6

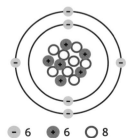

CARBON 14
This carbon atom has six protons and eight neutrons. Six plus eight is 14, so we call this form, or isotope, carbon-14. Carbon-14 atoms are unstable, or **radioactive**. Over time, they will change, or **decay**, into more stable types of atoms.

- 6 + 6 ○ 8

WHY ARE SOME ELEMENTS RADIOACTIVE?

Some elements have lots of different isotopes where the number of neutrons in their atoms doesn't match the number of protons. Atoms of these isotopes are less stable—meaning that they tend to break apart over time. When an unstable atom breaks apart, some of the energy that was holding the atom together is released in the form of **radiation**. The radiation can be harmful to living things, including humans, but it can also be useful. Many different "**radioactive**" isotopes are used by doctors to help diagnose and treat diseases. Radioactive elements are also used in **nuclear power** stations to help generate **electricity**. They are even found in smoke alarms in our homes!

HOW DO ELEMENTS FORM COMPOUNDS?

To understand how elements combine to form new substances, called **compounds**, we need to know more about electrons, and how they are arranged inside atoms. Electrons have a negative electrical charge, and protons have a positive electrical charge. Particles with opposite charges are attracted to each other, and this is what keeps the electrons attached to an atom. We can imagine the electrons orbiting the **nucleus** at the center of the atom, like the planets of our solar system. The positive charge of the protons exactly cancels out the negative charge of the electrons, so a normal atom has no electric charge.

As scientists learned more about atoms, they discovered that electrons don't all orbit the nucleus in the same way. They are arranged in a pattern of different energy levels, known as **shells**. Each shell can hold a set number of electrons. Once one shell is full, they start to fill the next shell. Atoms are most stable when their outer shell of electrons is full. The only atoms that naturally have a full outer shell are atoms of the noble

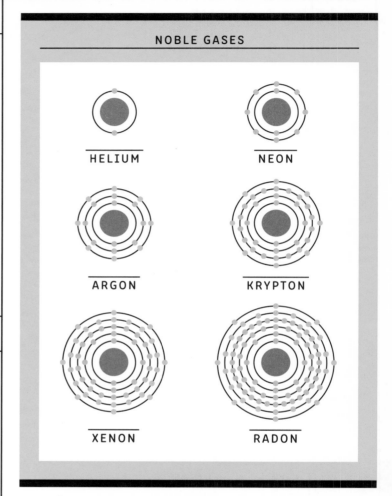

NOBLE GASES

HELIUM

NEON

ARGON

KRYPTON

XENON

RADON

gases (see page 158). This explains why these elements are so unreactive—they are totally stable and happy on their own.

Chemical **reactions** happen because atoms are on a mission to try to fill their outer shells and become as stable as possible. The only way that atoms can do this is by giving, taking, or sharing electrons with other atoms. As they do this, they form compounds.

Let's look at what happens when atoms of sodium and chlorine meet each other.

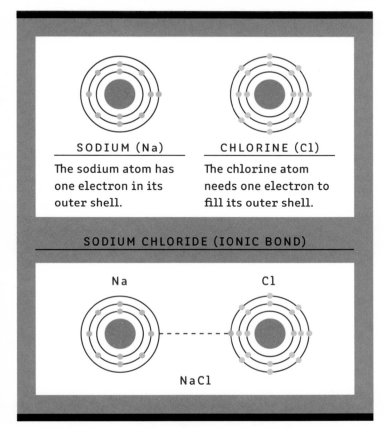

SODIUM (Na)

The sodium atom has one electron in its outer shell.

CHLORINE (Cl)

The chlorine atom needs one electron to fill its outer shell.

SODIUM CHLORIDE (IONIC BOND)

Na

Cl

NaCl

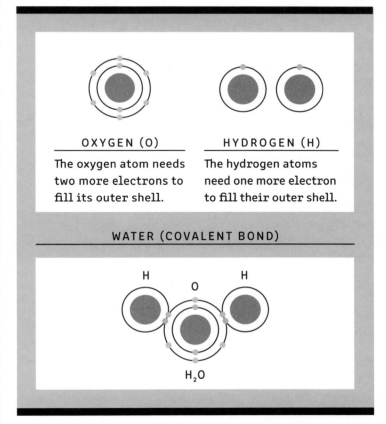

OXYGEN (O)

The oxygen atom needs two more electrons to fill its outer shell.

HYDROGEN (H)

The hydrogen atoms need one more electron to fill their outer shell.

WATER (COVALENT BOND)

H

O

H

H_2O

The sodium atom is happy to give up its outer electron, and the chlorine atom is equally happy to take it! Now both atoms have a full outer shell and are stable. However, each atom has changed in an important way. The sodium atom has given up an electron, so it now has more protons than electrons. It has become positively charged. The chlorine atom has gained an electron, so it now has more electrons than protons. It has become negatively charged. Opposite charges attract, so the sodium and chlorine atoms are now attracted to each other! They now hang out in a pair—as NaCl, the compound known as table **salt**.

Not all chemical reactions involve swapping electrons like this. There is another way that atoms can fill their outer shells—

they can share the same electrons. This is what happens when oxygen atoms meet hydrogen atoms.

Neither atom wants to give up its electrons. But if they cling together in a group of three, they can all share the same electrons. They have formed **molecules** of H_2O, the compound known as water! When oxygen and hydrogen atoms are part of water molecules they all have full outer shells, and they are very stable. It takes a lot of energy to break them apart.

The periodic table helps chemists to predict which elements will react together, and how—which elements will most likely give up electrons, grab electrons, or share electrons. The elements in each group have the same number of electrons in their outer shell, so they react with other substances in a similar way.

Properties of the Elements

THE THREE TABLES ON THESE PAGES SUMMARIZE SOME IMPORTANT PHYSICAL AND CHEMICAL PROPERTIES OF THE 92 ELEMENTS THAT ARE FOUND IN NATURE—THEIR MELTING AND BOILING POINTS, AVERAGE ATOMIC MASSES, AND DENSITIES. CHEMISTS USE THESE PROPERTIES TO EXPLAIN AND PREDICT HOW ELEMENTS AND COMPOUNDS BEHAVE.

MELTING POINTS AND BOILING POINTS

We are used to seeing liquid water boil and become a gas (water vapor) when it is heated, or freeze into a solid (ice) when it is cooled. All of the elements can exist as a solid, a liquid, and a gas too. These three forms are known as the three states of matter. The temperatures at which an element melts to become a liquid (its **melting point**) and boils to become a gas (its **boiling point**) are different for each element. At 68°F—average room temperature—most elements are solid, some are gases, and just two are liquids.

COMPARING TEMPERATURES

9710°F
Earth's inner core

6177°F
tungsten melts

4298°F
highest temperature ever reached on Earth's surface, when a meteorite struck 40 million years ago

2546°F
hottest part of a candle flame

1880°F
flowing lava

1220.58°F
aluminum melts

621.43°F
lead melts

136°F
highest air temperature ever recorded on Earth

98.6°F
average human body temperature

86°F
chocolate melts

68°F
average room temperature

36°F
inside a fridge

0°F
inside a freezer

−76°F
lowest temperature measured at the top of Mount Everest

−320.43°F
nitrogen boils

−380.2°F
average temperature on Pluto

−423.18°F
hydrogen boils

−452.07°F
helium boils

−459.7°F
lowest temperature ever produced in a lab on Earth

9941°F
surface of the Sun

6422°F
diamond (carbon) melts

5182°F
iron boils

3180°F
lead boils

2800°F
iron melts

1947°F
gold melts

1763.2°F
silver melts

752°F
wood-fired pizza oven

451°F
paper catches fire

212°F
water boils

122°F
asphalt begins to melt

91°F
butter melts

62.6 °F
average temperature of water at the surface of Earth's oceans

32°F
water freezes

−37.89°F
mercury melts

−128.2°F
lowest air temperature ever recorded on Earth

−346°F
nitrogen freezes

−464°F
lowest temperature in the solar system (on Earth's Moon)

−434.49°F
hydrogen melts

−459.67°F
absolute zero, the coldest it's possible for anything to be

No.	Element	Melting Point (°F)	Boiling Point (°F)	No.	Element	Melting Point (°F)	Boiling Point (°F)	No.	Element	Melting Point (°F)	Boiling Point (°F)
1	Hydrogen	-434.49	-423.18	32	Germanium	1720.85	5131	63	Europium	1512	2784
2	Helium	unknown	-452.07	33	Arsenic	sublimation: 1141		64	Gadolinium	2395	5923
3	Lithium	356.9	2448	34	Selenium	429.4	1265	65	Terbium	2478	5846
4	Beryllium	2349	4474	35	Bromine	19	137.8	66	Dysprosium	2574	4653
5	Boron	3771	7232	36	Krypton	-251.27	-244.15	67	Holmium	2682	4892
6	Carbon	sublimation: 6917		37	Rubidium	102.74	1270	68	Erbium	2784	5194
7	Nitrogen	-346	-320.43	38	Strontium	1431	2511	69	Thulium	2813	3542
8	Oxygen	-361.82	-297.33	39	Yttrium	2772	6053	70	Ytterbium	1515	2185
9	Fluorine	-363.41	-306.6	40	Zirconium	3369	7963	71	Lutetium	3025	6156
10	Neon	-415.46	-410.88	41	Niobium	4491	8566	72	Hafnium	4051	8312
11	Sodium	208.03	1621.29	42	Molybdenum	4752	8382	73	Tantalum	5463	9851
12	Magnesium	1202	1994	43	Technetium	3915	7704	74	Tungsten	6177	10031
13	Aluminum	1220.58	4566	44	Ruthenium	4231	7497	75	Rhenium	5765	10094
14	Silicon	2577	5909	45	Rhodium	3565	6683	76	Osmium	5491	9046
15	Phosphorus	111.47	536.9	46	Palladium	2830.6	5365	77	Iridium	4435	8002
16	Sulfur	239.38	832.3	47	Silver	1763.2	3924	78	Platinum	3214.8	6917
17	Chlorine	-150.7	-29.27	48	Cadmium	609.92	1413	79	Gold	1947.52	5137
18	Argon	-308.81	-302.52	49	Indium	313.88	3681	80	Mercury	-37.89	673.91
19	Potassium	146.3	1398	50	Tin	449.47	4687	81	Thallium	579	2683
20	Calcium	1548	2703	51	Antimony	1167.13	2889	82	Lead	621.43	3180
21	Scandium	2806	5137	52	Tellurium	841.12	1810	83	Bismuth	520.53	2847
22	Titanium	3038	5949	53	Iodine	236.7	363.9	84	Polonium	489	1764
23	Vanadium	3470	6165	54	Xenon	-169.15	-162.58	85	Astatine	572	662
24	Chromium	3465	4840	55	Cesium	83.3	1240	86	Radon	-96	-79.1
25	Manganese	2275	3742	56	Barium	1341	3353	87	Francium	70	1202
26	Iron	2800	5182	57	Lanthanum	1688	6267	88	Radium	1285	2732
27	Cobalt	2723	5301	58	Cerium	1470	6229	89	Actinium	1922	5792
28	Nickel	2651	5275	59	Praseodymium	1908	6368	90	Thorium	3182	8645
29	Copper	1984.32	4640	60	Neodymium	1861	5565	91	Protactinium	2862	7232
30	Zinc	787.15	1665	61	Promethium	1908	5432	92	Uranium	2075	7468
31	Gallium	85.58	4044	62	Samarium	1962	3261				

DENSITY

The density of an element tells us how much of that element fits into a certain space. This depends on how big and heavy its atoms are, and how they are arranged. It also depends on what state the element is in. Solids are denser than liquids, and liquids are denser than gases. In this table, the densities for each element are given at room temperature (68°F).

The densities are given in grams per cubic centimeter, so it tells you how much a lump of the element the exact size of this cube would weigh on Earth.

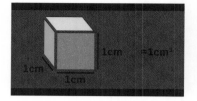

No.	Element	Density (g/cm³)	No.	Element	Density (g/cm³)	No.	Element	Density (g/cm³)	No.	Element	Density (g/cm³)
1	Hydrogen	0.00009	24	Chromium	7.15	47	Silver	10.5	70	Ytterbium	6.9
2	Helium	0.00016	25	Manganese	7.3	48	Cadmium	8.69	71	Lutetium	9.8
3	Lithium	0.53	26	Iron	7.87	49	Indium	7.31	72	Hafnium	13.2
4	Beryllium	1.848	27	Cobalt	8.9	50	Tin	7.3	73	Tantalum	16.4
5	Boron	2.34	28	Nickel	8.91	51	Antimony	6.684	74	Tungsten	19.3
6	Carbon	3.51	29	Copper	8.96	52	Tellurium	6.24	75	Rhenium	20.8
7	Nitrogen	0.00115	30	Zinc	7.14	53	Iodine	4.93	76	Osmium	22.59
8	Oxygen	0.00131	31	Gallium	5.907	54	Xenon	0.00537	77	Iridium	22.56
9	Fluorine	0.0016	32	Germanium	5.323	55	Cesium	1.873	78	Platinum	21.45
10	Neon	0.0009	33	Arsenic	5.75	56	Barium	3.62	79	Gold	19.5
11	Sodium	0.971	34	Selenium	4.79	57	Lanthanum	6.16	80	Mercury	13.53
12	Magnesium	1.738	35	Bromine	3.103	58	Cerium	6.78	81	Thallium	11.8
13	Aluminum	2.702	36	Krypton	0.00343	59	Praseodymium	6.77	82	Lead	11.34
14	Silicon	2.33	37	Rubidium	1.53	60	Neodymium	7.0	83	Bismuth	9.807
15	Phosphorus	1.82	38	Strontium	2.6	61	Promethium	7.26	84	Polonium	9.2
16	Sulfur	2.07	39	Yttrium	4.47	62	Samarium	7.54	85	Astatine	unknown
17	Chlorine	0.0029	40	Zirconium	6.52	63	Europium	5.248	86	Radon	0.00907
18	Argon	0.00163	41	Niobium	8.57	64	Gadolinium	7.895	87	Francium	unknown
19	Potassium	0.89	42	Molybdenum	10.2	65	Terbium	8.27	88	Radium	5
20	Calcium	1.55	43	Technetium	11	66	Dysprosium	8.536	89	Actinium	10
21	Scandium	3.0	44	Ruthenium	12.2	67	Holmium	8.8	90	Thorium	11.7
22	Titanium	4.50	45	Rhodium	12.4	68	Erbium	9.05	91	Protactinium	15.4
23	Vanadium	6.1	46	Palladium	12.02	69	Thulium	9.33	92	Uranium	19.1

MORE ABOUT THE ELEMENTS AND OTHER RESOURCES

AVERAGE ATOMIC MASS

The average atomic mass of an element is the weight of one atom of that element compared to the weight of a "standard" atom with one proton and one electron. This standard atom is calculated as one-twelfth of the mass of an atom of carbon-12 (see page 209). Each element exists in different forms, known as **isotopes**, the atoms of which contain different numbers of **neutrons**. This means isotopes of the same element have slightly different average atomic masses. The average atomic masses in this table are therefore averages for all the isotopes of that element found in nature.

No.	Element	Average Atomic Mass	No.	Element	Average Atomic Mass	No.	Element	Average Atomic Mass	No.	Element	Average Atomic Mass
1	Hydrogen	1.008	24	Chromium	51.996	47	Silver	107.868	70	Ytterbium	173.045
2	Helium	4.003	25	Manganese	54.938	48	Cadmium	112.414	71	Lutetium	174.967
3	Lithium	6.94	26	Iron	55.845	49	Indium	114.818	72	Hafnium	178.49
4	Beryllium	9.012	27	Cobalt	58.933	50	Tin	118.71	73	Tantalum	180.948
5	Boron	10.81	28	Nickel	58.693	51	Antimony	121.76	74	Tungsten	183.84
6	Carbon	12.011	29	Copper	63.546	52	Tellurium	127.6	75	Rhenium	186.207
7	Nitrogen	14.007	30	Zinc	65.38	53	Iodine	126.904	76	Osmium	190.23
8	Oxygen	15.999	31	Gallium	69.723	54	Xenon	131.293	77	Iridium	192.217
9	Fluorine	18.998	32	Germanium	72.63	55	Cesium	132.905	78	Platinum	195.084
10	Neon	20.18	33	Arsenic	74.922	56	Barium	137.327	79	Gold	196.967
11	Sodium	22.99	34	Selenium	78.971	57	Lanthanum	138.905	80	Mercury	200.592
12	Magnesium	24.305	35	Bromine	79.904	58	Cerium	140.116	81	Thallium	204.38
13	Aluminum	26.982	36	Krypton	83.798	59	Praseodymium	140.908	82	Lead	207.2
14	Silicon	28.085	37	Rubidium	85.468	60	Neodymium	144.242	83	Bismuth	208.98
15	Phosphorus	30.974	38	Strontium	87.62	61	Promethium	145	84	Polonium	209
16	Sulfur	32.06	39	Yttrium	88.906	62	Samarium	150.36	85	Astatine	210
17	Chlorine	35.45	40	Zirconium	91.224	63	Europium	151.964	86	Radon	222
18	Argon	39.948	41	Niobium	92.906	64	Gadolinium	157.25	87	Francium	223
19	Potassium	39.098	42	Molybdenum	95.95	65	Terbium	158.925	88	Radium	226
20	Calcium	40.078	43	Technetium	98	66	Dysprosium	162.5	89	Actinium	227
21	Scandium	44.956	44	Ruthenium	101.07	67	Holmium	164.93	90	Thorium	232.038
22	Titanium	47.867	45	Rhodium	102.906	68	Erbium	167.259	91	Protactinium	231.036
23	Vanadium	50.942	46	Palladium	106.42	69	Thulium	168.934	92	Uranium	238.029

FIND OUT MORE

Hundreds of sources were consulted to research, write, and illustrate this book. It is impossible to list them all here, but the following books and websites are particularly recommended to readers who would like to find out more about the elements.

WEBSITES

- American Chemical Society: https://www.acs.org/content/acs/en/education/resources.html
- International Union of Pure and Applied Chemistry: https://iupac.org
- Royal Society of Chemistry: https://www.rsc.org
- LiveScience Elements News: https://www.livescience.com/topics/elements
- Animated Science: The Periodic Table by Universitat de Barcelona: https://www.youtube.com/watch?time_continue=118&v=xcxZdl24ULo&feature=emb_logo
- TedEd's Interactive Periodic Table: http://ed.ted.com/periodic-videos
- Chemicool's Interactive Periodic Table: https://www.chemicool.com
- The Photographic Periodic Table of the Elements: https://periodictable.com

BOOKS

- *Nature's Building Blocks: An A–Z Guide to the Elements* by John Emsley (Oxford University Press, 2011)
- *The Elements: A Very Short Introduction* by Philip Ball (Oxford University Press, 2004)
- *The Secret Life of the Periodic Table* by Dr. Ben Still (Octopus Publishing Group Ltd, 2016)

GLOSSARY

ACID/ACIDIC: The pH scale measures how acid or alkaline something is. An acid (or acidic substance) has a pH less than 7. Acids share certain chemical properties such as the corrosive way they react with some metals. Vinegar and fruit juices are examples of acidic substances, with a low pH.

ALKALI/ALKALINE: The pH scale measures how acid or alkaline something is. An alkali (or alkaline substance) has a pH greater than 7. Alkalis have chemical properties that are opposite to those of acids. Baking soda and ammonia are examples of alkaline substances, with a high pH.

ALLOTROPE: Different forms of the same element, such as diamond and graphite (allotropes of carbon).

ALLOY: A mixture of two or more metals, or a metal and a non-metal.

ATOMIC NUMBER: The number of protons in each atom of an element.

AVERAGE ATOMIC MASS: The average weight of atoms of an element, compared to the weight of an atom consisting of one proton and one electron (also known as the relative atomic mass).

BOILING POINT: The temperature at which a liquid boils and becomes a gas.

BOND: An attraction between atoms, ions, or molecules that holds them together.

CAPACITOR: A device that stores electricity for a short time, before letting it flow again.

CATALYST: A substance that kick-starts or speeds up a chemical reaction, without being part of the reaction itself.

CELLS: All living things are made up of one or more cells. Each cell carries out certain jobs. Most cells are too small to see without a microscope.

CHLOROPHYLL: A green substance found in many plants, which soaks up sunlight energy so the plant can make its own food.

COMPOUND: A substance made from two or more elements that are chemically bonded together.

CONDUCT: Allow electricity or heat to travel along or through it.

CONDUCTOR: A substance that electricity and/or heat can flow through.

CORROSION: When a metal reacts with another substance, and is broken down or destroyed in the process.

CRUDE OIL: A common name for a mineral called petroleum, which is found in nature.

DECAY: When something that used to be alive rots away, as it is broken down by natural processes, such as microbes feeding on it.

DECAY (RADIOACTIVE): When unstable atoms of an element spontaneously change into atoms of a different isotope or atoms of a different element—often but not always by breaking apart—releasing energy in the process.

DENSITY: The mass (how much) of a substance that fits into a certain volume (or space).

DNA: Stands for deoxyribonucleic acid, a chemical with large molecules that is found in almost every living cell, and which carries the coded information that tells each cell how to work.

DUCTILE: Can be drawn or stretched out into a wire without losing strength.

ELECTRIC CURRENT: A flow of electrons (or sometimes a flow of charged atoms, which are known as ions).

ELECTRICITY: Energy in the form of an electric current that flows through wires and can be used to power things.

ELECTRON: A particle much smaller than an atom, with a negative electrical charge. Electrons are found in all atoms. To help us understand how electrons and atoms behave, we use an atomic model that shows electrons orbiting the nucleus of the atom at different distances. These layers or "shells" represent the different energy levels of different electrons.

ENZYME: A natural catalyst, which starts or speeds up chemical reactions in living things.

FERROMAGNETIC: Elements that are strongly attracted by magnets, and can form permanent magnets themselves.

FISSION (NUCLEAR): When the nucleus of an atom is split or broken up into smaller parts, releasing a large amount of energy.

FUSION (NUCLEAR): When the nuclei of atoms are joined together to form a single, larger atom.

HALF-LIFE: The time it takes for half of the unstable atoms in a sample of a radioactive material to decay (change into a different form).

HORMONE: Chemicals in our bodies that act as messengers, traveling around in our bodies and controlling the timing of different processes.

INSULATOR: A substance that heat and/or electricity cannot flow through.

ION: An atom or a molecule that has lost or gained electrons, and now has an electrical charge.

ISOTOPE: Atoms of the same element with different numbers of neutrons.

LUSTROUS: Reflects a lot of light, so shines brightly but gently.

MAGNET: An object that has magnetism (attracts other magnetic objects or is influenced by a magnetic field).

MAGNETIC: Can be attracted to a magnet, or can become a magnet itself.

MAGNETIC FIELD: An area around a magnet where its magnetic effects are felt by other magnetic materials.

MALLEABLE: Can be bent, hammered, or pressed into shape.

MELTING POINT: The temperature at which a solid melts and becomes a liquid.

MICROBE: A tiny living thing that can only be seen under a microscope, such as a bacterium.

MINERAL: Solid compound found in nature, made from a particular set of elements; the rocks, soils, and sands of Earth's crust are made up of different combinations of minerals.

MOLECULE: The smallest piece of a compound, made up of two or more atoms bonded together. Some pure elements also form molecules, when their atoms combine in pairs or threes.

NEUTRON: A particle smaller than an atom, with no electrical charge. Neutrons are found in the nucleus of most types of atoms.

NUCLEAR ENERGY: Energy released by changes to the nuclei of atoms themselves, in nuclear fission and fusion reactions, and by radioactive decay.

NUCLEAR POWER: Electricity generated using nuclear energy.

NUCLEUS: The central part of an atom, made of protons and neutrons. Plural is nuclei.

ORE: A rock or mineral that is found in nature, and is used by humans as a source of one or more elements; most of the elements we use are extracted from ores.

PARAMAGNETIC: Elements that are weakly attracted to magnets, but don't form permanent magnets in their pure form.

PARTICLE: A tiny piece of matter, or a building block of matter such as an atom, proton, or electron.

PARTICLE ACCELERATOR: A large machine that uses strong magnets and electrical currents to get particles traveling at very high speeds, before smashing them into other particles. These machines are used for research and to create certain elements that don't exist naturally on Earth.

PHOTOSYNTHESIS: The process by which plants convert carbon dioxide and water into food, using energy from sunlight.

PROTON: A particle smaller than an atom, with a positive electrical charge. Protons are found in the nucleus of all atoms. The number of protons in the nucleus of an atom determines what kind of atom, or element, it is.

RADIATION: Energy in the form of electromagnetic waves (such as light, heat, X-rays, or gamma rays) or in the form of moving particles (such as neutrons).

RADIOACTIVE: Naturally gives out energy in the form of particles and radiation, as its atoms break apart.

REACTION: A chemical reaction is when the atoms of one or more substances rearrange themselves to make new substances with different properties. A nuclear reaction is when atoms themselves are changed into new types of atoms.

SALT: A compound made up of positively and negatively charged atoms (ions), which are attracted to each other due to their opposite charges. The numbers of the ions are balanced so that the compound has a neutral electrical charge. Salts are formed by reactions between acids and alkalis. The salt we are most familiar with is table salt, NaCl.

SEDIMENTARY ROCKS: Rocks formed when layers of sand, silt, or other tiny pieces (sediments) settle on the floor of an ocean or lake, and slowly turn to rock.

SEMICONDUCTOR: A substance that conducts electricity in certain conditions, but not in others.

SHELL: A term used to model and describe the different energy levels of the electrons in an atom.

SMELTING: The process of heating ores (certain kinds of rocks) to melt them and allow a chemical reaction, in order to extract metals from minerals inside.

SOLAR CELL: A device that changes solar radiation (sunlight) directly into electricity.

SOLDER: An alloy that melts at a fairly low temperature, which can be melted and used to fuse other metals together.

SPECTROSCOPY: Analyzing substances by investigating and measuring the types of radiation (including light) that they absorb, emit, or scatter.

SUBLIMATION: Changes from a solid straight into a gas, without melting first.

SUPERALLOY: Alloys that can stand up to extreme conditions, such as high temperatures, stretching or squashing forces, or corrosive chemicals.

SUPERCONDUCTOR: A substance that conducts electricity extraordinarily well (and usually at very low temperatures).

SURFACE TENSION: An effect caused by molecules at the surface of a liquid clinging together tightly, creating a sort of stretchy "skin."

TARNISH: A thin layer of oxide that forms on the surface of certain metals, as the atoms on the surface react with oxygen, water, or other substances. Tarnish makes metals look dull, stained, or discolored.

TOXIC/TOXICITY: Toxic means poisonous to a living thing. Toxicity describes how toxic or poisonous a substance is to living things.

UV (ULTRAVIOLET): A type of electromagnetic radiation (light) that we can't see. UV radiation is a part of sunlight.

WELDING: Joining two pieces of metal together by heating them to their melting points, and pressing or hammering them together.

X-RAY: A very high-energy form of radiation with many practical uses. The effects of X-rays led to the discovery of radioactivity.

INDEX

Phaidon Press Inc.
65 Bleecker Street
New York, NY 10012

Phaidon.com

First published 2020
© 2020 Phaidon Press Limited
Text © Isabel Thomas
Illustrations © Sara Gillingham

Text set in Karelia, Clone Rounded and Adapter PE Display

IBSN 978 1 83866 231 8 (US edition)
Printer code 004-0820

Designed by Meagan Bennett
Edited by Maya Gartner

Printed in China